Essays on
American
Music

Essays on American Music

GARRY E. CLARKE

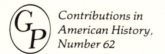

Contributions in
American History,
Number 62

GREENWOOD PRESS
WESTPORT, CONNECTICUT • LONDON, ENGLAND

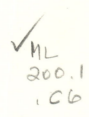

Library of Congress Cataloging in Publication Data

Clarke, Garry E
    Essays on American music.

    (Contributions in American history ; no. 62)
    Bibliography: p.
    Includes index.
    1. Music, American—Addresses, essays, lectures. 2. Composers, American. I. Title.
ML200.1C6   781.7′73   76-52606
ISBN 0-8371-9484-9

Library of Congress Catalog Card Number: 76-52606
ISBN: 0-8371-9484-9
ISSN: 0084-9219

First Published in 1977

Greenwood Press, Inc.
51 Riverside Avenue, Westport, Connecticut 06880

Printed in the United States of America

TO MY MOTHER
and to the memory of
MY FATHER
and
MY BROTHER

It is requisite for the ideal artist to possess a force of character that seems hardly compatible with its delicacy; he must keep his faith in himself while the incredulous world assails him with its utter disbelief; he must stand up against mankind and be his own sole disciple, both as respects his genius and the objects to which it is directed.

—**Nathaniel Hawthorne**
"The Artist of the Beautiful"
(*Mosses From an Old Manse*)

CONTENTS

PLATES

**Early publications and composers' manuscripts
in facsimile reproductions**

PREFACE

The beginnings of this book can be traced to 1962 when I first heard John Kirkpatrick's recording of Charles Ives's *"Concord" Sonata,* the 78 RPM version on Columbia Records. Although the copy was much scratched from library use, my hearing of the music sparked an intense interest in Ives. During the 1963-1964 academic year at Cornell College, a tutorial with Winifred Van Etten on American literature, and transcendental literature in particular, led to undergraduate study on Charles Ives, which was completed under the devoted guidance of Delinda Roggensack. At Yale University I came into contact with the Ives Collection, and in 1966 I began working with the manuscripts. One result of these studies was the editing and performing of one of Ives's piano works, the *Varied Air and Variations,* and the eventual further reconstructing and editing of the work with John Kirkpatrick, who by the late 1960s had become a friend and an important influence in my ever-growing interest in American music.

I began to play the music of Gottschalk, Griffes, Ives, and contemporary American composers. In the summer of 1970, a grant from the National Endowment for the Humanities allowed me to work in the Ives Collection at Yale and to obtain much of the information which has found its way into Chapter 5 of this book. During the 1971-1972 and 1973-1974 academic years, I taught a course in American music at Washington College. My enthusiasm for much of this music was by that time very great, and reflections on America's music in the form of a book became a necessity.

In discussing America's music—and I have used the term through-out this writing in reference to music in the colonies and the United States—a limited amount of material is covered. With few exceptions I have discussed one kind of music—from the so-called culti-vated tradition. And even that coverage is limited to topics that involve only some important figures and movements. But a com-plete chronology has not been my intention. Rather, I have chosen certain subjects and from these I have evolved essays, framed by general comments that form the beginning and the ending of the book. The omissions are numerous: Elliott Carter, Aaron Copland, Kenneth Gaburo, Walter Piston, Carl Ruggles, Roger Sessions, and a host of others. The significant American music in the vernacular tradition—jazz, for example—goes for the most part undiscussed. It is to the credit of the subject that there is so much of it, and it is exhilarating to know that there are so many likely prospects for a book of selected essays.

Whenever possible, I have tried to ascertain *how* a composer wrote, through his own words, by examining manuscripts (some of which may be found as facsimile reproductions in this book), and through clues in the music itself. Above all, I have tried to discover and to document the achievement of the particular composer and of his music. I have often expressed my judgments, despite the fact that anyone who indulges in criticism creates more problems for himself than a writer who deals primarily with historical data.

The concept of the "cultivated" and the "vernacular" traditions has been employed for some time under various labels—*educated* and *popular* culture, *elite* and *mass* art, or even the unfortunate *classical* and *popular* music. Although the term *cultivated* has been used on occasion (Henry Cowell, in a 1955 article in *The Score* comes to mind), my source is H. Wiley Hitchcock, whose fine com-prehensive study, *Music in the United States: A Historical Intro-duction* (Englewood Cliffs, N.J.: Prentice-Hall, 1974), cites the two major traditions in nineteenth-century American music as "culti-vated" and "vernacular" and then traces them. The terms work es-pecially well for that century. But they can also be used in connection with other periods and music, although in eighteenth- and twentieth-century American music the distinctions between them are often blurred.

Many people and institutions have aided me in one way or another with my project. The libraries of Harvard University and various librarians there were an invaluable help. At the Eda Kuhn Loeb Music Library I was assisted in particular by John Snyder, who was very helpful on numerous matters. At the Houghton Library of Harvard, Carolyn E. Jakeman located a number of rare books, periodicals, and manuscripts for me. The staff of the Boston Public Library and the Allen A. Brown Music Collection was kind and helpful. I am indebted to Harold E. Samuel and Alfred B. Kuhn of Yale University's John Herrick Jackson Music Library and to the staff of the Sterling Memorial Library at Yale. At The New York Public Library at Lincoln Center, I was aided by the Americana Collection and by Richard Jackson, its curator. The various divisions of the Library of Congress were an invaluable source of information. I appreciate the assistance of William L. Joyce of the American Antiquarian Society and Katherine H. Snell of the Hubbard Free Library, Augusta, Maine.

Lois Porter, John Cage, Robert Morris, and Virgil Thomson gave me lengthy and enlightening interviews, while James Drew and George Rochberg answered my queries by mail, thus providing me with important information.

In addition to Winifred Van Etten, Delinda Roggensack, and John Kirkpatrick, four other early influences are responsible for my general preparation for this writing: Earle B. Armil, Alf Houkom, Louise King, and Pauline Trotter. The book itself has been read carefully by my Washington College colleagues and students: Ormond Andrew, Richard Brown, Leo Dulin, Ronald Garrett, Joseph Getty, Kathleen Mills, John Klaus, and Dale Trusheim, all of whom have given me sound advice and constructive criticism. I wish to thank Erika Salloch, also of Washington College, for finding the poem "Märzschnee in München" by Marie Luise Kaschnitz, and for her translation.

Catherine P. Naul and Samuel Hope provided a number of excellent suggestions. The choir of Christ Church, Chestertown, Maryland, sang Billings, Belcher, and Swan with wonderful enthusiasm and with great beauty, helping me to arrive at many of the concepts that are expressed in the chapter on Yankee tunesmiths. My students at Washington College deserve my greatest thanks, for it is they who have contributed the most to my own development.

Stephen Lacey provided numerous and indispensable editorial readings of the manuscript. Jon Wakelyn, editor of the Contributions in American History series, has encouraged me throughout the months I was writing this book. I wish also to thank Jeannette Lindsay, James Sabin, and the editors at Greenwood Press.

I appreciate the hospitality of John Snyder in Boston and of Mrs. Franklyn D. Berry and Wilton Berry in South Dartmouth, Massachusetts. In Woodbridge, Connecticut, Dr. and Mrs. Gordon S. Haight gave my wife and me the use of their home during June and July of 1975 while they were abroad. That beautiful location provided the peace and seclusion necessary for the completion of the book.

Two final appreciations are in order, first to Washington College, a wonderful institution, which, in addition to so many things, awarded me a sabbatical for the spring term 1975. Finally, to my wife, Melissa, I owe thanks for the beautiful musical examples, as well as for much that has only a peripheral relationship to this book.

Garry E. Clarke
Woodbridge, Connecticut

ACKNOWLEDGMENTS

The author wishes to express his gratitude to the music publishers who granted permission to reproduce extracts from various works. Specific information is noted with the appropriate examples. Prose and poetic extracts are reprinted by permission of the following publishers and societies:

The excerpt from E. Webster's "Timothy Swan" reprinted by permission of the American Antiquarian Society, 185 Salisbury Street, Worcester, Massachusetts 01609.

The description of *Central Park in the Dark* by Charles Ives is used by permission of the publishers, Boelke-Bomart, Inc., Hillsdale, New York 12529.

The strophe of the poem "Märzschnee in München" by Marie Luise Kaschnitz from "Kein Zaberspruch" © 1972 by Insel Verlag, Frankfurt am Main.

Extracts from Louis Moreau Gottschalk, *Notes of a Pianist*, edited by Jeanne Behrend © 1964 by Alfred A. Knopf, Inc. are reprinted by permission of the publisher.

Excerpt from liner notes to CRUMB: Makrokosmos, Vol I (Twelve Fantasy-Pieces after the Zodiac, for Amplified Piano) (H-71293). Used by permission of Nonesuch Records.

Extracts from Charles Ives, *Essays Before a Sonata*, edited by Howard Boatwright © 1962 by W. W. Norton & Company, Inc. are reprinted by permission of the publisher.

The description of *The Unanswered Question* by Charles Ives. Copyright 1953 by Southern Music Publishing Co., Inc. Used by permission.

Thanks are due to Lois Porter, John Cage, Robert Morris, and Virgil Thomson for permission to publish information obtained in interviews; to John Cage for permission to reprint sections of his description of *Etudes Australes;* to Lois Porter and the John Herrick Jackson Music Library at Yale University for permission to publish material from the Quincy Porter Collection; to Robert Morris for permission to publish selections from his writings; and to James Drew and George Rochberg for permission to quote sections of their letters written to the author.

Essays on American Music

PROLOGUE

A culture is in its finest flower before it begins to analyze itself.
—Alfred North Whitehead, *Dialogues*

Nobody becomes an American composer by thinking about
America while composing.
—Virgil Thomson, *Music Reviewed*

Much of America's musical history is significant: an active American musial life, discernible since the early days of the colonies, has
produced works of importance and of greatness. This might well
seem an optimistic beginning to a topic that has historically been
subjected to negative treatment. But the myth of American musical
inferiority lingers; it is as real as the romantic myths of a positive
kind that have been a vital part of the foundation and evolution of
the American experience. Myths are an important, indeed essential,
aspect of any culture, and they are necessary for the development
of a national identity.[1] Myths may be found in many aspects of
American life, from the way American history has been recounted
to myths concerning social aspects of American culture. The tendency to deify the Washingtons and Lincolns while ignoring many
unfortunate aspects of their careers exemplifies the American collective national mythology at work. Music has suffered from a myth
of a different sort: the idea that America's music is for the most part
of little value.

The subject of American music, then, has not always aroused enthusiasm. Arthur Mendel, reviewing John Tasker Howard's *Our American Music* in 1931, echoed many fellow musicians when he wrote that "American music seemed to me a dull and trivial subject, of more interest to historical societies and Sons and Daughters of the Revolution than to those whose musical interests outweighed the patriotic."[2] Mendel then went on to say, however, that he was mistaken in such an assumption. Unfortunately, many who read the review probably felt that he was not. More recently, the important composers who have emerged in America have made us more receptive to our music, although some musicians still suggest that America has not yet produced a really great composer.

To some extent the early days of America have always had the reputation of being culturally insignificant and musically barbarous. The misconceptions are many and are frequently reprinted. George Hood's *A History of Music in New England*, published in 1846, begins: "The history of music in New England, for the first two centuries, is the history of Psalmody alone."[3] Writing only a few years ago, Virgil Thomson remarked that "American music has too short a history to be considered as a series of scenes; there is scarcely enough of it even to make a narrative. I have already sought to identify it as a twentieth-century show beginning about 1910."[4]

Hood and Thomson are inaccurate. Hood's comments can be understood as simply an early and misinformed commentary on American music, because modern research has found that there is much more than psalmody in the first two centuries of New England's music. And, although American music written prior to 1910 may not have been as significant as that composed later, Thomson's opinion illustrates a curious and general tendency to ignore positive aspects of early American music. The "show" did begin long before, and with the production of important works. Yet to present concerts of this significant music creates problems, even in 1975. "Can't you offer some more *serious* programming?" is a usual response to an evening of early American music.[5]

Nevertheless, American music is an exciting and often a profound literature despite its very difficult beginnings. Its growth lagged behind more immediate American goals of wealth and political solidity, and thus, while it is now achieving maturity, it is a maturity that still leaves a large part of the American population musically deficient. American music is optimistic in many ways, a result of the deep-rooted and intangible optimism that played a part in the founding of the country and in its early emergence as an important nation.

It is common practice to mention the work of a composer as if language were being discussed, for in a general sense, music is a kind of language. Schumann's music has a "German accent," at least to some critics. The "Parisian" operas of Rossini, Donizetti, and Verdi are really Italian works, stated in a musical language that remains Italian despite a French format. Chopin, at home with mazurkas and polonaises—part of the musical language of his Polish-French background—was uncomfortable with a bolero. Mozart's language, on the other hand, is an international European dialect, a result of the composer's years of travel outside Austria—and of Austria's own cosmopolitan and multinational character.

American music, or any national musical style for that matter, is not easy to discuss. Music is a language that is considered to be universal—an art form with properties transcending political, social, and cultural boundaries. This is true, of course, yet within music's international language are various dialects that make enormous differences in what is produced in particular areas. Music can be explained as organized sound—the exposition and treatment of ideas organized around such elements as pitch and duration—and the method of organization produces the different dialects. For example, the use of quarter-tones and *rāgas*, common elements in Indian music, have only rarely been a part of Western music.

Although music differs from language in that language is denotative in a way that music is not, for music cannot be translated into a system of reference different from itself with anything like completeness, yet in discussing music an allusion to language is nevertheless appropriate and helpful. Just as words evolve into certain patterns and sounds in a particular country, so do musical gestures. The gesture may be a combination of a number of elements: a rhythm that becomes associated with a particular region, a melodic formula, a certain scale, a harmonic combination, or even a dynamic level or an accent of particular distinction. If some of these entities com-

bine in a singular way, and if this combination comes to be frequently utilized on a broad scale, a regional musical dialect is developing.

Music, then, is universal—but it is not so universal that it cannot
be divided into national idioms. Not only is the use of national
musical dialects important here, but the very process of composition,
often an unconscious one on the part of the composer, can itself be
the result of a number of environmental or geographical factors.
Political boundaries influence the music that emerges from within
them. The fact that great music is written in some nations and not
in others suggests that a number of elements must combine in a
particular way to produce a significant artistic achievement. A
stable political system contributes to a social atmosphere that, in
turn, may encourage the development of the arts. Economic sta-
bility within a country—with its consequent freeing of leisure time—
will normally encourage people to direct their energies toward
aesthetic goals. The cultural heritage of a people also influences their
interest in music. A distinguished tradition of folk music, for example, can evolve into a cultivated music that can then become a tradition itself. Music is a vital activity, and the musical language that
develops in a nation cannot be divorced from the general complex
and multifaceted life of a people.

One of the most obvious ways to discern differences in the music
of nations is through the dance rhythms and folk tunes of particular
countries. An observer of Western culture soon learns that the
bourrée is French or that a certain well-loved folk song is English.
Sometimes the use of instruments helps determine a work's possible
source: a gamelan suggests that the music is East Indian; a balalaika,
that it is Russian. Or an astute listener may note the use of a Hun-
garian minor scale and assume with some justification that the work
is from that country, or at least from Eastern Europe.

However, uncertainty soon arises when the piece of music is more
abstract and offers less obvious clues. In such an instance, the listener's training and background are especially important. To one
whose experience is minimal, a composition such as the Saint-Saëns
Concerto No. 2 for piano and orchestra may not sound particularly
French. To the cultivated listener, employing many different skills
in his apperception of the work, the composition will sound unde-

niably French, even Parisian. There are reasons that we have such specific responses to a particular composition. An awareness of French culture will enable the listener to form associations in his mind between the music and his fundamental understanding of things French—even though there are no French songs or other obvious elements within the composition. The music simply speaks with a French accent—an intangible musical element. This might best be described as a felt insight, as an associative process that is not finally reducible to an intellectual statement.

The question is: how does such a quality in music arise? Basing his argument loosely on Hegelian dialectic, Olin Downes wrote in 1918 that there are three principal periods in the evolution of a nation's musical culture: the imitation of foreign sources; a revolt against this imitation, sometimes in the form of utilizing folk elements; and finally the evolution from these earlier periods to the "highly specialized expression of a leading composer."[6] In a 1903 essay, "An Affirmation of American Music," Arthur Farwell suggests that steps cannot be eliminated in the evolution of an art form. In noting that there must be "periodic action and reaction,"[7] Farwell indicates why music develops slowly: the process simply cannot be rushed. Great art is a result of this process, although an evolution is not just a series of stable moves toward a goal. Of course, art may also result from a cultural explosion, or even from turmoil. Stress can mold an artist; personal and cultural anxieties are sometimes as important as quiet reflection. It is when the symbolic absolutes which make a culture cohesive are faulted, through reflection or turmoil, that progress in an art form very frequently takes place. Yet great music has seldom been produced without major periods of personal reflection that help bring it into being. An important style of music will benefit from a fine composer who is the product of a long evolutionary process. He, in turn, will influence others, and more and more successful works in that style will be created.

Downes was correct in suggesting that imitation is an important first step, because as a composer imitates his sources, he develops technique. But the idea of utilizing folk sources to achieve a national identity is problematic. Folk materials can be deceptive. Many "American" folk tunes, especially early ones, have European origins. And it is not always possible for a folk tune to create an individual national style. For example, a symphony by a nineteenth-century American which quotes a folk tune or two may otherwise employ the musical language representative of nineteenth-century Germany. It is constructed by an American, but it is written for all practical purposes in German. A national language develops more subtly than this; the use of folk tunes is but an early step in the evolution, and this preliminary step alone cannot constitute such a language.

Be he a musician or a poet, it is that writer who rebels against or revolutionizes his models in a drastic manner who helps achieve a singular national language. In American literature, for example, Edgar Allan Poe, finding the established literary formulas of his time artistically inadequate, rebelled against them. As a consequence of his innovations, the short story was established as an acceptable and influential literary form. In music, the composer John Cage has achieved a rebellious musical language of international significance. At first, such writers or composers are usually thought of as being too radical to be important artists, yet their discoveries may have an influence beyond the work of the writers themselves. Their methods initially may not even be regarded as "nationalistic," but in time they may become characteristics of a particular region or school. Ultimately, perhaps their innovations will reach beyond these purely national origins as the language is synthesized and made universal. This synthesis is an important factor in the production of great works of art. For music that has as its fundamental conception the depiction or expression of nationalistic elements rarely achieves the profundity of music that has only the internal synthesis of musical materials as its goal. In the Western musical repertory, the composers who are placed in the highest positions are those who were not fundamentally interested in giving expression to national idioms. Those who pushed for nationalism in music, the Russian "five" for instance, are relegated in most cases to the second or third rank. As Downes argued, it is the composer who has evolved beyond mere nationalism, the "highly specialized expression" of a Josquin, Monteverdi, Bach, Mozart, or Stravinsky which really constitutes a significant musical contribution as Western minds usually define it.

How, then, does one actually define American music? In the words of one critic: "The way to write American music is simple.

All you have to do is to be an American and then write any kind of music you wish."⁸ Actually, this is a rather good prescription. American music is, simply, music composed by Americans. Some of it is good, some bad; some original, some derivative. Not all American music is American in style, for music and musical style do not always coincide—and style is at any rate difficult to delineate. There was, in fact, American music long before there was the possibility of an American musical style. And this raises a related question: who is an American composer? In the early days, many important American musicians were born in Europe. It is useful to say that an American composer is a composer who makes his career in America. Yet Stravinsky came to America, as did Schönberg, Bloch, and a host of others. Their music is not usually thought of in "American" terms, for their careers were established elsewhere. However, each of these men influenced American composers in varying degrees. Stravinsky had a number of followers from the 1940s through the 1960s whose music is Stravinskian in almost every sense of the word. From a standpoint of style, Stravinsky's American compositions are not American, whereas his followers' Stravinskian works are. The many neo-classical works that Americans produced as a result of Stravinsky's influence, in fact, represent one of America's stylistic norms at midcentury. From an historical perspective, however, Stravinsky's was an international career. Classification of style leads to one set of conclusions; historical classifications lead to others.

There are other problems which emerge as one tries to determine what constitutes American music. The earliest *Bay Psalm Books* are European in content, yet they are considered to be the first American music. Did the source become American when it crossed the Atlantic Ocean? What of the opposite situation: a composer such as John Knowles Paine, who went to Europe to acquire the musical language of nineteenth-century Germany? Of course, it is impossible to unravel all of the cultural ties between Europe and America. From the beginning the colonists attempted to transplant much of what had existed in the Old World. The Puritans wished to retain most aspects of their English life, but desired freedom of religious expression. The Virginians wanted to establish a feudal system parallel to that of the English manor tradition. The ties to Europe became more complex as the colonies grew and the European immigrants of the nineteenth century brought further historical models and influences. Consequently, American culture is an outgrowth of European culture and will always retain certain aspects of that culture.

When we examine the development of American music, we find composers who emerged from the European tradition to discover a new solution to a particular compositional problem. The works of Louis Moreau Gottschalk may be a part of the nineteenth-century European virtuoso tradition, but Gottschalk's use of North and South American melodies and his concept of rhythm remove the music from the mainstream of European tradition. Charles T. Griffes' early music shows his German schooling and his preoccupation with impressionism. In these works there is a hint of an originality that was to appear later, and in Griffes' last compositions the European elements have been synthesized into his own, original style. Yet there is a bit of Europe in almost every American composer, even in Charles Ives. If one casts aside all of the innovative qualities and visionary thinking found in his works, many of his compositions show a mind steeped in the tradition of late nineteenth-century Germany.

This European influence, never in itself negative, was the necessary first step in America's artistic evolution. However, it was a difficult influence to transcend if a truly American music were to emerge. European models were particularly influential because a feeling existed in nineteenth-century America that Europe represented "culture" whereas the United States represented the "backwoods." These prejudices had their culmination during the "Gilded Age" and resulted musically in the refinement of a derivative American-European style. German influences dominated this style, and the general opinion held that anything non-German was inferior. John Sullivan Dwight, one of the most militant of the German enthusiasts, expounded frequently on this subject in his famous *Dwight's Journal of Music*: "We confess we *are* partial to German music. We find more food for thought, more inspiration of the higher sentiments, more outlet of emotion, more enduring satisfaction, in the works of Handel, Mozart and Beethoven than in the operas of Donizetti and of Verdi. . . ."[9]

Of course, there were a few critics who thought differently. Some

believed that European music composed by Americans was not
entirely appropriate, and that a nation interested in "culture" should
develop its own. In a *New York Musical Review* article in 1854, a
writer on American psalmody noted: "Neither the heavy choral
[sic] of the German Protestant, the florid mass of the Romish Church,
nor the staid ecclesiastical music of England, nor all of these together,
entirely meet the wants of the American intellect and heart. . . .
We need a style of our own, avoiding the intricacy and difficulty of
the one school, and the tedious sameness of the other; but possess-
ing adaptation to our national peculiarities."[10] Such a style needs a
tradition to develop, and it was precisely tradition that the nineteenth century lacked. Gottschalk summarized this problem in his
journal: "We have no tradition in America. Archaeology, the worship of the past, could not exist in a society born but yesterday, that
has not yet had time to think of resting in order to dream, occupied
as it still is with providing for its material requirements."[11] Elsewhere in his journal the pianist writes that "in the United States,
cookery, like music, painting, and many other branches of a high
civilization, has hardly yet been called into being."[12]

In the preface to *The Marble Faun* (1859), Nathaniel Hawthorne
spoke of America similarly: "No author, without a trial, can conceive of the difficulty of writing a romance about a country where
there is no shadow, no antiquity, no mystery, no picturesque and
gloomy wrong, nor anything but a commonplace prosperity, in
broad and simple daylight. . . ." Hawthorne went on to contend,
rather wistfully, that "romance and poetry, ivy, lichens, and wall-
flowers need ruin to make them grow."[13]

In art a comparable dilemma existed, exemplified by the Hudson
River School, a group of nineteenth-century painters searching for
an American style. But as there was no lengthy American tradition
in painting, the artists had to look to Europe for a precedent. There
was an awareness, then, in all forms of the arts, that the creative
mind in America could not reach a depth of expression supported
as it was by only a thin veneer of tradition.

Yet by the last years of the nineteenth century, composers and
compositions suggested that a positive musical development was
taking place. In 1893, an English critic noted that progress had been
made in the direction of an American style. Before reviewing Horatio

Parker's *Hora Novissima,* this critic wrote that "commercial pursuits seemed to engross them [the Americans] utterly, leaving no room for the flowers of civilisation. But with the creation of a leisured class came the desire for art, and during the past ten years the Americans have made distinct progress in the cultivation of music."[14] The critic went on to discuss the problem of American composers' studying in Germany, for as late as the turn of the century, Germany continued to dominate Western music, and any alternative to the German tradition was met with skepticism. Yet some thought that such an alternative might be both possible and positive. When Vincent d'Indy once asked the American author and musician Henry Bellamann, "Why don't your American composers inspire themselves from their own landscape, their own legends and history, instead of leaning forever on the German walking-stick?"[15] he was expressing a sentiment that became more and more common as the desire for an American music became increasingly apparent. Nor was the United States the only country that felt the Germanic influence. Aaron Copland has argued that the entire history of twentieth-century music is a gradual pulling away from the Germanic tradition of the nineteenth century.[16]

Not all of the attributes of America's music can be traced to Europe; African rhythmic characteristics brought new life to the vernacular and ultimately to the cultivated traditions. In the twentieth century, the model of the Far East has frequently helped shape the works of Lou Harrison, John Cage, Harry Partch, Alan Hovhaness, and, to a lesser extent, those of Charles T. Griffes. When these non-European elements began to surface, a further development of a distinctive American music emerged. The most important event in this evolution is that Americans also learned to turn their vision inward, to reflect and to synthesize. This has been a compositional phenomenon of the twentieth century, a process that began with men such as Griffes and Ives, and that was continued by many who followed them.

Although it is difficult to describe "American" melodic and harmonic formulas productively, a study of the singular qualities of American rhythm is revealing. In one sense rhythm has a relationship to the spoken language of the country itself, not only in vocal music, in which the rhythm of the words has an effect on the rhythm of the music, but also in a general sense, since the basic linguistic rhythm of the spoken language influences a country's composers. American speech, then, necessarily relates to the way the rhythm of America's music has developed. Andrew Law recognized this when he wrote in 1814 that a musician must be acquainted with his language and "must feel the power of poetic numbers, and be able to unite these with those of music. . . ."[17]

A comparison between American and French music and language will help elaborate this idea. American rhythm, first of all, is firm and has, in general, enormous vitality. Just as there have been few American composers who have strived for Debussy's "orchestra with no feet," so, too, are there major differences in the rhythmic pattern of the spoken languages. Unlike French, American speech, in terms of inflection and rhythm, is characterized by strong accents and depends for both movement and stress on the varying length of the vowel sounds.

This quality of our speech suggests a reason for the American reliance on German musical formulas. A similarity exists in the rhythmic accents of the American and German languages as well as in the rhythmic accents of the music of Germany and the United States. In both language and music, strong accents are not avoided and there is a certain crispness of rhythmic structure. The rhythmic structure of Germanic languages differs from that of Romance languages, and the same may be said of the rhythmic structures of the music of a Germanic nation in comparison with that of a Romance nation.

Whatever may be the similarities of the rhythmic lives of nations, few countries have achieved the kind of rhythmic firmness and vitality that may be found in American music. Aaron Copland believes that some of this vitality can be ascribed to the rhythmic contribution of black music. He speaks of the ". . . conception of rhythm not as mental exercise but as something basic to the body's rhythmic impulse."[18] Many times this vitality alone will identify a work as being American. Although it would be a logical assumption to think that all music contains such emphases, this is not the case. There are many composers—Delius, Schönberg, Scriabin, and Sibelius among them—whose music to some extent lacks a truly vital rhythmic life. American composers, by comparison, normally write music whose most immediately arresting feature is strong rhythmic gestures.

Roy Harris has noted that Americans in general have a less symmetrical concept of rhythm than do Europeans. Harris feels that Americans "do not employ unconventional rhythms as a sophistical gesture; we cannot avoid them."[19] In the vernacular tradition, destroying the thirty-two bar form in some rock and roll music gives an indication of the asymmetrical patterns that tend to be a part of American rhythmic thinking. This "form" had dominated popular songwriting since the turn of the twentieth century. The fact that many rock and roll tunes employ odd-numbered formations gives this music structural interest and a rhythmic uniqueness.[20]

Americans have even developed revolutionary rhythmic innovations. Elliott Carter's "metrical modulation" is an example, a device that changes the basic tempo of a work not in a haphazard fashion, but by using mathematical relationships. Such elements as *accelerandos* and *ritards* are thus governed precisely. The rhythmic life of Carter's compositions is enormously rich and varied because of this innovative rhythmic practice. Another general rhythmic device, noted by Virgil Thomson, is seemingly the antithesis of the unconventional rhythm: a steady ground rhythm of equalized eighth notes, expressed or not expressed.[21] Winthrop Sargeant elaborates on what is basically the same procedure: "The jazz musician has a remarkable sense of subdivided and subordinate accents in what he is playing. . . . This awareness of minute component metrical units shows itself in all sorts of syncopative subtleties that are quite foreign to European music."[22]

The execution of these rhythms points out another national difference. The way they are *played* may give an indication that the performer is or is not an American. One need only listen to certain of America's most ingenious rhythmic innovations—such as ragtime—played by Europeans to note the difference in rhythmic concepts. A European's ragtime performance probably will be rigid and "by the book," and will not reflect the subtle rhythmic nuances and fluctuations that an American puts into his interpretation, simply as a matter of an instinctive cultural inheritance.

Rhythmic factors and their performance thus distinguish American music, yet these alone cannot make a national musical style of profound distinction. In *Music and Imagination,* Aaron Copland discusses the conditions for the creation of what he terms "an indigenous music of universal significance." Copland argues that the nation in which such music is created must have a profile of its own, and that the composer must be a part of that profile. Here is a more natural situation than the kind of groping that accompanies the early and usually embarrassed cultural efforts of a nation. Copland also notes that a composer must have some sense of musical culture, and that ". . . a superstructure of organized musical activities must exist. . . ."[23]

In 1930, Daniel Gregory Mason believed that America was finishing its musical childhood and entering the "awkward self-conscious stage of adolescence."[24] Of course, most of America's greatest music has been produced in the last half century. This could not have taken place much sooner, for Americans first had to experience the usual birth pains and obstacles that hinder the development of any art form in a young society—obstacles that are factors in its evolution into a mature form. American music in some ways is still a young music. As late as 1933, Roy Harris wrote that one could tell an American in Europe: "He has no poise, he is searching for something, he is concerned about his destiny and the appraisal of his people and his country, he is willing and eager to discuss homely social philosophy with you, he is naïvely receptive and easily browbeaten, and yet he radiates a fresh vitality and an unlimited reserve of energy; one feels within him a reticent ego which dares not emerge yet."[25] Harris' "American" is reminiscent of the kind of characters Henry James created in such works as *The American* and *Daisy Miller* and in his later writings, which describe conflicts between American and European culture. Harris' description is one of youth, and of a youthfulness filled with the wonderful quality of optimism that Americans demonstrated in their formative years. From this beginning a remarkable early period of American music was achieved that provided solid bases for a profound musical maturity.

In the final analysis, the concepts discussed in these pages reveal that although it is an enticing possibility to search for an American style in music, the American style is at best elusive. Some ideas of Constance Rourke, although centering on literature and art, may be felicitously applied to a discussion of music:

In our more hopeful moments we have supposed that something vaguely called the American spirit may infuse our art and literature and make this recognizably our own. At another tangent we have thrown the idea of nationalism out of the window and have insisted that art is an international language. So it often is: but no art has ever reached the point where it could speak a world language or even a hemispheric language without an ancestry of local or provincial expression behind it.[26]

One cannot hope for a tidy, inclusive list of elements that comprise our local or provincial expression, our American style. We must return to the concept of music by Americans as our definition of American music, observing that a stylistic definition cannot be an exact one. In *The Shape of Time*, George Kubler says it well: "Style is like a rainbow. . . . We can see it only briefly while we pause between the sun and the rain, and it vanishes when we go to the place where we thought we saw it."[27]

chapter 1

THE YANKEE TUNESMITHS

Laws are made for imitators. Creators make laws.
—John J. Becker, "Imitative Versus
Creative Music in America"

In the early years of America's history, most men who wrote music were only incidentally composers. Their lives were filled with other activities that left them with little time to develop a sophisticated compositional technique. Nevertheless, some of these men evolved a style that became an important contribution to the literature of music. H. Wiley Hitchcock has called these composers "Yankee tunesmiths," and the fact that their music shares a number of similar characteristics has led him to identify them further as the "First New England School."[1] This is an effective label; the writers, all living in New England during the second half of the eighteenth century, produced a body of literature that achieved positive and original solutions to the problems of musical composition.

The music of the "First New England School" culminates a tradition of vocal music that developed in the New England colonies during the seventeenth and eighteenth centuries. Psalms were an important part of church services from the earliest days, as indicated by the numerous editions of the *Bay Psalm Books*, published during the first years of the settlement of New England. Early attempts at the execution of these psalms, whether by speaking or singing, were no doubt far from accurate. The colonists' level of performance was so amateurish, in fact, that as in rural England, the procedure of "lining out" or "deaconing" was common. A line of the psalm would be read by the deacon or precentor and would be repeated by the congregation, who tried to sing what had just been read. Very rarely the psalm would be "set," or sung by the deacon as well as by the congregation, using the same basic format. This seems to be the only way by which singing in any ordered fashion could be achieved. Because this method continued from the last part of the seventeenth century until post-revolutionary times, it suggests that the general level of congregational singing was rather low for many years.[2]

Some progressive signs of musical activity can be found in the early colonial period, among them the publication in 1721 of Thomas Walter's *The Grounds and Rules of Musick Explained: Or, an Introduction to the Art of Singing by Note. Fitted to the Meanest Capacities.* In addition to being one of the earliest music books printed in the colonies, Walter's work contained the first American music with bar lines. Its many editions, the last in 1764, were important to the development of church music in New England. By the 1760s and 1770s others were writing on the same subject, among them William Billings, whose first publication, the *New-England Psalm-Singer,* appeared in 1770. In addition to music, these volumes contained instructional prefaces describing the rudiments of music along with comments on how to perform it. The authors even made tentative forays into the philosophy of music.

Another progressive element was the singing school, which first appeared in Boston as early as 1714 and which became common by the later 1720s. As in the case of musical publications, singing schools did much to develop a tradition of vocal music. A "learned" singer would be called into a community for several weeks or months to instruct those who were interested in the art of singing, particularly in its relationship to the worship service. The singing societies had a positive effect on both the community and the instructor. The social implications were considerable, for not only was making music a pleasurable activity, but people were able to form new social groups based on common interests. And, in addition to his gaining a reputation and spreading useful information, the instructor was paid for his services.[3]

This instruction helped bring about the formation of the church choir, and various parish records of the 1770s and 1780s contain references to the choir's growing importance. Eventually "artistic" music as opposed to "people's" music—the conflict between the church choir (or quartet) and the congregational singing—became a problem. An account published in 1891 by Alice Morse Earle shows that even in the late nineteenth century the controversy still existed:

I attended a church service not many years ago in Worcester, where an old clergyman, the venerable "Father" Allen, of Shrewsbury, then too aged and feeble to preach, was seated in the front pew of the church. When a quartette of singers began to render a rather operatic arrangement of a sacred song he rose, erect and stately, to his full gaunt height, turned slowly around and glanced reproachfully over the frivolous, backsliding congregation, wrapped around his spare, lean figure his full cloak of quilted black silk, took his shovel hat and his cane, and stalked indignantly and sadly the whole length of the broad central aisle, out of the church, thus making a last but futile protest against modern innovations in church music. Many, in whom the Puritan instincts and blood are still strong, sympathize internally with him in this feeling; and all novelty-lovers must acknowledge that the sublime simplicity and deep piety in which the old Puritan psalm-tunes abound, has seldom been attained in the modern church-songs. Even persons of neither musical knowledge, taste, nor love, feel the power of such a tune as Old Hundred; and more modern and more difficult melodies, though they charm with their harmony and novelty, can never equal it in impressiveness nor in true religious influence.[4]

But whatever the conflicts involved in such a controversy, the elevation of music as something to be "studied" had an overwhelmingly positive effect. People started writing music, and as they composed, they gained a surer hand. The "First New England School" is the culmination of this early period of musical activity in America.

Most of the Yankee tunesmiths were from Massachusetts and Connecticut. Such names as Asahel Benham, Supply Belcher, William Billings, Jacob French, Oliver Holden, Andrew Law, Justin Morgan, Daniel Read, and Timothy Swan are the best known of a large number of writers who contributed to the development of the First New England style. And in each case, music was only one of their several interests or occupations. Morgan, who was Vermont's

most important composer, was the breeder of the famous Morgan
horse. Read was a New Haven merchant, Swan a hatter, and Law a
minister with an impressive number of college degrees. Billings was
a tanner. Belcher was a tavernkeeper for some years. He was also a
town clerk and selectman, a justice of the peace, and a representative to the Massachusetts legislature. Acquainted with the mercantile
life of Boston, he was commissioned by General Washington as a
captain during the Revolutionary War. Belcher was also a teacher and
an amateur physician.[5] But he is remembered today for his musical
contributions; his love of music and his very real ability enabled
him to achieve considerable distinction as a singer, violinist, and
composer.

Example 1: William Billings: North Providence *from the* Singing
Master's Assistant *(Boston: Draper and Folsom, 1778).* *

---

*Some of the examples in this chapter have been slightly modified from the origi-
nal sources to facilitate reading. In particular, clefs and time signatures have been
altered in certain cases. Plates 1 and 2, reproduced from the original publications,
give points of comparison.

(ex. 1 cont.)

Example 2: Supply Belcher: Harmony *from the* Harmony of Maine
(Boston: Isaiah Thomas and Ebenezer T. Andrews, 1794).

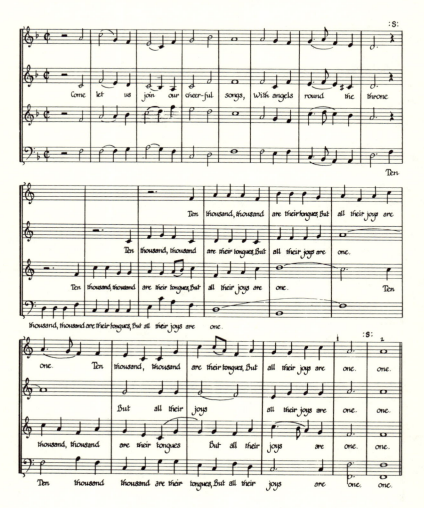

Example 3: Timothy Swan: Vermont *from the* New England Harmony (*Northampton, Mass.: Andrew Wright, 1801*).

These examples provide a solid introduction to the style of the Yankee tunesmiths. Billings' *North Providence* from the *Singing Master's Assistant* (1778), Belcher's *Harmony* from the *Harmony of Maine* (1794), and Swan's *Vermont* from his *New England Harmony* (1801) all employ the same text. The similarities of treatment are obvious and striking. In each case, after an initial homophonic passage, we find a section of "fuging" where the voices enter one by one in a quasi-imitative fashion. The three composers employ exactly the same form and almost identical rhythmic structures, in part because each has followed the natural accents and rhythms of the text itself. Yet Belcher and Swan undoubtedly were influenced by Billings, as they had come into direct contact with the composer, and because the *Singing Master's Assistant* was a generally important work for early American musicians. The similarity of these particular works gives us a sound basis for grouping the late eighteenth-century New Englanders together into a "school."

By describing general characteristics of the Yankee tunesmiths' music, we can bring the works more effectively into focus. With very few exceptions, this music is choral, the majority of it written in four parts. However, the distribution of the parts makes the sound of this music differ from the kind of soprano, alto, tenor, and bass ordering so familiar to twentieth-century ears. The Yankee tunesmiths' arrangement of treble, counter, tenor, and bass placed the melody in the tenor during homophonic passages. The treble worked as a kind of countermelody or descant to the tenor line. It was common practice to mix voices on the various parts. Thus, if there were enough singers, two or three of the treble voices sang the tenor line, which would then sound in octaves with the tenors singing the same music. Some of the men sang with the women on the treble. In the *New-England Psalm-Singer*, William Billings describes the process of exchangings and doublings:

A Man cannot sing a proper Treble without counterfeiting a Woman's Voice, which is very unnatural, and in the Ears of most Judges very Disagreable: Neither can a Woman sing a proper Tenor without counterfeiting a Man's Voice, which is also unnatural and disagreeable: But a Man may sing a Treble the Eighth below, and a Woman a Tenor the Eighth above, and then they will act upon Principles of Nature, and may make good Music, for every Eighth or Octave in Effect is the same.[6]

Plate 1: William Billings: North Providence *from the* Singing Master's Assistant *(Boston: Draper and Folsom, 1778). Music Division, Library of Congress.*

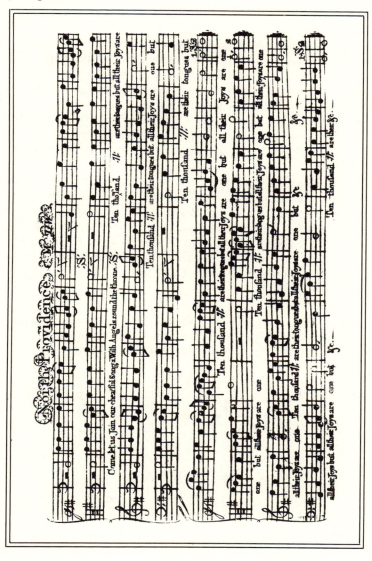

The resulting sound is a singular one. That lines in octaves produce a variety of voice leadings that are not evident by simply looking at the four parts as they are written indicates the ingenuity of musical texture.

Contemporary performances have varied widely, some to the detriment of the music, because many musicians are not familiar with eighteenth-century New England performance practices. There has been a widespread and unfortunate tendency to "rearrange" the voices, both in published modern editions and in performance, so that the tenor line of the original is placed in the soprano line and the treble line is shifted to the tenor. The sound of four-part writing as twentieth-century ears define it is created by this arrangement, but it has little to do with the music as the early New Englanders conceived it.[7]

An example of how important correct doubling is for an adequate performance of the music of the Yankee tunesmiths may be seen in a reexamination of the opening passage of Billings' *North Providence*. Example 4a shows the work as it will sound if the voices are doubled according to the custom of the time. Example 4b is the same music in a "modern" adaptation, with the treble and the tenor reversed and without the vocal doublings. This considerable transformation

Example 4: William Billings: North Providence. *(a) doublings according to performance practices of Billings' time, (b) a "modernization," without octave doublings and with treble and tenor reversed.*

changes the piece to such an extent that the composer's intention is lost in the so-called modernization.

These peculiarities of four-part writing are only one of the music's characteristics. The melodies of the New England tunesmiths are usually simple, direct, and uncomplicated, although unexpected melodic turns give them an interest. The melodic rhythm, for example, may do something unanticipated after establishing a set of probabilities that gives little indication that anything particularly unusual would occur. A flowing melodic line might suddenly become angular. The harmony is predominantly diatonic. Unusual harmonic progressions, including modal writing, a general love of the sound of a chord without its third, unorthodox voice leadings by cultivated standards including frequent parallel fifths, and unusual cadences give the music a harmonic distinction. Example 5, from an anthem of Billings, is one of these progressions. The chord that has been marked with an asterisk is usually considered to be a secondary dominant, which should resolve in this case to a B-major chord, the dominant of E major. Yet Billings, with the help of a passing note, moves the progression to the tonic. It is an arresting progression and actually quite a successful one:

Example 5: William Billings: An Anthem taken from sundry Scriptures for Charity meetings *from the* Psalm-Singer's Amusement *(Boston: The Author, 1781), measures 120-123.*

The tunesmiths' rhythmic approach, in general, also achieves unique gestures that are not found in other music of the time. This often results in an indigenous rhythmic vitality.

The compositional process that produced these works is important. Billings' preface to the *Continental Harmony* shows that his was basically a contrapuntal approach:

SCHOLAR. Sir, I should be glad to know whether you have any particular rule for introducing discords, in musical composition; I think you say that you have not tied yourself to any rules laid down by others, and I want to know whether you have formed a set of rules in your own mind, by which you are governed in some measure.

MASTER. Musical composition is a sort of something, which is much better felt than described, (at least by me) for if I was to attempt it, I should not know where to begin or where to leave off; therefore considering myself so unable to perform it, I shall not undertake the task; but in answer to your question, although I am not confined to rules prescribed by others, yet I come as near as I possibly can to a set of rules which I have carved out for myself; but when fancy gets upon the wing, she seems to despise all form, and scorns to be confined or limited by any formal prescriptions whatsoever; for the first part is nothing more than a flight of fancy, the other parts are forced to comply and conform to that, by partaking of the same air, or, at least, as much of it as they can get; But by reason of this restraint, the last parts are seldom so good as the first; for the second part is subservient to the first, the third part must conform to first and second, and the fourth part must conform to the other three; therefore, the grand difficulty in composition, is to preserve the air through each part separately, and yet cause them to harmonize with each other at the same time.[8]

In these pieces the treble worked in counterpoint with the tenor and the bass was enormously important, as demonstrated by the fact that it was not uncommon to double the line with a cello. A composer, in fact, did not think simply in terms of melody and harmony even in homophonic passages, but rather in terms of single lines that combined effectively. An unpublished memoir by E. Webster, written in 1842, discusses Timothy Swan's method of composition in a similar manner:

His rule in composition was to make the air, and throw as much music & melody into it as he was able, then make the other parts to harmonize; not forgeting [sic] to give *them* a good share of melody.[9]

This method of writing continued in America many years after Billings and his contemporaries. The same basic procedure is explained by John G. McCurry in his preface to the *Social Harp*, published in the mid-nineteenth century. Although McCurry is speaking of three-part vocal writing, his method is similar to that used by some of the colonial American composers. McCurry states that one first composes the tenor, and he lists a number of considerations that govern the writing of a successful tenor line. Then he discusses the composition of the other voices:

After you have written your tenor, then commence your bass by placing your notes a proper distance from the tenor, and be careful always not to place any note within one degree of the corresponding note in the other part, or within seven degrees, it being within one degree of the octave. Also avoid ninths, as they have the same effect as seconds and sevenths. Any two notes of the same name will make an agreeable sound, you may place notes in unison if you see proper. The intervals that produce harmony, (when sounded together,) are thirds, fourths, fifths, sixths, and eighths, or unison. Those that produce a disagreeable sound are seconds, sevenths and ninths. . . . After having written the bass and tenor, commence the treble by observing both parts already written; be careful not to place any note on the next sound to the notes in either part that is already located. . . .[10]

The differences between this process and that used by the composers of the "First New England School" are minimal. The New Englanders generally employed a consonant harmonic language, with seconds or sevenths serving a passing or otherwise transient function in the music. McCurry also describes what is fundamentally a "point against point" compositional procedure.

The music of Billings, Belcher, Swan, and their contemporaries is not the simple four-part writing it superficially appears to be, and the process that created it is not strictly a homophonic one. Some verses by Increase Mather's grandson, Dr. Mather Byles, set to music by Billings and Daniel Read and printed at the beginning of Billings' *New-England Psalm-Singer*, Belcher's *Harmony of Maine*, and elsewhere, expresses poetically the independence of voices sought by these composers:

Down steers the Bass with grave majestick air,
And up the Treble mounts with shrill career;
With softer sounds, in mild melodious maze,
Warbling between the Tenor gently plays:
But if th' aspiring Altus joins its force,
See! like the lark, wings its tow' ring course;
. . . .
Then rolls the rapture thro the air around
In the full magick melody of sound.

If we view this practice in relation to general harmonic movement, in particular that which results in open fifths and unisons, we discover that the music of this "school" has a curious relationship in terms of sound to the kind of vocal writing that is characteristic of the Renaissance. There are differences, of course: The New Englanders did not, for instance, generally employ the suspension as an expressive device. Nevertheless, the similarities speak for themselves. One possible explanation for this relationship is the Yankee tunesmiths' lack of familiarity with the current European style—that they were too distanced for it to influence their compositional process. They were "behind" in a sense, and their models would have typified those of an earlier period. The New England process of composition even suggests a period earlier than the Renaissance, for the independence of lines and temporary linear wanderings sometimes bring about clashes similar to those found in the music of the *Ars Nova* of the fourteenth century, music that was also constructed line upon line.[11]

There are other indications of reliances on earlier or atypical European composers. That Belcher was once referred to in a newspaper article as the "Handel of Maine" (or "Handell of Maine" as the journal quaintly put it)[12] rather than as the "Haydn of Maine"— this almost forty years after Handel's death—is another indication of the historical disparity between America's compositional practices and those of Europe. Haydn and his contemporaries were not as familiar to New Englanders as were earlier generations of European composers and the English composers popular in early America, the unskilled Tans'urs and Williamses who wrote outside of the mainstream of late eighteenth-century European music and who often influenced music produced in the New England colonies in the early days.[13]

The concept of "fuging," one of the most important elements of the Yankee tunesmiths' style, has been noted in reference to Examples 1, 2, and 3, for the text with its reference to "ten thousand, thousand are their tongues" is exactly the kind that would lead a composer of the time to insert a fuging section. A "fugue" and a "fuge" are different entities.[14] There are isolated examples of "strict" counterpoint for a measure or two in some of the works of the New Englanders, which they employed if the material was simple enough. For the most part, however, the contrapuntal writing is far removed from the textbook concept of counterpoint. Billings, in the *Singing Master's Assistant*, defined "fuge" or "fuging" as "Notes flying after each other, altho' not always the same sound. N.B. Music is said to be Fuging, when one part comes in after another; its beauties cannot be numbered, it is sufficient to say, that it is universally pleasing[.]"[15] In the *New-England Psalm-Singer*, he wrote that "fuging is accounted the most ingenious and generaly the most grateful both to Performers and Auditors, of any Part in Composition."[16] And in one of his long footnotes in the *Continental Harmony* he argued that there is variety in fuging, much more than in other kinds of texture.[17]

The composition process in the case of fuging passages was much different from the "normal" writing of counterpoint. A composer undoubtedly started one voice and then fit other notes with it as best he could, which resulted in a short passage where the voices entered one after another before returning to homophonic texture. The relationship of the material between the lines was not particularly important. More urgent was the problem of simply getting the voices going simultaneously. There is, in other words, a distinct relationship to what the composers did in homophonic writing and in fuging passages. Billings' indication of "Notes, flying after each other" is appropriate, for if a composer achieved this effect, he felt that he had made his point.

Example 6 contains a short section where the voices enter one by one. Although imitation between the bass and tenor remains strict for a few notes, in general the associations are of a free nature. The entry of the treble brings about a return to four-part texture that soon assumes homophonic characteristics: imitation has barely begun when it is suddenly completed. By comparison, the fuging section of *North Providence* (Example 1) assumes a more complex and sophisticated form. In that fuging passage, the melodic lines

Example 6: William Billings: Universal Praise: An Anthem for Thanks-
giving Day, taken from Psalm 149, &c. *from the* Continental Harmony
*(Boston: Isaiah Thomas and Ebenezer T. Andrews, 1794), measures
29-37.*

differ from one another, and the initial entries are rhythmically irregular. Once the motion begins, there is a constant rhythmic thrust
toward the final cadence. Billings was capable of extending his
material in such instances, for the *Continental Harmony* offers an
example of a twenty-eight-measure fuging section.[18] At times, therefore, it is possible to find a highly developed example of fuging.
The majority, however, are of the kind in which the imitation is
only suggested—the voices have staggered entrances, but the contrapuntal texture is not sustained. To write a long passage of strict
counterpoint was beyond the capabilities of the composers, who
could not write "by the rules"—or at least by established European
rules.

Indeed, much of the singular style of the New Englanders may easily be accounted for. They did not have enough training to write music that was free from such "errors" as the improbable voice leadings and unusual harmonic progressions that dominate the music. To learn these aspects of composing would have required procedured study, and the members of the "First New England School" composed more from instinct than from thorough musical training. Swan, for example, had briefly attended singing school, but this was certainly not the most impressive training for learning the technical complexities of writing music. These writers, then, learned in what can best be described as a relaxed, trial-and-error manner. One of Roger Sessions' comments on the creative process applies to the Yankee tunesmiths: ". . . a composer, like anyone else engaged in creative activity, is totally involved in *what he is doing:* only to a very peripheral extent, if at all, is he interested in *how he is doing it.*"[19] The philosophy expressed by Billings in the *New-England Psalm-Singer* seems almost to have anticipated Sessions. Concerning the rules of composition, Billings stated that "Nature is the best dictator." There is poetic license, he reasoned, so why not musical license? "I think it is best for every composer to be his own Carver"[20] has become his most famous pronouncement on the art of composition. This statement has been used to rationalize the music of Billings and the general style of the New Englanders, but no justification is needed. They were able to overcome their lack of formal training and to produce a literature that is original because they created their own methods of composition.

Historians and critics have not always been kind to the music of the Yankee tunesmiths. Reverend Francis Brown wrote in an essay published in 1810 that there was a time in New England when Billings was more popular than Handel. "Bad music has been preferred to good,"[21] he wrote, and there were many who agreed with this opinion. In 1834, William S. Porter declared Billings and his contemporary Oliver Holden to be "light and impious trash." "The great body of American psalm tunes," Porter continued, "which a few years since, were extensively used, and which abound in miserable attempts at fugue and imitation are entirely beneath criticism: they have noise and that is all."[22] Nathaniel D. Gould's *Church Music in America* (1853) terms the period of Billings and his contemporaries a "dark age."[23] And even though Billings is considered by most critics to be the finest composer of the "First New England School," as late as 1939 his music was said to be only of historical interest.[24] MacDougal's opinions in *Early New England Psalmody* (1940) are typical:

. . . Billings like all the Colonial composers who tried their hand at the anthem, can not give continuity to the musical line, nor does he have any idea of how to unify anything longer than a psalm tune; he relies entirely on a succession of more or less long phrases defined by strong cadences and separated by long rests. The usual errors made by music students in their first harmony are common with Billings. . . .[25]

Fuging, too, has been criticized mercilessly. Oliver Holden in the preface to the *Union Harmony* (1793) wrote: "Fuging music in general is badly calculated for divine worship; for it often happens that music of this description will not admit of a change of words without injuring the subject."[26] There is evidence that Holden's personal preference was for a quieter, less complicated sound, a preference that was undoubtedly shared by many of his contemporaries. In his essay, "pronounced before the Middlesex Musical Society" at Dunstable, Massachusetts, in 1807, John Hubbard ended his talk by blasting the New England composers and the confusion in their fuges, which he termed a "perversion." Hubbard's idea of a composer of distinction was Handel.[27] Critics in succeeding generations also remembered the "confused" passages of writing in the music of the Yankee tunesmiths. In Hastings' *Dissertation on Musical Taste* (1822), a section entitled "Of Fugue and Imitation" mentions "those senseless productions, which formerly found their way into our American churches."[28]

Criticisms such as these were once common, and only recently have careful examinations of the best examples of the New England musical style shown these opinions to be for the most part ill-founded. In fact, the New England composers wrote music of considerable achievement. Released from European "standards," the music works well on its own terms.

The compositions of Supply Belcher (1751-1836) are representative of the "First New England School," although his work is relatively unknown. John Tasker Howard, in his voluminous *Our American Music*, makes no mention of this composer. Other writers and

Plate 2: Supply Belcher: fuging section of Winthrop *from the* Harmony of Maine *(Boston: Isaiah Thomas and Ebenezer T. Andrews, 1794). Music Division, Library of Congress.*

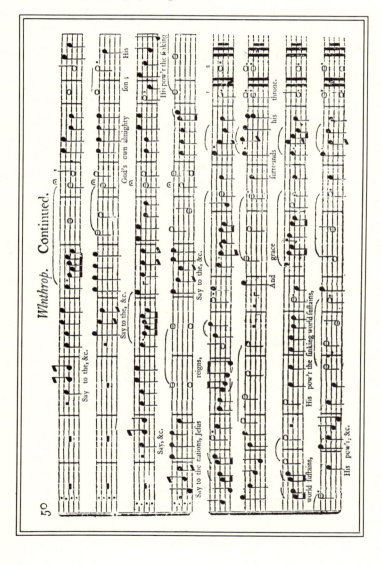

critics, unimpressed by Belcher's writing and accepting its alleged crudity, have found little to admire.[29] Yet there are positive qualities in his music, and some of it is very effective. Belcher's works appeared in several collections and in the *Harmony of Maine*.[30]

Handsel (Example 7) is one of the simple homophonic settings in Belcher's publication. It begins with the open sound of a B and an E; the second syllable of the word *Jesus* is placed on the first down-

Example 7: Supply Belcher: Handsel *from the* Harmony of Maine.

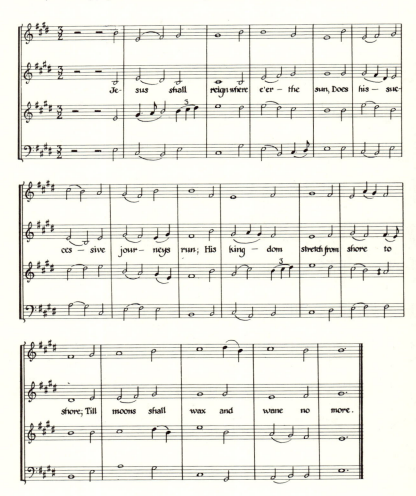

beat of the composition. Thus, two characteristic qualities are immediately evident. The rather awkward setting of the word *Jesus,*
combined with the open sound of the first chord, gives an idiosyn-
cratic quality to the opening gesture. A successful performance will
have to stress the anacrusis, so as to present a feeling of angularity
in the rhythmic pulse. Yet aside from the opening gesture, where
the word setting and not the music creates the angularity, the rhythm
works in conventional patterns. The voices move effectively, and
the setting of the opening words with the rhythmic "push" of the
triplets leading to the word *reign* demonstrates a characteristic
rhythmic thrust. There is linear movement resulting in unexpected
crossings and surprising chord connections. Belcher is clearly concerned with both the vertical and the horizontal aspects of the work.
All of the lines are smooth, with the tenor demonstrating especially
admirable melodic qualities. The opening progression and round-
ing off of musical ideas in the second half of the composition give
symmetry to a small work that starts at one point and moves ef-
ficiently to another point.

Example 8: Supply Belcher: Ocean *from the* Harmony of Maine.

(ex. 8 cont.)

Ocean (Example 8) is more complex. The fuging section, in which each of the parts enters in a loose kind of counterpoint, is highlighted by descriptive writing on the word *rolling* which, when pitted against the heavily articulated accents on "billows sleep," creates a turbulent and exciting musical texture. The structure of *Ocean* is ABB, the usual form for a fuging tune: an initial homophonic section is followed by a repeated fuging section. Symmetry is achieved by having the contrapuntal writing merge into homophonic texture at the end of the B sections. What should be noted in relationship to this particular example is the enormous vitality and rhythmic thrust of the fuging section that resolves itself only at the final cadence, in itself an instance of an open fifth placed at an important moment in a work. The linear writing that results in the crossing of the tenor and bass, and the exciting combination of pitches (on the first syllable of "billows"), are each striking. And there are several other moments in the piece when the independence of each voice results in clashing dissonances.

"Word painting" is evident in much of the music of Belcher and his contemporaries. Example 9, taken from the composer's *Winthrop* is typical. Some writers have felt that there is nothing very clever about setting "sinking" and "sustains" in such a manner. John Hubbard, complaining about this kind of writing in an essay on music published in 1808, argued that ". . . very few distinct ideas can be represented by any arrangements of notes. The language of music, when destitute of words, must ever be ambiguous. What natural connexion can possibly subsist between a low note and the word

Example 9: Supply Belcher: Winthrop *from the* Harmony of Maine, *measures 22-30.*

hell? or a high note and the word *heaven?* Imitations of this kind are a burlesque on common sense, and a species of musical buffoonery."[31] Yet most composers have felt that such connections do exist; from a very early time they have been a part of Western music. Word painting, in fact, is one of the devices that can give meaning to music. Belcher, like so many of his contemporaries, was a master of this technique and employed it in a sophisticated manner.

The work of Timothy Swan (1758-1842) (see Example 3) illustrates how similar writings of the New Englanders were. Swan's *Poland* (Example 10) is one of his most famous compositions, and the common aspects of this work and Belcher's *Handsel* (Example 7) are numerous and obvious. The relationship of the keys of the two works is unimportant in itself. The use of the same meter, however, is noteworthy, especially since both composers begin curiously, in

Example 10: Timothy Swan: Poland *from the* New England Harmony.

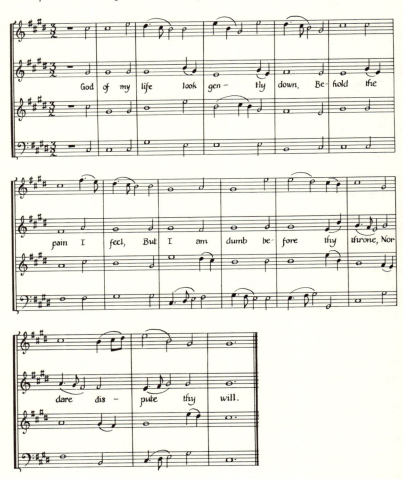

Swan's case by the placement of the rather unimportant word *of* on the first downbeat. The rhythmic similarities in each case are evident, but Swan's use of a phrase construction of 4 + 3 gives *Poland* a rather asymmetrical structure. Swan was a melodically oriented composer, and although individually the lines in *Poland*

are almost awkward, it is their interrelation that causes the four parts to be effective.

Perhaps the greatest composer of early American music was William Billings (1746-1800). Although many of the other New Englanders of the late eighteenth century wrote excellent music, Billings' reputation is well justified. His publications of collected works [the *New-England Psalm-Singer* (1770), the *Singing Master's Assistant* (1778), *Music in Miniature* (1779), the *Psalm-Singer's Amusement* (1781), the *Suffolk Harmony* (1786), and the *Continental Harmony* (1794)] constitute a large body of literature—over five times as much as any of his contemporaries. (There are over 300 surviving pieces.) Most of the other composers published only a volume or two, which hardly gave them opportunity for significant musical growth. In Billings' case, the development of a style from the *New-England Psalm-Singer* to the *Continental Harmony* is unmistakable. Had he published only his first collection, Billings would probably languish in relative obscurity.

In addition to the fact that his music had distinction, Billings was his own best sales representative, and he succeeded in making his music known. His reputation throughout civilized New England was considerable, and his work as a singing master gave him the opportunity to teach his compositions and make them known to a large audience. He had a high opinion of his work, which is apparent from a reading of any of the prefaces to his publications. Billings wrote his music with a sure hand and did not worry about his lack of training, and this rash optimism is reflected in the music he produced.

The fact that the "Musical Tanner," as Billings was called, had a number of peculiar physical and personal characteristics contributed to his reputation as an eccentric artist. Gould's discussion of these characteristics in his volume on American church music reveals the legendary status Billings had achieved by the 1850s:

Billings was somewhat deformed in person, blind with one eye, one leg shorter than the other, one arm somewhat withered, with a mind as eccentric as his person was deformed. To say nothing of the deformity of his habits, suffice it to say, he had propensity for taking snuff that may seem almost incredible, when in these days those that use it are not very much inclined to expose the article. He used to carry it in his coat-pocket, which was made of leather; and every few minutes, instead of taking it in the usual manner, with thumb and finger, would take out a handful and snuff it from between his thumb and clenched hand. We might infer, from this circumstance, that his voice could not have been very pleasant and delicate.[32]

Even though Billings has been much criticized, he did exert a considerable influence on his own generation of composers as well as on future writers. William Schuman's *New England Triptych* and Otto Luening's *Prelude to a Hymn Tune by William Billings* are works from the twentieth century that use tunes by Billings as their source material. Henry Cowell and Lou Harrison have been fascinated with fuging tunes and have composed a number of them, turning an eighteenth-century practice into a twentieth-century one.

An examination of some of the characteristics of Billings' music demonstrates why it can be called the crowning achievement of the "First New England School" and why Billings has influenced composers of the twentieth century. Like his contemporaries, Billings was almost exclusively a writer of choral music. Billings' own voice was loud and enthusiastic, and a reflection of Reverend Dr. Pierce, quoted by Gould, recalls it: "He [Pierce] said Billings had a stentorian voice, and when he stood by him to sing, he could not hear his own voice; and every one that ever heard Dr. Pierce sing, especially at Commencement dinners, at Cambridge, knows that his voice was not wanting in power."[33]

Billings' enthusiasm for the human voice was such that, in works such as the *Singing Master's Assistant*, he gave some attention to how vocal music should be performed: "Be sure not to force the Sound thro' your Nose; but warble the Notes in your Throat."[34] In the *New-England Psalm-Singer*, Billings elaborated on the problem of solo singing: "Much Caution should be used in singing Solo, in my Opinion Two or Three at most are enough to sing it well, it should be sung as Soft as an Eccho, in order to keep the Hearers in an agreeable Suspense till all the Parts join together in a full Chorus, as smart and strong as possible."[35] Billings' attitude toward the solo voice is patently negative, and this preference for a combined sound stands out from standard English practice of the time. Billings' interest in vocal problems is one of the factors that led him to the composition of a large and solid body of choral music.

For the most part, Billings' harmony is diatonic, although there are a few augmented triads and diminished sevenths in his work. Diatonicism is evidenced, for instance, by Billings' unfamiliarity with augmented sixth chords, even though they may be found in some of his contemporaries' works. Modulations are rare. The progressions in his early pieces often resulted in an awkwardness (the move from III to II, for example), although these tendencies are less evident in Billings' later pieces. He does not rely entirely on the usual dominant-tonic formulas at cadences, but rather on the linear movement of different voices leading to a point of resolution. Sometimes this intuitive contrapuntal approach results in momentary harmonic clashes. Billings eventually learned to use inversions effectively, and gradually an ever-improving compositional technique helped him to write smooth progressions.[36]

Billings' rhythm is noted for its lack of symmetry. He juxtaposes different kinds of rhythms in combination with asymmetrical phrase structures that make the music rhythmically arresting. His writing also frequently contains stereotyped rhythmic patterns, for example, the use of a dotted note followed by a shorter note:

Example 11a: William Billings: Marblehead *from the* Singing Master's Assistant, *measures 1-4 (tenor line only).*

Example 11b: William Billings: Great-Plain *from the* Continental Harmony, *measures 1-8 (tenor line only).*

Example 11c: William Billings: Roxbury *from the* New-England
Psalm-Singer *(Boston: Edes and Gill, 1770), measures 1-8 (tenor line
only).* *

When Billings employs duple or quadruple meters, the music
often assumes a dancelike character, with a beginning on a weak
beat. *North Providence* (Example 1), *Boston, Shiloh,* and *East Sudbury* are typical:

Example 12a: William Billings: Boston *from the* Singing Master's
Assistant, *measures 1-5 (tenor line only).*

Example 12b: William Billings: East Sudbury *from the* Continental
Harmony, *measures 1-5 (tenor line only).*

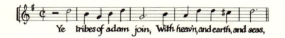

Example 12c: William Billings: Shiloh *from the* Suffolk Harmony
(Boston: J. Norman, 1786), measures 1-5 (tenor line only).

Despite the fact that some of his pieces show curious settings of
words, there is in general a happy union of text and music. Billings
insisted on a strong treatment of words, and the only times con-

---

*The composer notes, concerning the lack of a text: "No doubt the reader will
excuse my not adapting words to all the tunes as it is attended with great incon-
veniency[.]"

fusion arises, it occurs because of the notation. If the barring is adjusted in certain of the compositions, Billings' intention becomes clear.[37] Because he tended to think in asymmetrical terms a good deal of the time, his music often has the feeling of groups of fives and sevens. Yet to notate them as such would have been unthinkable to a composer of Billings' time. The bar line was a hindrance for him, as it is for most composers who treat rhythm asymmetrically.

Like his contemporaries, Billings was aesthetically fascinated by the suggestive qualities of words, as we can see in the following example from *Creation:*

Example 13a: William Billings: Creation *from the* Continental Harmony, *measures 45-53 (tenor line only).*

In *Deliverance* there is a descriptive passage on the word *shake:*

Example 13b: William Billings: Deliverance, An Anthem *from the* Continental Harmony, *measures 31-34.*

"Everlasting" receives the following rather Handelian treatment in one of Billings' anthems in the *New-England Psalm-Singer:*

Example·13c: William Billings: An Anthem Suitable to be sung at a Charity meeting *from the* New-England Psalm-Singer, *measures 129-133 (tenor line only).*

And in *Brunswick* the word "pants" is set graphically:

Example 13d: William Billings: Brunswick *from the* Singing Master's Assistant, *measures 19-26 (tenor line only).*

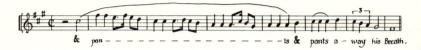

*Words such as *laugh, fly, roll,* and *shooting* also provided Billings with material for word painting, and he seldom failed to make the most of such instances. One of the most amazing of these passages is from *An Anthem: Psalm 18* and is certainly a singular instance of a "melisma" in a section marked *Grave:*

Example 13e: William Billings: An Anthem, Psalm 18 *from the* New-England Psalm Singer, *measures 33-41 (tenor line only).*

It is a tribute to Billings' real abilities that his music achieved such distinction when so much of it is plain writing, for the most part unadorned by ornamentation. And this is another indication that his music is far removed from the general kinds of composition characteristic of the late eighteenth century in Europe. Although there are ornaments in certain passages of Billings' music, and although performers might add ornamentation not in the score, his writing was really too vigorous most of the time to tolerate what the colonial composers called the "little notes" in music.[38]

Billings' originality and indeed that of the "First New England School" is evident if we compare its music to that written elsewhere in the colonies. The Moravians, for example, were overwhelmed by European influences. The rhythmic and melodic structures, the harmonic and formal aspects, and even the use of German in many of the Moravian works, all illustrate that any significant Moravian achievement, although important, was predominantly a European one. Surviving musical examples of the Philadelphia Quakers and those of the Virginians do not show a marked individuality when compared to European models. Colonial Charleston, too, boasted a sophisticated musical life, but compositions written there reflected the patrician South's cultural reliance on Europe. The Yankee tunesmiths achieved an originality not found elsewhere in the colonies.

When the contemporary composer Ned Rorem states that Billings' ". . . music was rough-hewn as an old church door,"[39] he refers not to the gates of a cathedral or even to the doors of a large cosmopolitan church, but to the door of a colonial New England meeting house. The sounds within are American. They are sounds that are an original solution to the compositional problem, carved out effectively and with distinction. Billings and his New England contemporaries were all carvers.

chapter 2

LOUIS MOREAU GOTTSCHALK

[Art] has always taken on a special native fiber before it
assumes the greater breadth.
  —Constance Rourke, *Charles Sheeler: Artist in the
  American Tradition*

The history of American music in the first decades of the nineteenth
century cannot be considered apart from the economic and social
contexts that made music possible. Two important developments
were the increase in musical publications and the refinement of the
piano as a virtuoso concert instrument. By the end of the century's
second decade, over 15,000 musical publications had already been
made available in America.[1] The production of pianos also began
to increase, so that in 1852 the United States commissioner of patents
could report that about 9,000 pianos had been made the year before,
almost doubling the quantity produced in 1829.[2] The production of
21,000 pianos in 1860 represented a 133 percent increase over the
1851 figure.[3] Richard Hoffman, the pianist, noted in his musical
memoirs that in the 1840s it had been difficult to find even one piano
in some of the small towns where he had given concerts. By 1895
the change had been so phenomenal that Hoffman was amazed.[4]

Not only did the number of pianos increase, but the American
piano achieved a superiority that by 1860 made it as fine an instrument as any of its European rivals. The Chickering piano was a distinctive instrument, and the growing reputation of the Steinway

contributed to the company's emergence as an American institution. When an exhibit of pianos was displayed at the Centennial celebration in Philadelphia, it was noted that the American pianos were far superior to the European models.[5]

The evolution of the piano and the increasing importance of musical publications are two of the factors that contributed to the prominence of Louis Moreau Gottschalk (1829-1869), a musician whose music hovers between the cultivated and the vernacular. In his curious synthesis of these traditions, Gottschalk produced a large but flawed piano literature that achieves a distinctive American identity.

The biographical aspects of Gottschalk's life are fascinating and are crucial for an assessment of his various compositional styles. Gottschalk was born in New Orleans, a city whose exotic qualities provided an important early influence on him. It was a city in which the cultivated and the primitive—Italian operas, Creole tunes, South American and African rhythms, and French gavottes—existed side by side. Dancing was vital to life: "The story of music in New Orleans must begin with dancing."[6] One of Gottschalk's earliest biographers, H. D.,[7] gives a vivid account of the dancing for which New Orleans was famous:

Let a stranger to New Orleans visit, on an afternoon of one of its holydays, the public squares in the lower portions of the city, and he will find them filled with its African population, tricked out with every variety of a showy costume, joyous, wild, and in the full exercise of a real saturnalia. As he approaches the scene of an infinite mirth, his ear first catches a quick, low, continuous, dead sound, which dominates over the laughter, hallo, and roar of a thousand voices, while the listener marvels at what it can be doing there. This is the music of the Bamboula, of the dance Bamboula; a dance which takes possession of the negro's whole life, transforms him into a savage of the banks of the Congo, and reinvests him with all the instincts, the sentiments, the feelings which nature gave to his race, to sleep for a while, to be partially obliterated by the touch of civilization, but to remain forever its especial mark.

Upon entering the square, the visitor finds the multitude packed in groups of close, narrow circles, of a central area of only a few feet; and there, in the centre of each circle, sits the musician, astride a barrel, strong-headed, which he beats with two sticks, to a strange measure incessantly, like mad, for hours together, while the perspiration literally rolls in streams and wets the ground; and there, too, labor the dancers, male and female, under an inspiration or a possession, which takes from their limbs all sense of weariness, and gives to them a rapidity and a durability of motion that will hardly be found elsewhere outside of mere machinery. The head rests upon the breast, or is thrown back upon the shoulders, the eyes closed, or glaring, while the arms, amid cries, and shouts, and sharp ejaculations, float upon the air, or keep time, with the hands patting upon the thighs, to a music which is seemingly eternal.

The feet scarce tread wider space than their own length; but rise and fall, turn in and out, touch first the heel and then the toe, rapidly and more rapidly, till they twinkle to the eye, which finds its sight too slow a follower of their movements. Ah! the *abandon* of the Bamboula; the transformations of the Bamboula; no wilder scene, no more exciting exhibition of the dominancy of sheer passion, uncultivated, savage, is to be found in the tales of travelers.[8]

Such memories of the New Orleans streets were vital for the evolution of Gottschalk's style. Equally important was the music he heard elsewhere. Gottschalk's parents introduced him to the cultivated tradition at an early age, and he thus became acquainted with the works of European composers.

Gottschalk was sent to Paris in 1842, a journey that initiated a life of travel that took him through much of the world and brought him into contact with numerous nineteenth-century luminaries. Generally, an American in Paris in the 1840s was viewed with disdain. Yet the young musician managed to make his way, and his studies led to concerts where his playing and his compositions caused a sensation. *Bamboula, Le Bananier,* and *La Savane:* the titles as well as the contents of the works breathed a curious exoticism. Paris responded feverishly to the "different" sound of Gottschalk's music, recognizing for the first time in serious music the sounds of an American genesis. For Gottschalk had taken memories of New Orleans' dance rhythms and folk tunes and had woven them into a musical fabric typical of European nineteenth-century virtuoso playing. It was this outwardly bizarre synthesis that created a new kind of music. Gottschalk's compositions impressed many of France's finest musicians—Chopin, Saint-Saëns, Berlioz, and Bizet. The young artist also began his concert travels at this time, playing in various

parts of France, Switzerland, and Spain. Spanish tunes became the
basis of a number of compositions written during his stay there in
1851 and 1852, and the Spanish influence remained with him for
some years.

When Gottschalk returned to the United States in 1853, after
eleven years of European study, travel, and concertizing, he was a
seasoned and accomplished artist. He traveled, gave concerts, and
wrote and published his music. By the late 1850s Gottschalk needed
a respite from this peripatetic existence. The years 1857-1862 found
him living in the tropical atmosphere of the Caribbean. The accounts of Gottschalk in the early 1860s, improvising in the moonlight near an extinct volcano in Guadeloupe, are the kind that made
him a legendary romantic personality. Part of this impression comes
from Gottschalk himself:

I again began to live according to the customs of these primitive countries,
which, if they are not strictly virtuous, are nonetheless terribly attractive.
I saw again those beautiful *trigueñas,* with red lips and brown bosoms,
ignorant of evil, sinning with frankness, without fearing the bitterness of
remorse. All this is frightfully immoral, I know, but life in the savannas of
the tropics, in the midst of a half-civilized and voluptuous race, cannot be
that of a London cockney, a Parisian idler, or an American Presbyterian.[9]

When Gottschalk returned to the United States again, in 1862, it
was to another hectic schedule of concerts throughout the country.
He had played for presidents at various times in his career: Martin
Van Buren once abandoned a performance of Bellini's *La Sonnambula*
to go next door to hear one of Gottschalk's New York concerts, and
Millard Fillmore was an admirer. On March 24, 1864, Gottschalk
performed (badly he said) for President and Mrs. Lincoln, including
his composition *Union.* Although some of these incidents are documented in his writings, the main journal entries concern his experiences in such obscure places as Dayton, Nevada, where miners in
flannel shirts had what might have been their first exposure to serious
music.[10] Such concerts, together with the publication of his music,
brought cultivated music to a wider audience than ever before. Yet
not everyone agreed that this was Gottschalk's intention. His harshest
criticism came from the Bostonian John Sullivan Dwight, who
blasted Gottschalk whenever possible in the influential *Dwight's*

Journal of Music. Dwight, a divinity student from Harvard, had been an unsuccessful Unitarian minister. His great love was music, and the formation of *Dwight's Journal* gave him editorial space to expound his theories. Dwight was credited with having "a fair ear" and a general aesthetic sensibility. One source mentions that "he could read notes," although his perception was not keen enough to be disturbed by technical errors.[11] Dwight's knowledge, although superficial, had a certain validity; he argued that music was an intellectual activity and insisted on the importance of the spirit in which a work was performed.[12]

Gottschalk was a Southerner, neither intellectual nor Germanic, and this resulted in some scathing notices in the *Journal.* When Gottschalk first returned to the United States from Europe, an early issue of *Dwight's Journal* (February 19, 1853) reprinted a generally negative review that had appeared in the *New York Courier and Inquirer* of February 12. Gottschalk later played in Boston in October 1853, and Dwight wrote that his works bore no more resemblance to Liszt, Chopin, or Thalberg "than the lightest magazine verses with the inspired lyrics of the great bards." Dwight continued: "Could a more trivial and insulting string of musical rigmarole have been offered to an audience of earnest music lovers?. . ."[13] Gottschalk played a second Boston concert, and while the review of that performance was less critical, it did attack Gottschalk's own compositions: ". . . Who could think for a moment of comparing them with such fine inspirations as any of the little mazourkas or notturnos of Chopin; the 'Invitation' of Weber; the little tone-poems of Henselt, Stephen Heller, &c. . . ."[14] Dwight did not realize that Gottschalk had substituted a Beethoven bagatelle for one of the "Gottschalk" pieces listed on the program and Dwight, a Beethoven worshiper, had not recognized it!

The Gottschalk controversy continued in *Dwight's Journal.* The November 19, 1853, issue carried both a commentary concerning Dwight's prejudices and a reply by Dwight. The November 26 issue contained a reply to the reply by a "Lover of Music and Justice." Gottschalk had become well known and was causing consternation among the critics.

A problem that particularly bothered many centered on the general literature that was a part of Gottschalk's concert programs. His preference was his own music rather than the works of Bach or Beethoven. Gottschalk did know how to play the masters, at least in private. William Mason wrote to William L. Hawes (reprinted in *The Musician*, October 1908) that Gottschalk played Bach well and that he had performed other classical compositions. Mason thought that Gottschalk's playing of the Chopin *Fantaisie in F Minor* was unequaled.[15] George P. Upton recalled an afternoon in 1864 when Gottschalk played, "in his dreamy way," Beethoven's *"Moonlight" Sonata* and some of Mendelssohn's *Midsummer Night's Dream* and *Songs Without Words*. But Gottschalk usually did not play these compositions in public. He felt that, while many could play Bach or Beethoven well, he was himself the supreme interpreter of his own music. Said Upton: "In reality, the music which he played was not a fair test of his taste or ability."[16]

However, when Gottschalk did play familiar works of other composers in public, there is evidence that his performances could have been more effective. A Chicago reviewer wrote negatively in December 1864 concerning performances of violin and piano sonatas of Mozart and Beethoven in which Gottschalk had participated, concluding that "these sonatas were not given as they should be."[17] An account of Gottschalk's performing the Henselt *Concerto in F Minor* describes what happened on at least one occasion when he was confronted with a work of immense difficulty:

Mr. Gottschalk *attempted* to play the first part of Henselt's Concerto, Op. 16. We say "attempted," not because he substituted for the difficult runs of the middle part his usual easy ones, leaving out entirely those for the left hand, nor because he dropped a good many notes; but because, in spite of these abbreviations and simplifications, the remaining difficulties of the piece appeared to be so immense to him, that he could not afford to show the least expression, nor any thing of an artistic-like conception or treatment.[18]

Yet even John Sullivan Dwight had to admit that "Mr. Gottschalk's touch is the most remarkable we ever heard. . . ."[19] In concert Gottschalk was obviously uneven, but at its best his playing was probably enormously effective.

Accounts of Gottschalk performing show him to be the typical nineteenth-century virtuoso showman: ". . . why does he always make a 'ninny' of himself, whenever he takes his place at the Pianoforte before an audience—by the nervous attempts to disrobe his fair fingers of those close-fitting 'kids'—giving them (his fingers) an imaginary plunge-bath—rubbing and wringing the while—and then turning them out for a general 'airing' over the keys?"[20] Another account complained: "When the difficulties of execution do not require him to watch his hands, he has a glance ever ready to wander lazily about the concert-room, scrutinizing the audience."[21]

There is evidence to suggest that Gottschalk found performance to be distressing. He confides in his diary that audiences gave him nausea: "I am pleased to think that beyond the tomb concerts exist only in the memory, like the nightmare that we recall to ourselves confusedly in the morning and that has painfully disturbed our sleep."[22] This complaint seems to have been only part of a more general dissatisfaction. *Dwight's Journal* of March 4, 1865, quotes a "lugubrious card" being passed out at Gottschalk's concerts that finds the artist in a melancholy mood:

To my *friends and the public:*
On the eve of my departure from this country—my native land—the land of my earliest affections—I feel that I must express my heartfelt regrets on parting with the public, whose kindness has sustained me throughout my public career. To all my friends, who have given me so many proofs of warm interest, I bid a fond farewell. The clouds that conceal the future are transparent and bright only in the morning of life. I have already come to the age when they show more deceptions than joys. Even, as I say to you all, farewell, methinks a distant echo faintly answers "adieu!" A last, a long—farewell.[23]

Before leaving the United States, Gottschalk traveled to California, where in addition to concertizing he found time to indulge in one of his favorite pastimes—visiting insane asylums. But a number of circumstances on the West Coast, in particular a questionable incident with a young lady, prompted him to embark for South America. Gottschalk found himself in Peru in the midst of the November 1865 revolution. His accounts of this event are as absorbing as those of his travels through the United States during the Civil War. Between 1865 and 1869 his wanderings led him to other South

American countries—Chile, Argentina, Uruguay, and Brazil. His pace was too frantic, and the culmination of many years of hectic living began to cause a deterioration of his health.

One aspect of Gottschalk's death is as "romantic" as the legends surrounding his life. Despite extreme fatigue, he agreed to play in Rio de Janeiro on November 25, 1869. He was in the midst of playing one of his recent compositions, the "lamentation" entitled *Morte!!*, when he collapsed. Carried from the concert hall, he lingered for some days and died on December 18, 1869.

With such an inconsistent yet evocative life, it is not surprising that Gottschalk's music should be an uneven but fascinating conglomeration of styles. His most important works, his piano pieces, can be divided into several categories: the virtuoso compositions of a general nature; those that use themes of the United States, Spain, the West Indies, or South America; and the salon music of the *Last Hope* variety. Simply to make money, Gottschalk wrote compositions under pseudonyms such as Seven Octaves, A.B.C., Oscar Litti, and Paul Ernest. Some of Gottschalk's music—piano pieces, songs, and even operas—is missing. Many works that Gottschalk "improvised" for specific occasions were never committed to paper. "Indeed, the published pieces are but as a shadow of his entire creations," according to N. R. Espadero, one of Gottschalk's Havana friends.[24]

Despite the problem of dealing with an incomplete *oeuvre*, the piano works that do survive are a valuable indication of Gottschalk's achievement. The pieces were utilitarian, for they provided Gottschalk with a popular repertory for the audiences he found in his travels. The music has a kind of appeal that made it immediately accessible to nineteenth-century audiences. Roger Sessions has written that ". . . the artist's values are not, and cannot be, those of the market."[25] Certainly Gottschalk wrote for the market, and not an entirely sophisticated one at that. Yet the accusation that Gottschalk was "playing down" to his audiences is not entirely fair. As William Mason observed concerning the caliber of audiences in the 1840s, and it applied to later audiences as well: "It is difficult to realize the crudity of musical taste in the early days."[26]

Gottschalk felt music to be a sensuous activity, more a physical than an intellectual pursuit, and this philosophy influenced the kind of music he produced: "Art is the ardent aspiration for the beautiful. It is voluptuousness sublimed by the spirit; it is an irresistible transport that makes us burst the bonds of material space, through the ideal, and transports us to the celestial spheres."[27] He was a romantic who abhorred confining musical structures: "Poesy and youth are by nature vagabonds; they are butterflies. Shut them up in the cage of reason, and their transparent wings are broken against the prison bars. Regulate their flight and you take from them their scope and boldness—two qualities that often are found in inexperience and whose loss is not always compensated by maturity of talent."[28]

Another passage in Gottschalk's journal centers on compositional problems of freedom and form:

If I write, my imagination takes the wings of Iris, traverses space, and shows me fairylands. As soon as I want to put it down on paper, from being a butterfly it becomes a bat. The wings become weighty under the burden of my phrases and fall heavily. The mischievous thing tempts me, draws me on, intoxicates me, offers me a thousand encouragements to follow it. With pen in hand I try to give a form framed in my own words to the beauties she permits me to have a glimpse of, but, like the will-o'-the-wisp that the belated traveler pursues, it vanishes into the darkness at the moment when I think I have grasped it.[29]

Thus, the music of this nineteenth-century romantic can be more easily understood through insights into his nature revealed in his journals, for, like so many romantics, the locus of his art is fundamentally biographical and self-expressive.

Gottschalk was, in fact, a romantic in the grandest sense of the word, as the following journal entry discussing a "monster concert" indicates:

. . . I composed a *Triumphal Hymn* and a *Grand March.* My orchestra consisted of six hundred and fifty performers, eighty-seven choristers, fifteen solo singers, fifty drums, and eighty trumpets—that is to say, nearly nine hundred persons bellowing and blowing to see who could scream the loudest. The violins alone were seventy in number, contrabasses eleven, violoncellos eleven!

You can imagine the effect. No one can have any idea of the labor it cost me.[30]

Gottschalk's additional romantic qualities include a melancholy, an "undercurrent of sadness" as one writer has described it, which may be found in much of his music.[31] There is even a romantic pre-occupation with the macabre—with bats—a fascination reminiscent of Edgar Allan Poe: "I liked to follow with my eyes their wild flight, whose circles, always narrowing, had my lamp for their center. I liked, also, their sharp little cry, which people the immense depths of my chamber."[32]

This romanticism could be Gottschalk's own worst enemy. He was overly fond of literary associations, and the "programs" attached to many of his works are typical of romantic music. Extra-musical factors can easily lead to exaggeration, and exaggeration to sentimentality. This is true of Gottschalk's most famous work, *The Last Hope*, which he termed a "religious meditation." The "new and only correct edition" of this work carried a preface, reprinted from *La France Musicale:*

One of the most charming pianists of this city having observed—the ladies observe everything—that Gottschalk never passes an evening without executing, with profound religious sentiment, his poetic reverie "The Last Hope," asked of him his reason for so doing.

"It is," replied he, "because I have heart-memories, and that melody has become my evening prayer."

These words seemed to hide a mournful mystery, and the inquirer dared not question the artist further. A happy chance has given me [Gustave Chouquet] the key to the admirable pianist's reply to his lovely questioner.

During his stay at Cuba, Gottschalk found himself at S——— [Santiago], where a woman of mind and heart, to whom he had been particularly recommended, conceived for him at once the most active sympathy, in one of those sweet affections almost as tender as maternal love.

Struck down by an incurable malady, Madame S——— mourned the absence of her only son, and could alone find forgetfulness of her sufferings while listening to her dear pianist, now become her guest and her most powerful physician. One evening, while suffering still more than usual—"In pity," said she, making use of one of the ravishing idioms of the Spanish tongue—"in pity, my dear Moreau, one little melody, the last hope!" And Gottschalk commenced to improvise an air at once plaintive and pleasing, —one of those spirit-breaths that mount sweetly to heaven, whence they have so recently descended. On the morrow, the traveller-artist was obliged to leave his friend, to fulfil an engagement in a neighboring city. When he returned, two days afterwards, the bells of the church of S[antiago] were sounding a slow and solemn peal. A mournful presentiment suddenly froze the heart of Gottschalk, who, hurrying forward his horse, arrived upon the open square of the church just at the moment when the mortal remains of Senora S——— were brought from the sacred edifice.

This is why the great pianist always plays with so much emotion the piece that holy memories have caused him to name "The Last Hope," and why, in replying to his fair questioner, he called it his "Evening Prayer."[33]

Many, including the composer Mrs. H. H. A. Beach, were brought to tears by *The Last Hope*. Rev. Edwin Parker, a Hartford, Connecticut, Congregational minister, transformed the melody into a hymn, *Mercy*. John Sullivan Dwight, on the other hand, noted that "religious meditation" was hardly an appropriate indication: ". . . there were jack o'lantern freaks in it."[34] Of course, a work with programmatic implications may have many interpretations, some of them inadvertently humorous. When Gottschalk received the proofs prior to one of the work's first publications (William Mason remembered the incident as having taken place in 1854 or 1855), he was astonished that the engravers had printed the title as *The Latest Hops*.[35] Whatever musical connotations this piece brings to the listener, it is appropriate for performance in a parlor or salon: its sentimental, inordinately romantic gushings illustrate one kind of writing for which Gottschalk was famous.

An obvious aspect of Gottschalk's writing is the conglomeration of native American and traditional European elements, presented in a virtuoso framework. This is produced by a number of characteristic devices: octaves, double notes, ornate passage work, interlocking figures of various kinds, trills, tremolos, scale passages, and arpeggiations. And although they appear and sound difficult, the pieces are in reality not as demanding as those of Chopin or Liszt. Gottschalk's music "fits" well into a pianist's hands. Playing Gottschalk gives the pianist an indication of why the composer did not admire the piano writing of Beethoven. Everything had to "work" pianistically, and pianistic awkwardness was not tolerated. One particular characteristic is Gottschalk's placing many of the right-hand passages in the highest registers of the piano to produce a continuously brilliant timbre.

Melodically, the composer was at his best when he was using the tunes of others. The pieces with an original melodic invention are his least effective:

Example 14: Louis Moreau Gottschalk: The Dying Poet, Meditation *(Boston: Oliver Diston & Co., 1864), measures 9-16 (melodic line only).* *

This example, from one of the "Seven Octaves" pieces, became one of the composer's most popular works, yet it suffers, not only because of its sentimentality but also because the melody contains numerous clichés. At other times Gottschalk's melodic structures deteriorate into mere passage work, for he does not usually draw a series of complex relationships from a motive or a phrase. Rather, he spins out his thoughts with whatever invention occurs to him at the moment of conception.

Harmony in Gottschalk's music is usually diatonic with a large number of major and minor chords, dominant and tonic relationships: *The Banjo* does not deviate from F-sharp major in all of its 224 measures. On occasion, however, Gottschalk does depart from the diatonic to achieve some unusual harmonic results. *The Last Hope* (Example 15) contains passages reminiscent of Wagner, with sequential repetitions and enharmonic transformations:

---

*Although a number of libraries have collections of original publications, the most accessible sources for Gottschalk's piano music are the *Piano Music of Louis Moreau Gottschalk*, selected and introduced by Richard Jackson (New York: Dover Publications, 1973) and *The Piano Works of Louis Moreau Gottschalk*, 5 vols., edited by Vera Brodsky Lawrence (New York: Arno Press and the New York Times, 1969). All of the examples in this chapter may be found in the Arno edition. The Dover publication contains all of the examples with the exception of *Columbia* (Example 20).

Example 15: Louis Moreau Gottschalk: The Last Hope, Religious
Meditation (New York: Firth, Pond & Co., 1854), measures 14-18.

At times chromatic elements give an unusual color to the music:

Example 16: Louis Moreau Gottschalk: Morte!!, Lamentation (New
York: William Hall & Son, 1869), measures 68-70.

Here, the chord marked with an asterisk serves as a momentary
linear movement away from the diatonic harmonies that dominate
the rest of the phrase.

Sometimes Gottschalk employs enharmonic change, for example
in Souvenir de Porto Rico, where he modulates from E-flat minor
to G-flat major, which is transformed immediately into its enharmonic equivalent, F-sharp major. At other times, the use of an
enharmonic transformation results in a chromatic modulation.
Danza contains a passage where B-flat is altered to A-sharp. The
B-flat or A-sharp, a common tone between E-flat major and F-sharp
major, serves as the link between the two keys and provides a smooth
connection. The fact that E-flat and F-sharp are an augmented second
apart is a characteristic quality of the Gottschalk modulation.
Many of Gottschalk's works contain similar relationships: El Cocoyé,
for example, moves from F-sharp major to E-flat minor. Bataille, a
work in E-flat major, contains a section in F-sharp major. The similarity of sectional harmonic movement between these compositions

and *Souvenir de Porto Rico,* with its movement from E-flat minor to F-sharp major, is striking.

Occasionally, Gottschalk's works achieve harmonic relationships that give a strong structure to the work. *Danza* is a rambling piece on first examination. Gottschalk begins in E-flat major, moves to F-sharp major and then to E-flat minor before returning to E-flat major. Initially, the coda of the work appears to be merely a routine conclusion to the several pages of writing. Yet the structure of the last page, with its movements through E-flat major, F-sharp major, E-flat minor, and E-flat major mirrors the harmonic events of the rest of the piece, compacting and synthesizing them.

Gottschalk's works that use Creole, West Indian, or South American sources incorporate rhythms representative of the vernacular music of these exotic areas. These rhythms, it must be remembered, were not what "respectable" music contained. One reason they found their way into his pieces is that Gottschalk, in taking vernacular rhythms for concert use, chose not to conceal the popular nature of his sources. Of further importance was his close affinity to dance music, and although he was most excited with tropical dance rhythms, such as the "bamboula," in a piece such as *Pasquinade* Gottschalk could work effectively with the European gavotte. Even so, it is tropical rhythms that gave Gottschalk the most inspiration, among them the habanera, usually expressed as follows: ♩. ♪ ♫ and the tresillo: ♩. ♩. ♩ .[36] Many of Gottschalk's works employ these devices, among them *Ojos Criollos:*

Example 17: Louis Moreau Gottschalk: Ojos Criollos, Danse Cubaine, Caprice Brillant *(New York: William Hall & Son, 1864), measures 21-24.*

One of the composer's most famous works, *Bamboula*, is based on habanera rhythms. A representative passage follows:

Example 18: Louis Moreau Gottschalk: Bamboula, Danse de Nègres *(Mainz: B. Schott, n.d. [1847?]), measures 17-20.*

Formal structures in Gottschalk's music are often handled without sophistication. Normally he was content to use simple ternary forms, uncomplicated rondos, or themes with variations. At other times a number of tunes strung together in a free fantasia-like form are the basis for a composition. The complexities of logic involved in more intricate forms were foreign to Gottschalk's compositional temperament. As he wrote in his journal:

The form! O pagans of art! The form! When, then, will the time come, routine fetish worshipers, when you will have the courage or the talent to avow that there is more genius in the pretty waltzes of Strauss than in five hundred pages of schoolwork; in eight notes of genius, wholly without ornament, ignorant of their nakedness, but beautiful in their ignorance, than in a logarithmic problem?[37]

The labor that most composers experience in the evolution of an intricate formal structure, the working out of a development section in a sonata form, for example, the "logarithmic problems" of music, meant little to Gottschalk. This helps to explain why his music is almost entirely homophonic. Although he had studied composition as a youth in Paris, Gottschalk had not made a thorough and systematic study of counterpoint. One of the few works that does employ contrapuntal writing is the patriotic tour de force *Union*, where he joins *Yankee Doodle* and *Hail Columbia*, first placing *Yankee Doodle* in the right hand with *Hail Columbia* in the left hand, then reversing the process. Nineteenth-century audiences found such tricks exciting, and the procedure was actually a common one. (In a similar vein, William Mason once joined *Yankee Doodle* and *Old Hundred* in counterpoint at a concert, which led some members of the clergy to hiss. When asked to do the same thing some years later, Mason warned the audience that by joining the two tunes he meant no disrespect to *Yankee Doodle.*)[38] These instances illustrate the state of counterpoint among nineteenth-century American pianist-composers. Lacking carefully evolved formal structures, and disinclined to undertake the rigors of counterpoint, Gottschalk's compositional process betrays an essentially elementary nature. That he did not have the time or the genius to overcome his casual approach to writing is perhaps the reason much of his music does not achieve real significance.

Gottschalk's position improves immensely if he is analyzed not just as a composer but also as an arranger, for his best works are those in which he develops themes by others. His arrangements are many, and they cover every aspect of his art except the salon pieces. The early works that captivated Europe all elaborate material that Gottschalk heard in New Orleans as a youth. The settings of Spanish and West Indian sources, and such patriotic works as *Union* and *Battle Cry of Freedom*, are transcriptions similar to the nineteenth-century opera fantasias which every virtuoso had in his repertory. It is true that certain works which do not employ quotations are frequently effective. *Pasquinade*, with its reminiscences of the gavotte and cakewalk, and *Minuit à Séville*, with its flamenco rhythms and guitar-like figurations, are "original" works of quality. But in Gottschalk's most effective compositions, the treatment is of already existing material that he has transformed masterfully into a new setting.

Some pieces are arrangements that quote tunes literally within the virtuoso framework: *La Savane, Union, Battle Cry of Freedom, La Jota Aragonesa,* and *Souvenirs d'Andalousie*, for instance. Others represent brilliant transformations of the borrowed material. Among these is *Le Bananier* with a tune developed from a Creole air, *En avan' Grénadié.* Example 19a is the melody more or less as it would have been heard in the Creole source. Gottschalk's first statement,

Plate 3: Louis Moreau Gottschalk: *a section of* Minuit à Séville *(manuscript). Music Division, The New York Public Library at Lincoln Center, Astor, Lenox and Tilden Foundations.*

however, differs from the original, for he has stretched the rhythmic values to create an asymmetrical structure (5 + 5):

Example 19a: Creole air: En avan' Grénadié, *from Clara Gottschalk Peterson, comp. and arr.:* Creole Songs from New Orleans in the Negro-Dialect *(New Orleans: L. Grunewald Co., 1902), measures 1-5 (vocal line only).*

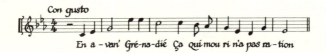

Example 19b: Louis Moreau Gottschalk: Le Bananier, Chanson Nègre *(Boston: Oliver Ditson, n.d.), measures 4-8 (melodic line only).*

Another kind of thematic transformation can be found in the "Caprice Américaine," *Columbia.* The material in this case is Stephen Foster's *My Old Kentucky Home, Goodnight.* Example 20a is Foster's original version (transposed and rhythmically adjusted to facilitate comparison). Gottschalk's adaptation (Example 20b) is curious in the way it works around the original to form a general kind of association with it. This is also true of Examples 20c and 20d:

Example 20(a) and (c): Stephen Foster: My Old Kentucky Home, Good Night *(New York: Firth, Pond & Co., 1853), measures 8-12 and 25-28 (vocal part only); original a half-tone lower. (b) and (d): Louis Moreau Gottschalk:* Columbia, Caprice Américaine *(New York: Firth, Pond & Co., 1860), measures 2-10 and 27-30 (melodic line only).*

A

B

C

Weep no more my la-dy, oh weep no more to - day!

D

marcato il canto

Sometimes Gottschalk's treatment of a source moves beyond arranging. His masterpiece, *Souvenir de Porto Rico,* is based on a Puerto Rican Christmas song, a simple and repetitious melody. Gottschalk's original statement follows:

Example 21: Louis Moreau Gottschalk: Souvenir de Porto Rico, Marche des Gibardos *(Mainz: B. Schott, 1859), measures 17-24.*

Gottschalk employs a theme and variations format for the development of this material. After its initial, hushed appearance, the theme begins a process of slow transformation and careful growth until it reaches its climax (Example 22). This statement is masterful, not only

Example 22: Louis Moreau Gottschalk: Souvenir de Porto Rico, *measures 173-188.*

because it culminates the material that has been stated before and is, simultaneously, a logical outgrowth of it but also because Gottschalk transforms the mode from minor to major at the height of the development and accompanies this change with a metamorphosis, both rhythmic and thematic, of what has taken place earlier. The composition to this point has been one of steady growth, both dynamically and thematically, from a *pianissimo* to the thunderous statement at the climax. A subsidiary theme (functioning as a "chorus") and its development (Examples 23a-c) works in conjunction with the evolution of the main theme, a further indication of Gottschalk's skill in the transformation of material in *Souvenir de Porto Rico*. Once the climax is reached, Gottschalk backtracks in an abbreviated way to the *pianissimo* of the opening bars of the work. This material mirrors the first part of the piece—producing a beautiful arch form. Here Gottschalk overcame his compositional problems

Examples 23a-c: Louis Moreau Gottschalk: Souvenir de Porto Rico,
measures 49-58, 100-108, and 164-172.

C

admirably, and although these strengths are not the rule, *Souvenir de Porto Rico* is not the only instance of such success. Pieces such as *El Cocoyé,* another work that treats already existing themes, also identify Gottschalk as an artist who occasionally rose above his usual standard.

At times Gottschalk wrote compositions that were his own impressions, using original themes. In such cases a note was sometimes inserted at the beginning of the piece to assure the public that the work was not an arrangement. *Suis Moi!* and *O, Ma Charmante, Epargnez Moi!* are both prefaced by an introduction not only by Gottschalk but by the publisher as well. The latter states: "The author in this morceau (which is entirely original) has endeavored to convey an idea of the singular rythm [sic] and charming character, of the music which exists among the Creoles of the Spanish Antilles. Chopin it is well known transferred the national traits of

Poland, to his Mazurkas and Polonaises, and Mr. Gottschalk has endeavored to reproduce in works of an appropriate character, the characteristic traits of the Dances of the West Indias."[39] The fact that these words appeared in the published edition indicates that one of Gottschalk's normal procedures was to arrange rather than to write original music.

In their day Gottschalk's works were very successful. *Le Bananier* was so popular that it was made into various transcriptions, including an arrangement by Offenbach for cello and piano. Bizet performed it as a child. Even in Russia, Borodin had actually written out a copy of *Le Bananier* by hand.[40] Gottschalk's hold on the imaginations of many musicians was so substantial that Filippo Filippi, the dean of Italian critics, was reminded of Gottschalk's music at the 1872 *La Scala* premiere of Verdi's *Aida*.[41]

However, the first biography published after Gottschalk's death, by Mary Alice Ives Seymour, writing under the name Octavia Hensel, a former student and evidently a former mistress, gave the distinct impression that Gottschalk was a shallow, simpering, and foolish man. His music, too, received lamentable attention. Of Gottschalk's *La Gallina*, the authoress gushed: " . . . [it] caused even little children to say, 'oh, hear the chickens pick up corn!'"[42] And by 1883, when Ritter's *Music in America* was published, only one page in a book of over 400 was devoted to Gottschalk. In a chapter entitled "Progress of Instrumental and Vocal Music in New York," Ritter wrote of Gottschalk's one-sidedness and the repetitiousness of his music. "He spent his best force while endeavoring to entertain musically inexperienced and uninspiring audiences,"[43] Ritter wrote, and this negative assessment gradually became generally accepted. Gottschalk was remembered chiefly because of his personality and he was even called, somewhat appropriately, the first of the American matinée idols.[44]

Much of Gottschalk's music, of course, shows that some of the important aspects of composition eluded him. I have mentioned his lack of care with formal matters, and often the proportions of his works create problems. Development and contrasts within the thematic material are not always evident, so that transformations of material are omitted in favor of showers of brilliant yet empty passage work, which function as filler material rather than as a positive structural aspect of the piece. Gottschalk did not always investigate the possibilities of modulatory progression, but rather relied on a few stock procedures that he handled well, but that tend to give an impression of sameness to some of his compositions. He was, in fact, often content to reach an event in the most direct way without prolonging or delaying. Norbert Wiener's observation that "clichés . . . are less illuminating than great poems"[45] is appropriate to Gottschalk's art. Too often he employed the cliché, rather than another, more meaningful method of expression.

The "great poem," however, was not what Gottschalk hoped to achieve. He simply composed, quickly and instinctively. He was too busy traveling and performing to reflect very much about how to delay the climax of a piece, how to achieve a new modulation, or how to relate the formal aspects of his work, although sometimes these things happened as a matter of course. In Roger Sessions' words: "The composer does not ask himself, apropos of what he is doing: 'Is this good,' 'is it beautiful,' or even 'is it interesting'; if he should do so he would be quite off the track. What he is really asking is whether what he is doing is right, in terms of its specific context, which is that of his conception, to which his musical ideas have led him."[46]

Gottschalk's approach to writing, hindered by his lack of intellectual commitment, also suffered because of his own sense of inferiority. He confided to his diary: "There is within me a want of equilibrium between my aspirations and my aptitudes. The former desire to soar toward regions of incomparable sublimity; the latter tend toward the lowest depths of reality, fettering in some way the flight of my aspirations and keeping me prisoner. From that come my lack of confidence in myself and my irritability when I am criticized."[47]

Yet, despite all of its problems, there is something in Gottschalk's music that makes it appealing. The style is so individual, so *original*, that there is seldom any doubt that a piece is Gottschalk's. Gottschalk invested his music with a "special native fiber"—with the tumultuous life and sounds of the cultures he knew personally and evolved these into his own unique musical style. Here lies his ultimate achievement and his music's value.

chapter 3

THE AMERICAN-EUROPEANS

The great young American composer will not appear suddenly out of the West with an immortal masterpiece under his arm. He will come out of a long line of lesser men—half geniuses perhaps, each one of whom in his own way and with his own qualities, will prepare the way for our mature music.
—Aaron Copland, *The New Music*

The American imitations of Europe will always lack interest and vitality, as all derivations do.
—Alfred North Whitehead, *Dialogues*

On July 24, 1838, Ralph Waldo Emerson addressed the literary societies of Dartmouth College on the subject of literary ethics. One of his comments from this lecture has become a classic critique of American gropings toward culture: ". . . the mark of American merit in painting, in sculpture, in poetry, in fiction, in eloquence, seems to be a certain grace without grandeur, and itself not new but derivative, a vase of fair outline, but empty,—which whoso sees, may fill with what wit and character is in him, but which does not, like the charged cloud, overflow with terrible beauty, and emit lightnings on all beholders."[1] The problem of the "empty vase" was *what* should fill it. America was, in a very real sense, searching for an identity in the nineteenth century. As the century progressed, the search became more and more problematic.

In the latter part of the century, America was a country of numerous and confusing crosscurrents. But it was during these years, the "Gilded Age" as Mark Twain called it, that a national identity finally began to emerge. Americans accumulated wealth, and the new materialism laid the foundations for a more secular way of life. Existence was certainly different from the early days in New England, where the church was the central focus of community structure. The United States was entering a secular age where leisure and an appetite for the good things of life would influence the arts as well as other aspects of the American condition.

This new secular emphasis led to a search for sophistication in which European influences on American taste were to be of vital importance. The prejudiced opinions on art, society, and culture of Charles Eliot Norton, a professor of art history at Harvard in the last quarter of the century, had widespread influence. Norton worshiped the Parthenon and deplored the lack of any similar architectural perfection in America. He believed that America's heritage was not suitable for significant cultural experience. To Norton, an Italian sunset was superior to a California sunset because the latter was not infused with history. Norton also noted the aspects of materialism that rapidly were becoming prevalent in America. As he expressed it, Americans were people "seeking material comfort in a brutal way."[2] A large number of Americans who could not accept the possibility of a purely American cultural distinction shared these feelings.

To some, refinement was classicism. Horatio Greenough thought that sculpture must be based on ancient Rome to constitute a significant art. His famous statue of George Washington, clad in a toga, is representative and shows the influence of his Italian training. America's reliance on antiquity has its European parallels: many painters of the mid-nineteenth century in France, for instance, relied mindlessly on classical subjects and on an earlier technical achievement they learned by rote. Paintings of Jean Louis Ernest Meissonier, François Joseph Heim, and Thomas Couture show technical mastery depicting trivial and often insipid ancient themes—as in Couture's *The Romans of Decadence.*

American architecture was also influenced by Europe, in particular by Great Britain in the Georgian and later the Greek Revival styles. By the late nineteenth century, buildings in various styles were appearing in America—Tudor dwellings, Gothic churches, French châteaux, and Italian palazzi. Because the quest for affluence had made some Americans enormously rich, and because such institutions as the income tax had not yet appeared to curtail the accumulation of wealth, the "great" families of America built houses suitable for an American "royalty." In the 1880s and 1890s, George Washington Vanderbilt II built what he hoped would be the finest country estate in America. After purchasing 125,000 acres of land near Asheville, North Carolina, he constructed "Biltmore," a 250-room house reminiscent of the French Renaissance. It was all very grand and all very derivative. The house itself was inspired by some of the great châteaux: Chambord, Chenonceaux, and Blois. Vanderbilt, however, infused this inspiration with his own ideas. In addition, he traveled throughout Europe, purchasing tapestries, statuary, porcelains, paintings, and other items to furnish his estate. The result is impressive, yet not on a standard with the European originals that inspired the American derivation.

In music, too, Americans were searching, and their quest usually led them to Germany to acquire a compositional or even a piano technique based on German principles. Unlike the Yankee tunesmiths, who wrote music in an original style because European study for an eighteenth-century New Englander was unthinkable, the cultivated late nineteenth-century musician could not imagine any possibility other than European preparation. Amy Fay's *Music Study in Germany* documents the experiences of one such American. The final words of the book, ". . . that marvellous and only real home of music—Germany,"[3] simply echoed a popular sentiment, and the American composers of the late nineteenth and early twentieth centuries who accepted this assumption were numerous. Charles Ives, in fact, is the only musician who followed the path of the "First New England School," carving a compositional method at home. The others were European-trained, mostly in Germany.

A number of these late nineteenth- and early twentieth-century composers have been grouped together like the New Englanders of the late eighteenth century by H. Wiley Hitchcock, who has termed them the "Second New England School." These composers have also been known as "Boston Academics" and "Boston Classicists."[4] These last two categories seem inadequate, however, because the music was not exclusively written by "academics," nor was the mind of a "classicist" always at work.

Because not all of the composers of the era fit effectively into these divisions, I will employ the more generalized classification of American-European to describe the Americans of this period who studied in Europe or who wrote in a European manner. This term encompasses a large number of writers including non-New Englanders, non-Bostonians, non-academicians, and non-classicists who in a general sense shared the similar traits of European training or European outlook (which, in this period, is synonymous with German training and outlook) and a conservative approach to composition. The tradition of the American-European is for that matter a long one: John Knowles Paine, one of the earliest of the prominent musicians to fit the mold of an American who adopted European methods after study in Germany, was born in 1839. One of the latest, John Powell, a Virginian whose method, despite many quotations of American sources, was not significantly different from Paine's, died in 1963. Mrs. H. H. A. Beach, George Whitefield Chadwick, Frederick Converse, Edward Burlingame Hill, Edward MacDowell, Daniel Gregory Mason, and a host of others lived in the years between Paine and Powell and wrote from similar assumptions.

There is a difference between these composers and the Americans who went to Europe in the 1920s and 1930s. The Coplands, Thomsons, and Porters studied abroad but returned to write music that did not attempt to transplant European compositional styles. Rather, their music went in other directions, eventually becoming for the most part free of European influences. The earlier composers talked of being Americans, but they were too impressed with the virtues of cultured Europe to escape being predominantly derivative.

The American-Europeans are important, for they produced a solid body of literature. Chadwick composed in all of the major forms, including operas, symphonies, miscellaneous orchestra works, string quartets, a sizable body of choral literature, and over one hundred songs. Because of such creative output a feeling emerged in America that there were distinguished composers at work writing "classical" music. The *Boston Globe* in 1905 called Chadwick's *Symphony No. 3* "the best of all that have been written since Brahms."[5]

Chadwick and many of his contemporaries were thoroughly trained composers who produced works that could at least be compared to their European models. And they were full-time musicians: the professional American artist was emerging.

After the Civil War, an upsurge in publishing brought about a demand for literary works, enabling some men to earn a living entirely by writing. In music, the professional became more common after universities formed music departments, as symphony orchestras established themselves, and as more and more Americans found themselves needing the services of musicians—professional piano teachers, for example. David Stanley Smith's recollection of Horatio Parker's schedule during Parker's years at Yale is revealing, for it shows that Parker was in every sense a professional:

Late Saturday afternoon, choir rehearsal in New York; Sunday, service morning and evening; Monday afternoon and evening in Philadelphia for rehearsals of the Eurydice and Orpheus Clubs; night train to New York, thence to New Haven for two classes on Tuesday; Tuesday evening, by trolley to Derby for a rehearsal of the Derby Choral Club, arriving in New Haven at midnight; Wednesday, a lecture on the History of Music and a class in composition; Thursday, again two classes; Thursday evening, rehearsal of the New Haven Oratorio Society; Friday morning, rehearsal of the New Haven Symphony Orchestra; Saturday, off again for New York. Naturally these rehearsals culminated in frequent concerts. Then there was the inevitable grind of the Dean's office, with conferences and letter-writing.[6]

During Parker's first year of teaching at Yale, he formed what was to become the New Haven Symphony Orchestra. This group, composed of Yale students and members of the New Haven community, presented its first concert in 1895. The program consisted of the *Overture Rosamunde* of Schubert, Bruch's *Concerto in G Minor* op. 26 for violin and orchestra, the *Two Elegiac Melodies* op. 34 of Grieg, and a Haydn symphony. The *New Haven Journal and Courier* reported that "New Haven and Yale now boasts the best symphony orchestra in New England outside of Boston."[7] One year later the same newspaper claimed that the New Haven Symphony was "firmly and permanently established."[8] These accounts suggest the new and frequent ventures that introduced great music to American audiences. And the professional European-trained American musicians were responsible for many of the innovations.

Musicians worked hard, for there was much to be done in America, and at times they were able to enjoy the very American materialism that had helped create their lives as professional musicians. Music could pay handsomely. Horatio Parker had a number of important prizes to his credit, including the two $10,000 awards he won for his operas *Mona* and *Fairyland*. Mrs. H. H. A. Beach's summer house on Cape Cod was bought and paid for entirely from the royalties she received from one song, *Ecstasy* op. 19.

In examining the American-Europeans' music, an obvious characteristic is its derivative nature. The writers worshiped the past, and in a figurative sense their music found expression in Greenough-like works, clad in a pseudoantiquity. Paine wrote music for Sophocles' *Oedipus Tyrannus*. Chadwick returned to the mythology of Greece for many of his compositions, including the symphonic poem *Aphrodite*, inspired by a head of the goddess that Chadwick saw in the Boston Art Museum. The work is preceded in the published score by verses that speak of wandering in the moonlight on a far-off Grecian shore. The evocation is of antiquity and represents a kind of quasi-Greek Revivalism in music.

Other periods, of course, were also consulted by these composers for possible inspiration. The cultivation of medieval sources was evident in Paine's *Azara* and Parker's *Hora Novissima*, and the composers relied in addition on contemporary Europe. Paine wrote a Germanic "Spring" *Symphony* (no. 2, *"Im Frühling"*) that caused musical Boston of 1880 to shout and wave handkerchiefs. John Sullivan Dwight, usually dignified, stood in his seat and opened and closed his umbrella as a sign of approval.[9] Paine's work is remarkably similar to a "Spring" *Symphony* (no. 8, *"Frühlingsklänge"*) composed in 1878 by the German composer Joachim Raff, so Dwight's excitement is understandable. The venerable critic must have been thrilled by the fact that a Germanic symphony composed by an American had come to Boston.

Another characteristic of much of this music is its often bombastic and pedantic quality. Alexis de Tocqueville, visiting the United States in the 1830s, had noted the bombastic style typical of American speakers and writers.[10] This "inflated" quality was a characteristic of much of the music produced by the Americans and was a typical late nineteenth-century characteristic as well. Music, in a figurative sense, sprawled in as many directions as George W. Vanderbilt's "Biltmore," Thoreau's journals, or Whittier's poems. But from the many "directions" there are two binding forces that make the music a coherent group of works: European influence and conservatism.

The work of John Knowles Paine illustrates both forces. It has been said that ". . . as a creative artist he was something of a pedant, . . ."[11] and many of his works have a certain pedantic quality. One of these is a piece with the promising title *Fuga Giocosa* (1884). Paine's subject is excellent and American with its allusion to "Over the fence is out:"[12]

Example 24: John Knowles Paine: Fuga Giocosa *op. 41 no. 3 (Boston: A. P. Schmidt, 1884), measures 1-4.*

But the treatment is dull, stodgy, and—well, pedantic. There are numerous sequences and other stock procedures, among them these lifeless passages:

Example 25a-b: John Knowles Paine: Fuga Giocosa *op. 41 no. 3, measures 21-27 and 61-68.*

A

B

This is a fugue in which the possibilities of the material are not imaginatively realized. Paine relies on contrapuntal clichés to achieve a result that is anything but *giocosa*. It is an American work, for it is by an American. Its subject is even American in character. The style of the rest, however, is European, and inferior European. The coda is reminiscent of passages from Brahms's *Sonata* op. 1, not one of that composer's strongest utterances. The piece is an effective example of the derivative and conservative American-European style.

The mixture of periods and of pasts is evident in another work, John Powell's *Sonate Noble* op. 21, published by G. Schirmer in 1921 at the time Schirmer was printing privately Charles Ives's *"Concord"* Sonata. Powell's work follows a four-movement plan that the composers of the late eighteenth century found useful. His style is reminiscent here of Brahms' Vienna, there of a Virginia plantation, and elsewhere of Appalachia. The title page quotes Sidney Lanier's "The Symphony":

> Vainly might Plato's head revolve it,
> Plainly the heart of a child could solve it.

The sonata form of the first movement is straightforward, Brahmsian, yet somehow unimaginative despite excellent material. The theme and variations that form the second movement suffer both

Plate 4: John Knowles Paine: opening of Fugue op. 15 no. 3 (manuscript). By permission of the Houghton Library, Harvard University.

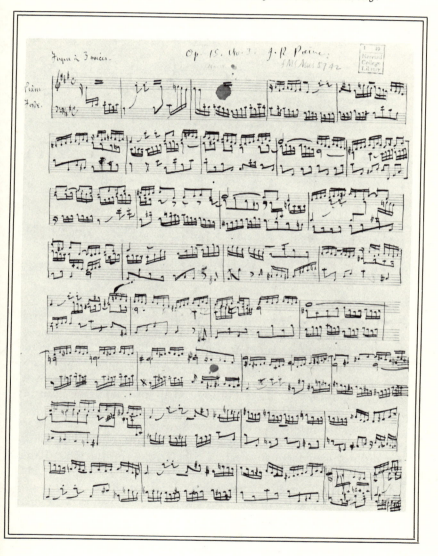

because of the theme and because of its treatment. But the opening of the minuet is promising, with its folkish overtones:

Example 26: John Powell: Sonate Noble op. 21, Minuetto, measures 1-19. Copyright © 1921 G. Schirmer, Inc. Used by permission.

Soon, however, the style returns to Europe, to Vienna (where Powell had studied composition and piano). The concluding rondo is classical in its proportions and in its textures. The piece was written some years after Paine's fugue, yet remains conceptually similar and represents a further example of the American-European approach. Both composers only leave Europe for an instant: Paine with his fugue subject, Powell with the first section of his minuet.

The central problem with these works is that their composers were earnest but limited musicians who thought, but whose thinking did not lead them to original conclusions. In the 1880s Paine wrote a *Nocturne* à la Chopin (with a few hints of Field, Schumann, and Liszt), and Powell composed an orchestral work, *Natchez-on-the-Hill*, which was the music of the late nineteenth century, written in 1931. Always these musicians searched for a "usable past," as Van Wyck Brooks has called it, but the way the past was employed left the result *in* the past and lacking any real distinction.

The American-Europeans were noble men and women. Parker wrote in his diary: "Every man should contribute to the advancement of the human race, should train himself carefully for work, should do some thing better than it has ever been done before. . . ."[13] Unfortunately, Parker and most of his contemporaries were not equipped to do things better than ever before. They were still so confined by imitation and analogue that they could not yet think of evolving their own language; thus the distinction that was always a potentiality never really occurred, and they merely copied the romanticism of an earlier period. For European music in the last years of the nineteenth century began moving in directions that many American composers found impossible to comprehend. As Stravinsky and Schönberg contributed to the complexity of music, the conservative Americans became increasingly puzzled. The pianist Josef Hofmann wrote to Daniel Gregory Mason on July 25, 1918, about "the restlessness and discontent in music of the present day" (undoubtedly referring to the music of the avant-garde composers of the time) as being an unhealthy sign. Hofmann wondered if the musical climate would improve after the war. In his memoirs, Mason later glossed this passage by commenting that it was impossible to realize in 1918 how much worse musical matters would become.[14]

Mason wrote that American music is ". . . a sturdy offshoot of the great tree of European music. . .,"[15] yet he must have wondered where European music itself was going. He entered a work in the Pittsfield, Massachusetts, Festival in the early 1920s but the prize was won by Schönberg. *Music in My Time*, Mason's memoirs, contains passages showing that, for him, Schönberg's writing was incomprehensible, and expressing his irritation that Schönberg's "modern" work had won the award.[16] Mason did not believe that Schönberg and Hindemith could replace composers such as Schubert and Schumann. Music, Mason complained, had lost its sincerity and even its vitality.[17]

Like their avant-garde contemporaries, many of the conservative Americans suffered from what they felt was a misunderstanding on the part of the public. The neglect of Charles Ives in the first part of the twentieth century is well known. Audiences did not hear Ives's music because it was too difficult to be performed by most musicians of the time. (And audiences probably would have had difficulty understanding it anyway.) But unbelievably the conservatives were misunderstood, too. When John Powell played some of Mason's piano pieces at Carnegie Hall, he warned the composer not to worry if they didn't appeal to the audience. In contending that ". . . there is no real musical public, and . . . current fashions are all against music like yours,"[18] Powell reflected the complaints that a Stravinsky and a Schönberg would have had about the public's reaction to their music.

Mason lauds the conductor and pianist Ossip Gabrilowitsch's distaste of ". . . the ugliness of Schönberg, the wordliness of Strauss, the barbarism of Stravinsky. Above all he [Gabrilowitsch] made no pretense of any interest in the smart-Aleck cynicism so unescapable in the music that followed the war."[19] The new music, quite simply, was not understood by composers who worshiped the past, lamented the death of Brahms, and deplored the emergence of the musical language of a new century. These problems and misunderstandings were partly a result of the cultural climate in America at the time, for the influences and crosscurrents were many, and the "search" for a cultural identity resulted in chaos in some circles and order in others, and a lack of communication between the two. This climate helps explain some of the confusing aspects of American composers' music: despite the seemingly ordered lives and earnest efforts of the American-Europeans, their music is actually as confusing in its way as the works of the revolutionaries.

Edward MacDowell (1861-1908), who had one of the finest compositional techniques of the Americans writing in a European manner, is a case in point. In his day, and for decades after his death, MacDowell enjoyed an enormous reputation; critics held that America had finally produced a great artist. Henry T. Finck found MacDowell in some ways superior to Brahms, as these words from his memoir of 1926 indicate:

I find more original melody in MacDowell's songs as a whole than in the more numerous ones of Brahms; and in his piano pieces the American leaves the German so far behind that you can hardly see him.[20]

Lawrence Gilman's excited account of MacDowell's genius saw the music in a singular light:

His [MacDowell's] music is characterised by great buoyancy and freshness, by an abounding vitality, by a constantly juxtaposed tenderness and strength, by a pervading nobility of tone and feeling. It is charged with emotion, yet it is not brooding or hectic, and it is seldom intricate or recondite in its psychology. It is music curiously free from the fevers of sex. And here I do not wish to be misunderstood. This music is anything but androgynous. It is always virile, often passionate, and, in its intensest moments, full of force and vigour. But the sexual impulse which underlies it is singularly fine, strong, and controlled.[21]

Gilman's comments show that music-making had to be reinforced as a masculine expression in an age when composing was not considered as virile a profession as banking. And the statement might seem curious to those whose familiarity with MacDowell is based on *To a Wild Rose*, *To a Water Lily*, and the other miniatures for which he became famous. This other side of the composer is analyzed by Paul Rosenfeld:

The feelings entertained about life by him seem to have remained uncertain; and while fumbling for them he seems regularly to have succumbed to "nice" and "respectable" emotions, conventional, accepted by and welcome to, the best people. It is shocking to find how full of vague poesy he is.[22]

MacDowell's works represent the problems serious music in America faced at the turn of the century. Not surprisingly, he had lived in Europe, for the most part in Germany, from the age of fifteen until he was twenty-seven. Because he spent his early life sheltered by an upper middle-class New York family and lived in Europe before returning to America—to Boston—which Dwight, Paine, and others had molded into a German province of sorts, it is not surprising that MacDowell's music is stylistically European despite folksy titles that make some of his pieces American at least in name. Like his contemporaries, MacDowell was away from the mainstream of American life, and like them he had a busy schedule, teaching at Columbia for some years, touring as a pianist, working with private students, and composing.

MacDowell's early works are large-scaled romantic compositions in the grand manner of Liszt. The *Concerto No. 2* for piano and orchestra, especially, is written with a sure hand and demonstrates a fine compositional technique. With early works such as these, MacDowell should have reached a significant maturity. Yet this did not happen. His compositions grew smaller in size and simpler in conception, and he wrote no orchestral works after 1896.

MacDowell had misgivings about his own music. To visitors at the MacDowell summer place in Peterboro, New Hampshire, he once said: "I am going to the cabin to write some of my rotten melodies!" When he found that Teresa Carreño was playing one of his early works, the *Concert-Etude* op. 36, he sent her a telegram: "Don't put that dreadful thing on your programme."[23] MacDowell's mental collapse and early death (at age forty-six) were tragedies. His works, however, had dwindled from the impressive early efforts to small sentimental compositions suitable for the salon. Health problems certainly contributed to MacDowell's decline. Yet we might also speculate that MacDowell realized, perhaps unconsciously, that his kind of writing, the romantic gesture, was a dead end. The American-Europeans in general suggest the declining romantic style of Europe rather than the development of a cultivated tradition on which America's musical maturity could be built.

But these questions and speculations are part of the confusion surrounding the "Gilded Age" itself. America was moving in several directions. The staid, square music of the Paines and Powells is representative of an era that in music continued long after the "Gilded Age" had officially ended. Alexis de Tocqueville's observations in the early nineteenth century about the fine arts in America refer to artists who, "unable any longer to conceive greatness, . . . try for elegance and prettiness. Appearance counts for more than reality."[24] These words describe much of the music of the Americans who went to Europe and returned to write cultivated, conservative music. Yet through these musicians America was developing a compositional technique.

chapter 4

CHARLES TOMLINSON GRIFFES

And, like a yellow silken scarf,
The thick fogs hangs along the quay.
—Oscar Wilde, "Symphony in Yellow"

Although Charles T. Griffes lived when the American-European style was at its height, he achieved original solutions to musical problems. His compositional method can best be described as eclectic, employing various sources that synthesize into a unique music. Eclecticism was a possibility for musicians who were searching for an American style; it differed from the Germanic approach that dominated most of America's cultivated musical tradition at the turn of the twentieth century.[1] American painters at this time were borrowing from various other styles, and the artist William Merritt Chase exemplifies an eclectic approach in art. To some critics this eclecticism constituted the American style in painting in the late nineteenth century.[2] The same can be said of America's original, non-Germanic music of the early twentieth century, including the works of Griffes and of Charles Ives.

Griffes was born in 1884, when John Knowles Paine was being praised for his Germanic symphonies, and died in 1920, at about the time John Powell and Daniel Gregory Mason were deploring the "terrible" music of Stravinsky and Schönberg. Griffes' early life was spent in Elmira, New York, and he was graduated from Elmira Academy in 1903. During these years he studied with Mary Selma

Broughton, who became one of his greatest supporters during his brief career. After graduation from the academy, Griffes went to Germany, in the accepted manner, where he studied with a number of teachers, including about a dozen lessons in composition with Englebert Humperdinck. Griffes returned to the United States in 1907 and accepted a position at the Hackley School in Tarrytown, New York. He taught music at the boys' preparatory school, composed, and shuttled back and forth between Hackley and New York City, which was the center of his musical activities. His early death of empyema, in April 1920, was a tragedy for American music.

In the last months of his life, Griffes began to receive recognition for his music. His symphonic poem, *The Pleasure-Dome of Kubla Khan,* was played by the Boston Symphony Orchestra on several occasions late in 1919, including an enthusiastically received performance at Carnegie Hall. The New York Symphony and the eminent flutist George Barrère had performed his *Poem for Flute and Orchestra* at about the same time, again with positive results, and the Philadelphia Orchestra played four of Griffes' works shortly thereafter. Griffes' music for the dance pantomime *Sho-Jo* was performed as an orchestral work by the Cleveland Orchestra in February 1920. At the same time his songs were being included on various programs, and his *Sonata* for piano was arousing the interest of a number of pianists. G. Schirmer, the most important American music publisher, was issuing some of his compositions, and had been doing so since 1909. Griffes was gaining an important reputation in the final years of his life; yet after his death his works were curiously neglected. Even now, although his music has been catalogued authoritatively, the one full-length biography of Griffes is less than satisfactory.[3] Two of his most visionary works, *Sho-Jo* and *The Kairn of Koridwen,* have never been published. At this point many of Griffes' published compositions are out of print, and the current Griffes discography is modest. The most discouraging factor is that his music is performed only occasionally. Griffes' works are a distinguished contribution to American music; their neglect is unfortunate.

Griffes began with his contemporaries, in the world of late nineteenth-century German composition. His first published songs, in the style of Wolf, Brahms, or Strauss, were composed using German texts. These early works, which comprise a "first period," gave way to a "second period" of impressionism that stemmed from Debussy and Ravel. Ravel's *Jeux d'eau,* in particular, had made a great impression on Griffes early in his career, and this influence may be seen in such pieces as *The Fountain of the Acqua Paola* from *Roman Sketches.* Because so much of his music falls into this "second period," Griffes was remembered for many years chiefly as an impressionist. A related interest was the music of the Orient, and this influence may be found in some of Griffes' works. In the "third period," his style became much more experimental, bearing a resemblance in some ways to Stravinsky and Scriabin, but in most respects becoming a synthesis of numerous elements—German, impressionistic, Oriental—into a striking, original style.

The music represents a logical growth on Griffes' part. He undoubtedly realized that German music, which had been important for so long, and which was of such great consequence to his American and European contemporaries, was a style that could not renew itself. By 1900 so much had been said so profoundly that the late and in some ways decadent examples of the romantic style hardly represented a positive method of writing for one as sensitive as Griffes. His music in a quasi-German style consists of intimate *Lieder,* where even a composer such as Richard Strauss could work on a modest scale. And Griffes' impressionism was never a strictly French one, although like Debussy, he was "more interested in tints than in solid colors."[4] But Griffes' expression was his own impressionism, evolving from German influences as well as from his acquaintance with the French impressionists. His final works went even further from his earlier models. Rudolph Ganz said that the *Sonata* for piano ". . . . is free from all foreign influences,"[5] an assertion that would have been difficult to make concerning the music of Griffes' American predecessors and contemporaries.

Griffes' mature style includes characteristics that differ markedly from those of his contemporaries. The sweeping gestures and enormous thrust that may be found in much of his music are romantic traits, as is his frequent use of chromatic harmonic language. Sevenths, ninths, and elevenths are a part of Griffes' harmonic structures. There are passages of bitonality, a song cycle based predominantly on whole tone and pentatonic scales, and a *rāga*-like construction which Griffes employs in the *Sonata*. There are also "static" harmonies and ostinatos, two of the most frequently employed techniques of the composer.

Griffes' melodic structures are complex in the later pieces, with winding tunes that are made up of small intervals encompassing a large range. The rhythmic constructions are flexible, with irregular phrasings and complex cross rhythms that sometimes give the music a strong rhythmic profile, and at other times a nebulous one. Griffes' music shows a mastery of form, which is evident even in his earliest songs. Some works employ a free treatment of formal elements in a rhapsodic manner, the *Barcarolle* and *Scherzo* from the *Fantasy Pieces* being examples. The use of ternary structures may be seen in the *Three Tone-Pictures* or in the song *Symphony in Yellow*. The *Roman Sketches* could best be described as examples of "arch" form, for in each case the composer works into the central part of the piece and then out again. The *Sonata* contains a fine example of sonata form, and the *Poem for Flute and Orchestra* is evidence that Griffes was able to manipulate the material of a rondo in a masterful and unusual way.

The compositions of Griffes display an excellent contrapuntal technique that in most cases is more subtle than the counterpoint that characterizes the opening of the last movement of the piano *Sonata*. When Griffes is working within a homophonic framework, he is seldom content to revert to obvious solutions of texture.

Griffes' orchestration is original and expert, and the sonorities of his instrumental combinations are remarkable. He wrote for such "new" elements as orchestral piano, integrating it effectively into the general orchestral texture. The opening of *The Pleasure-Dome of Kubla Khan* is an example of Griffes' effective writing for orchestral piano. But the other elements in this passage—the divided violoncellos and double basses playing *sul ponticello*, the bass drum and the gong (kept vibrating by friction on the edge), and the trombones—create a combination of instruments and a resulting unique orchestral sound unlike that of any other American work composed prior to 1920. In most of his orchestral works, in fact, the combination of instruments produces singular results. *The Kairn of Koridwen* is scored for an ensemble of flute, two clarinets, two horns, harp, celeste, and piano, recalling some of the instrumental combinations Stravinsky was employing in such works as *L'Histoire du Soldat*, which was composed at about the same time as Griffes' work. Another aspect of Griffes' orchestration is his reliance on instruments other than the violin. Marian Bauer has provided an explanation for this characteristic. When Bauer asked the composer why he employed the violin so infrequently, he replied: ". . . I dislike the violin. I never use it even in my orchestral scores any more than I have to, and I would not want to write for it as a solo instrument."[6]

Griffes, in fact, approached composition in a fresh, new way. Even in his earliest songs, there is evidence of an original mind at work. One of the finest of these is *Auf geheimem Waldespfade*, a realization of Lenau's poem representative of the late nineteenth-century *Lied*. The purely accompanimental nature of the piano part is Brahmsian, and some of the melodic and harmonic turns are reminiscent of Richard Strauss. Yet there are certain characteristics that foreshadow Griffes' later compositional style, among them the opening chords, with their added sixths and statements of the minor dominant. The harmonic structure of the fifth and sixth measures is

Example 27: Charles T. Griffes: Auf geheimem Waldespfade, *measures 1-9; original a whole-tone lower. Copyright © 1909 G. Shirmer, Inc. Used by permission.*

(ex. 27 cont.)

also characteristic of Griffes' later style: the chromatic movement in the piano part and the enharmonic change in the vocal line bring about a smooth progression to the "climax" of the first section of the piece, but a climax that is stated in dynamic terms of *piano* and *pianissimo!* This moment (measure 8) is a $\frac{6}{4}$ chord, a device that gave such composers as Richard Strauss and Anton Bruckner many a climactic moment. In Griffes' case, a $\frac{6}{4}$ construction occurs at exactly the same point in the other two "verses" of the poem, helping to achieve a tightness of form.

Another passage that gives strength to this work is the beautiful harmonic change that ushers in the third verse (Example 28). The first measure of the example is the familiar $\frac{6}{4}$. The harmony introducing the words *"und ich mein' . . ."* is another $\frac{6}{4}$ construction, and the following chromatic progression is a typical late nineteenth-century gesture. But something exquisite happens during these measures that is surprising from a technical standpoint because of the previous $\frac{6}{4}$: one would not expect the two similar harmonies to be so near to each other. These few unconventional movements help to rationalize the return to a more conventional ending, which at the same time echoes the beginning of the piece.

Example 28: Charles T. Griffes: Auf geheimem Waldespfade, *measures 17-21.*

The achievement of *Auf geheimem Waldespfade* is considerable. Working within a homophonic framework, using a limited means, the composer achieves a number of meaningful gestures, which are always moving to a goal. And effectively, this process does not always take place in the same manner. For example, the middle section of the song consists of seven measures of pedal point on B-flat (measures 8-14) prolonging the progress to the conclusion of the second verse, suspending it in a beautiful and unresolved harmonic world. The progressions of the outer two sections work differently, with more frequent harmonic changes. The fact that events are reached in different ways is one indication of the song's strength and musical achievement. It is Germanic, certainly, but despite its style it emerges as a strong work with hints of an originality to come.

Griffes' "suspension" of musical elements is evident in *The Lake at Evening* and *The Vale of Dreams* from *Three Tone-Pictures* for piano, works in which Griffes' originality is becoming more pro-

nounced. These pieces, like so many of Griffes' compositions, exist
in a world far removed from reality, even in what might be termed
an "imaginary space," if the suggestive qualities of the music are
considered. From an analytical standpoint, this characteristic can
be confirmed by an examination of *The Lake at Evening.* A pedal
point on A gives a firm reference to the main tonality of the piece.
It progresses to a pedal point on B, which in turn paves the way for
the climax of the work, before subsiding to the original A again,
binding the work together as a typical ternary form. However, it is
what *surrounds* these pedal points that makes the music so "suspended"—so unresolved. One would think that there would be a
harmonic stagnancy and a lack of any firm direction with continuous pedal points, but this is not the case. In the outer sections of
the piece the A is always there, yet the harmony rarely places the
work within the framework of a tonic chord. Griffes uses a $\frac{6}{4}$ construction to avoid a confrontation with a simple A major chord,
much as he added a sixth to the first chord of *Auf geheimem Waldespfade.*

In *The Lake at Evening,* there are also augmented constructions
that figure prominently in many of Griffes' compositions. In addition to these unresolved chords, the rhythmic ostinato also suspends
the work in a strange unmoving musical world not unlike that of

Example 29: Charles T. Griffes: The Lake at Evening *op. 5 no. 1 from*
Three Tone-Pictures, *measures 1-10. Copyright © 1915 G. Schirmer,
Inc. Used by permission.*

Ravel's *Le Gibet* from *Gaspard de la Nuit.* The result of all of these technical elements is that harmonies, rhythms, and musical material in general help in achieving an effective impression of a lake at evening, and of stillness. The eminent critic James Gibbons Huneker called Griffes a "fantasist,"[7] and with good reason: much of his music seems to exist in a faraway, mystical world.

Another fascinating aspect of Griffes' music is the fact that despite the high levels of dissonance in some of the pieces, the *effect* is not always one of dissonance. Ernest Hutcheson once pointed out to Griffes "that *The Vale of Dreams* didn't have a single concord until the last note,"[8] and even the last chord is a $\frac{6}{4}$ that leaves the work curiously unresolved. And yet the concluding gesture of the piece gives the effect of a true resolution, and the pages of dissonance that have preceded it display a curious kind of consonance from the standpoint of the way they are perceived, despite the fact that technically they are dissonant constructions. It is to Griffes' credit that he was able to blur the two distinctions of consonance and dissonance, at least as they affect a listener's response to the music.

This blurring of distinctions, an almost mysterious quality in Griffes' music, is evident in many aspects of his art. It has been noted that his rhythms can be either straightforward or nebulous. Early critics complained about this, among them William Treat Upton, who contended that, had Griffes lived, his music might have developed "in the direction of an ever increasing wholesome rhythmic vitality. . . ."[9] A passage that Upton felt lacked this secure rhythmic quality may be found in the song *Thy Dark Eyes to Mine,* where Griffes establishes a steady triplet motion stated against syncopated duplets, creating a series of gentle cross rhythms. Example 30, a passage that evolves out of these triplets, which Upton called "vague,"[10] creates an illusion of nebulousness. In reality, the rhythmic structure is important for the effect Griffes is seeking. The motion in these measures is pointed toward the word *kiss,* and the cross rhythms, particularly in the first two measures, help to bring about a rhythmic "sweep" to the top of the phrase (although the vocal and piano parts give the effect of reaching a climax at different times, a further indication of the conceptual range of the passage). Another example of Griffes' rhythmic complexity may be

Example 30: Charles T. Griffes: Thy Dark Eyes to Mine *op. 11 no. 2*
from Three Poems of Fiona MacLeod, *measures 16-19. Copyright* ©
1918 G. Schirmer, Inc. Used by permission.

found in the *Sonata*. Once again, the cross rhythms create a complicated rhythmic structure; but each elaboration of this density is
important for the sweeping effect Griffes desires.

Example 31: Charles T. Griffes: Sonata, *measures 25-26. Copyright* ©
1921 G. Schirmer, Inc. Used by permission.

These visionary pieces confused Griffes' contemporaries. *WaiKiki*,
for example, was an "enigma" to William Treat Upton, who complained of the unvocal melodic line and the "uncouth" character of

Plate 5: Charles Tomlinson Griffes: final measures of **The White Peacock** (manuscript, with original ending followed by the composer's revision). Music Division, Library of Congress.

much of the harmonization. *Phantoms* was another abstruse piece
for Upton, who wrote that it was: "farfetched, difficult out of all
proportion to its value, [and] it seems—at least to me—a veritable
tonal nightmare."[11] The critic also complained that Griffes' work
never seemed settled in matters of melody and harmonic background.[12] And by the standards of the day it was not, except to
those few who were aware that difficult melodies, harmonies, and
rhythms were characteristics that created the Griffes originality
and effectiveness.

Part of this effectiveness results from Griffes' developmental
process—for his material usually evolves in meaningful ways. Sometimes it is a simple kind of procedure, as in *The White Peacock*,
where the opening gesture (Example 32a) becomes the final moment
of the piece, transformed and developed (Example 32c).

Example 32a: Charles T. Griffes: The White Peacock *op. 7 no. 1 from*
Roman Sketches, *opening. Copyright © 1917 G. Schirmer, Inc. Used
by permission.*

Example 32b: Charles T. Griffes: The White Peacock *(original ending,
after the Library of Congress manuscript).*

Example 32c: Charles T. Griffes: The White Peacock *(revised ending).*

Griffes' original ending (Example 32b) is more of a cadence in the conventional sense. But the composer realized that a finer effect was achieved by relating the last measures to the opening, creating both a sense of unity and a feeling of nebulousness in the unresolved conclusion. This relationship is actually a simple one. In the *Sonata* the evolution of material is more complex. Gilbert Chase has identified the source of the work: a scale with Oriental overtones, used like a *rāga* (Example 33a). All the material of the *Sonata* is derived from this source, and the intervals that form the "scale" create tritones and augmented intervals that are important in the melodic and harmonic evolution. Example 33b is an indication of the harmonic language of the *Sonata*. Every note of the work can be related to the source, an indication of the tightness of the material:

Example 33a: "Rāga." Adapted from Gilbert Chase, America's Music, 1st ed. (New York: McGraw Hill Book Company, 1955), p. 520.

Example 33b: Charles T. Griffes: Sonata, *measures 8-11.*

There are other examples of Griffes' unusual ability in employing his eclectic sources masterfully. The first of the *Two Sketches Based on Indian Themes* employs a farewell song of the Chippewa Indians, which Griffes uses in a setting for string quartet. *Five Poems of*

Ancient China and Japan employ five- and six-note scales effectively. *Sakura-Sakura* is a harmonization of a Japanese "cherry dance." Griffes also orchestrated a Japanese or Javanese lullaby, *Komori Uta.* The quasi-Orientalism of these pieces is also found in *The Pleasure-Dome of Kubla Khan,* with its winding melodies and lush orchestral sonorities. The *Poem for Flute and Orchestra* also has Oriental overtones, and in this work Griffes' eclectic approach is especially masterful.

Griffes had another important compositional strength—an ability to make something important *happen* in a piece of music. *La Fuite de la Lune,* a song based on a poem of Oscar Wilde, is an example. The poem follows:

> To outer senses there is peace,
> A dreamy peace on either hand,
> Deep silence in the shadowy land,
> Deep silence where the shadows cease.
>
> Save for a cry that echoes shrill,
> From some lone bird disconsolate;
> A corn crake calling to its mate;
> The answer from the misty hill.
>
> And suddenly the moon withdraws
> Her sickle from the light'ning skies,
> And to her sombre cavern flies,
> Wrapped in a veil of yellow gauze.

Any composer sensitive to the effective setting of words would note immediately that the first two verses of the poem suggest one kind of musical treatment, reminiscent of peace, silence, and mist. The moon's disappearance suggests another kind of music, and the problem is how to reconcile the two moods. Griffes' solution is to treat the first two verses (especially the second) as static entities. The music is suspended in Griffes' familiar "space," and the depiction of the words in musical terms is effective. His real mastery is evident in the transition between the second and third verses of the poem, a musical depiction of the moon's disappearance (Example 34). This is the moment that makes the piece "work," and the early static moments can be seen as a prelude to this particular event. Griffes' setting of the final line of the poem returns to the atmosphere of the beginning of the song, much as the final moments of *Auf geheimem Waldespfade* and *The White Peacock* make allusions to the beginnings of these works.

Example 34: Charles T. Griffes: La Fuite de la Lune op. 3 no. 1, measures 24-30. Copyright © 1915 G. Schirmer, Inc. Used by permission.

The *Sonata* is another composition that builds to an important event, in this case the positively ferocious conclusion of the work. The power of those measures is not surprising in view of the vigorous opening of the *Sonata*. Griffes, however, seldom approaches an event in the most direct way. In this work the excursions and detours, the powerful sections verging on violence and the moments of calm and outer tranquility lead to the final *apothéose*, creating a memorable experience for the listener. The same may be said of many of Griffes' works, for they possess elements that make them important musical entities: unity, variety, originality, suspense, surprise, and so many qualities common to great music.

In dealing with Griffes, we must consider his music's emotional impact, and here the composer leaves some listeners less than satisfied. Aaron Copland has noted that although many of his contemporaries sought refuge in academic institutions, Griffes escaped to an ivory tower.[13] This tower is reminiscent at times of the lines

from Samuel Taylor Coleridge's *Kubla Khan*, which was the inspiration for Griffes' *Pleasure-Dome:*

> It was a miracle of rare device,
> A sunny pleasure-dome with caves of ice!

Griffes' music may be beautifully written and may display the attributes of a sound construction. Yet the musical expression is a
cold tower to some listeners, despite the obvious passion of *Evening
Song*, the exuberance of *We'll To the Woods, and Gather May*, and
the intensity of emotions in the songs set to the poetry of Fiona
MacLeod. One of the composer's colleagues at Hackley expressed a
feeling concerning Griffes at the piano: ". . . he always left me completely cold. I was filled with utmost admiration for his utter *skill*
but he never reached my heart. . . . He seemed to me always a man
of intellect, living in an inner world of thought."[14]
    The same may be said of the effect of the composer's music, for
Griffes' singular expression is not the kind that will appeal to every
musician or audience. Griffes' biographer's comment that the *Sonata*
is "more generally respected than understood, and with a greater
reputation than audience," is true of Griffes' music in general.[15] On
the surface, Griffes' art *is* difficult to understand, and it does not
appeal to everyone. It is a paradox in so many ways: the pages of
dissonance that do not sound particularly harsh, the stretches of
static harmonies that still achieve direction, the musical gestures
that sound remote to some listeners and emotional to others. For
the right individual, however, Griffes' music is an important experience, and the ivory tower an inviting one. There is the possibility
that the Griffes dichotomy stems from the composer's eclectic approach and the singular musical language that resulted from his
method. This is the problem of Griffes' music, but also its reward: a
final dichotomy.
    Wilfrid Mellers sees Griffes in his final years as a case similar to
Hart Crane and Thomas Wolfe: "men of extreme nervous sensitivity
who also wore themselves out in youth: who uttered a yell of desperation because, opposed to the industrial society they lived in,
they were imprisoned within their own senses, as Griffes is imprisoned within his raga-chord."[16] The "raga-chord" of the Griffes
Sonata is not a stifling element for the composer, however, who

uses it effectively and far beyond what could be expected of it. Nor can it be said with any certainty that his "yell" is a cry of desperation. Just as one can dispute the assertion that Crane and Wolfe were "imprisoned" within their senses, so is Mellers' gloomy and exaggerated portrait of Griffes questionable.

Griffes may have been on the verge of greatness, as H. Wiley Hitchcock suggests,[17] but in actuality some of this greatness had been achieved already. One can lament the fact that Griffes would have written so much more had he lived, as Upton asserts in his 1923 study of the Griffes songs,[18] but it is possible to think of numerous composers who died prematurely. What a composer produces is important, not what he might have produced.

What is unfortunate is that Griffes' work at Hackley gave him only a limited time to compose. His correspondence is full of references to teaching and how it bored him. Unlike some of the composers who found themselves in the intellectual climate of a university, Griffes was not satisfied by the unchallenging position at the boys' preparatory school. His piano students there were not stimulating, and Griffes' required attendance at chapels and assemblies as a hymn player was annoying to him. The dates attached to some of his compositions suggest that his position probably hindered his composing. A notation on the *Sonata*—December 1917-January 1918—is revealing, for it suggests that Griffes wrote most of the work during the Christmas holiday when he was away for at least a few weeks from the drudgery of teaching.

Griffes was above all a sensitive man who, in addition to his music, was an artist, working with pen and ink and with watercolors. He was interested in photography; he did etchings in copper. He loved yellow and orange: flowers, fruit, draperies, porcelain, and sunsets.[19] This helps explain his preoccupation with the poetry of Oscar Wilde: *La Mer, Le Réveillon, Impression du Matin,* and *La Fuite de la Lune,* all of which Griffes set to music, contain references to yellow, and Griffes' setting of Wilde's *Symphony in Yellow* is his most famous and certainly one of his best-written songs. This sensitive composer is responsible for a significant body of music. John Tasker Howard has put it well: "It is such as he, great or small, who make for the advancement of art and of science."[20] For an American musician in the first years of the twentieth century, this is a notable achievement.

chapter 5

CHARLES EDWARD IVES

It takes two to speak the truth,—one to speak, and another to hear.

> —Henry David Thoreau, *A Week on the Concord and Merrimack Rivers*

Vom Plattenspieler kommt Musik aus Neuengland
Eine sanfte Tonmalerei
Mit Kirchenglocken Militärmarsch Tanz
Der ausgegrabene Charles Ives
Als er lebte kannte ihn keiner.*

> —Marie Luise Kaschnitz, "Märzschnee in München"

Charles Ives wrote his music at the height of the American-European enthusiasm. But unlike other composers of his time, Ives studied in the United States, receiving a musical training that reflected two approaches: the Yankee tunesmith method, suggested by his father, and the German method, related to him by Horatio Parker. This eclectic preparation resulted in a new music, little understood in its time, but ultimately of far-reaching consequence.

---

*On the record player music from New England
A gentle tone poem
With church bells military-march and dance
Charles Ives exhumed
When he was alive nobody knew him.

To some critics Ives is representative of his time—a New England
Protestant; a champion of the masses; a rugged Teddy Roosevelt; a
product of nineteenth-century America. One critic has contended
that Ives was deeply committed to the genteel middle-class life of
his time and his social class.[1] To others Ives was a visionary who
somehow rose above his background, or who *evolved* from it an
existence far removed from the general American life, developing
in the process a transcendental musical language. Although Ives's
music has enjoyed positive criticism in recent years, there are still
those who find that as a composer he was less than the complete
artist. Virgil Thomson has contended that Ives's music will be survived by that of MacDowell![2]

There is, however, much to substantiate the opinion that Ives is a
major composer. Ives, the man, is full of contradictions, and his
music is often contradictory. Yet these discrepancies are an essential
part of a singular musical expression that makes Ives the culmination of the years of preparation and the decades of half-geniuses
that were a necessary part of the American musical evolution.

Ives is a product of what Van Wyck Brooks has called New England's "Indian Summer." It was a time when numerous schools of
thought were contributing to a flowering culture. Transcendentalists,
Platonists, Hegelians, pragmatists, mesmerists, and Christian
Scientists were all a part of this renaissance, and such fields as psychology were a further source of enlightenment. Ives's music, another product of the New England thinking of the time, encompasses ideas that go beyond the narrow confines of the music itself,
creating relationships with many "nonmusical" concepts and disciplines.

Ives's philosophy, then, is a result of a number of New England
philosophies, in particular transcendentalism, an offshoot of Unitarianism. New England transcendentalists believed that all things
are interrelated. Thus, God, man, and nature are in a close association. This concept, the Over-Soul as Emerson termed it, was an
important aspect of transcendental thinking. In his first series of
Essays, Emerson wrote of ". . . that Unity, that Over-Soul, within
which every man's particular being is contained and made one with
all other." He continued: "We live in succession, in division, in parts,
in particles. Meantime within man is the soul of the whole; the wise

silence; the universal beauty, to which every part and particle is equally related; the eternal *one*."[3] These thoughts were influenced by German romanticism and in some ways are reminiscent of the mysticism of the Orient. Perry Miller describes the transcendentalists as "children of the Puritan past," emancipated from Calvinism by Unitarianism, finding "a new religious expression . . . derived from romantic literature and from the philosophical idealism of Germany."[4] The transcendentalists had a contempt for tradition, loved independence, and cultivated their own resources.[5] These sensitive, and in some ways impractical, utopians had a number of misgivings about American society, in particular a mistrust of the materialism that was becoming an essential part of American life with the expansion of the business and industrial worlds.

Within the transcendental movement there was a dichotomy between the active and the passive, between the scientific and the mystical. Life was an enigma to many of these nineteenth-century thinkers, and with the enigma came the problems and confusion that were the results of the questions of existence.

Many of the transcendentalists showed an interest in music. Margaret Fuller spoke of the "music of the universe" in her writing, and she felt that music was the greatest of the arts. "I will triumph," she proclaimed to her journal after hearing a performance of Beethoven's *Symphony No. 7.*[6] Her ideas of music were far-reaching, for in addition to Beethoven, she appreciated American Indian and Chinese music.

John Sullivan Dwight exhibited a transcendentalist's thinking in his contention, found throughout his writings, that music is *life*. Amos Bronson Alcott's journals contain references to mornings and evenings of music. The entry for May 2, 1839: ". . . conversation. Walking. Evening, a concert of vocal and instrumental music. Conversation of music;" and that of April 5, 1846, which found Alcott at 6 A.M. "Reading of a hymn, with Conversation. Music— Prepare wood—" and at six in the evening: "Supper. Music and Conversation;"[7] are representative. Alcott's diary entry of January 4, 1850, demonstrates his musical language and amazing verbosity, a trait some of his transcendental contemporaries shared: "For beauty, in its varied displays, is but the overflowing of life's tides, rising and spilling forth their forms and colours in rapture, in music,

and song."[8] As with Dwight, Alcott saw music as an activity synonymous with life.

Henry David Thoreau, an important influence on Ives, was a
transcendentalist whose love of music is expressed throughout his
writing and whose works contain numerous references to silence.
"To ears that are expanded, what a harp this world is!"[9] he wrote.
Thoreau's concepts of the universal drew him into the realm of pure
transcendentalism and even to the antiquity of ancient Greece.
According to Annie Russel Marble: "There seemed an aptness in
Thoreau's love for the flute,—the symbol of classic times and the
legends of Pan."[10] Thoreau's flute was an important part of his life,
and his accounts of sailing on a river with flute and water joining
each other in counterpoint demonstrate a transcendentalist's feeling
of oneness with nature.[11]

Thoreau's love of silence is important, for by "hearing" the un-
speakable musical qualities of silence, he was anticipating an entire
school of progressive American musical thought that influenced
not only Ives but also John Cage and other composers of the mid-
twentieth century. "Silence alone is worthy to be heard,"[12] Thoreau
wrote. He could see the relationship of music and nature: to think
of music as "the sound of the circulation in nature's veins"[13] brings
aspects of life into a oneness. Sounds fascinated him. The telegraph
lines in Concord were a source of music: "I hear something new at
every telegraph-post. I have not got out of hearing one before I
hear a new harp."[14]

Transcendentalism was not the only important school of thought
in nineteenth-century New England, however. Pragmatism was
another result of the American thinking of this period. The pragmatists viewed the universe as open and unfinished, and the pragmatic concern for the *consequences* that are the result of all ideas is
at the heart of their philosophy. William James stated that the pragmatic approach to questions such as "Is the world one or many?—
fated or free? material or spiritual?" was to trace the practical consequences of such concepts. "What difference would it practically
make to any one if this notion rather than that notion were true? If
no practical difference whatever can be traced, then the alternatives
mean practically the same thing, and all dispute is idle. Whenever a

dispute is serious, we ought to be able to show some practical difference that must follow from one side or the other's being right."[15]

These last words are representative of one of the most important aspects of New England thinking of the time: a search for truth. Ives wrote in *Essays Before a Sonata* that Emerson ". . . will not accept repose against the activity of truth,"[16] and for many years this search occupied the New England mind. Christian Science, a religion that is a logical product of the New England "Indian Summer," was another of the philosophical "schools" that tried to discover or ascertain truths. *Science and Health* (1875), the most important writing on Christian Science, is filled with references to truth, stated in language reminiscent of the transcendentalists: "We learn from science mind is universal, the first and only cause of all that really is; . . . The real is Truth, Life, Love and Intelligence, all of which are Spirit, and Spirit is God, and God, Soul, the Principle of the universe and man."[17] The final paragraph of the first edition of *Science and Health* proclaims that "Truth cannot be lost."[18] Mary Baker Eddy, the founder of Christian Science and the author of *Science and Health*, proposed to define truth, offering the following suggestion: "To learn the Truth of things, they must be explained from the basis of Soul, and not sense."[19] This thought, like the transcendentalists' view concerning materialism as a lamentable aspect of American life, displays a concept that the *soul* is all-important.

As with other New Englanders of the time, Mrs. Eddy's style of writing was one that included musical references. The allusion to the "harmony of being," "harpstrings," and "tones of the mind" and other such phrases are found throughout her works. In writing of the masters, Mrs. Eddy drew them into the transcendental community:

Touched by the Principle of his grand symphonies, a Mozart or a Beethoven experienced much more than he ever expressed in music; each was a musician before the world knew it; so to catch the divine harmonies of Soul, we must rise in the scale of being through the understanding of science, and experience, in order to demonstrate. Love gives forth its own concord, to correct the discords of sense; and whatsoever inspires us with Love, Wisdom or Truth, whether it be song, sermon, or science, will bless the human family; . . .[20]

Christian Science is but a representative movement, for the general New England thinking was similar; thoughts of the universal, concepts of the Over-Soul, and quests for truth were evident in one form or another in most of the philosophies of serious thinkers.

Ives, above all a transcendentalist, was in a more general sense a typical New England thinker of his time. Ives, too, sought to discover truth—in fact to him music itself was a form of truth—and his view of music was a universal one. In writing that ". . . it is better to hope that music may always be a transcendental language in the most extravagant sense,"[21] Ives was indicating that he saw music as one part of a kind of Over-Soul—reflecting the unity of his entire existence, and the existence of the universal itself. To Ives there was unity in chaos and chaos in unity. Thus, he emerges as a logical product of his age and locality.

Ives was born in Danbury, Connecticut, in 1874, a descendant of an old New England family. The setting of Ives's childhood was an influencing factor on his musical development; the small New England town with its village choir, barn dances, camp meetings, circus parades, town bands, and transcendental philosophers—an environment fast disappearing even in Ives's youth—is reflected in almost every work he composed. Another aspect of the New England town was Ives's father, George, an extraordinary man who directed the town band in Danbury and who created a musical atmosphere in the Ives home through which his son learned the elements of music. George Ives was in many ways a sophisticated musician who had studied music theory and related subjects. The elder Ives's musical notebooks are a clue to the musical influences he passed on to his son. Bach chorales and works by early Italian composers such as Lotti, Caldara, and Marcello find themselves next to tunes such as *Old Dan Tucker, Give Me the Girl That Is Ripe for Joy,* and *Yankee Doodle,* all copied out by hand. George Ives, in fact, loved all kinds of sounds and was fascinated by possibilities of making music that had not been examined by other musicians of the time. He trained his family to sing *Swanee River* in the key of E-flat while he played the accompaniment in the key of C. The elder Ives loved the sounds of a thunderstorm, which he tried to duplicate on the piano. He experimented with quarter-tones. He even found a positive musical experience from the off-key singing of one of the old men of the Danbury community:

Once a nice young man . . . said to Father, "How can you stand it to hear old John Bell (the best stone-mason in town) sing?" . . . Father said, "He is a supreme musician." The young man . . . was horrified—"Why, he sings off the key, the wrong notes and everything—and that horrible, raucous voice—and he bellows out and hits notes no one else does—it's awful!" Father said, "Watch him closely and reverently, look into his face and hear the music of the ages. Don't pay too much attention to the sounds—for if you do, you may miss the music. You won't get a wild, heroic ride to heaven on pretty little sounds.[22]

Philip Sutherland remembers how excited the elder Ives became when two bands approached each other from opposite directions: "They'd be going one way with the band, with another band going the other way 'round the park here [in Danbury] and the two would clash—that interested him very much, but people in Danbury didn't think it was very interesting to see the two bands blending and playing different tunes. They didn't take George Ives very seriously. He was only the band-leader."[23] Yet this bandleader, with his unique concept of what constituted a musical experience, had a profound effect on his son's philosophy of music. George Ives was a carver, and he taught his son the possibilities of such a method.

Charles Ives attended Hopkins Grammar School and Yale University. If his youth in Danbury had produced an invaluable exposure to visionary musical concepts, his studies at Yale with Horatio Parker produced another necessary ingredient: an intensive study of the methods of the "establishment." Ives had been introduced to these concepts by his father, who tried to put them into perspective with his own revolutionary musical views. At Yale Ives was given the possibility that the traditional approach was the only proper method for a serious American composer. This concept, of course, is found in the works of Parker, a composer whose music is notably undistinguished. It may be found in the curriculum Parker established at Yale, for music study there in the 1890s was a traditional approach, in which harmony, counterpoint, instrumentation, "strict" and "free" composition, music history, and "practical" music instruction were the normal fare. The combination of courses made it possible for a student to achieve a solid, if conservative, background.

In view of his traditional attitudes, it is surprising to find that Parker had been rebellious in his student days. His teacher George Whitefield Chadwick remembered that ". . . he was far from docile. In fact, he was impatient of the restrictions of musical form and rather rebellious of the discipline of counterpoint and fugues."[24] Parker, of course, experienced the same problems with Ives. He joked that his student had a habit of "hogging all the keys at one meal,"[25] and he found little to admire in Ives's fugues where the subjects were stated in four different keys. Actually, Parker had practiced a similar compositional approach in *The Legend of St. Christopher,* in which the voices enter in one contrapuntal passage at the interval of the fourth rather than in the "accepted manner."

Basically, however, Parker was a sincere and conventional teacher. He was convinced that music should be learned by absorbing the rules, which was the first step in acquiring a secure compositional technique. And although Parker has been portrayed as a villain in a recent Ives biography, there is little to substantiate such an assertion.[26] He helped Ives acquire a fine technique and brought him into contact with the American-European approach, just as Ives's father had shown him the merits of being a carver.

Ives graduated from Yale in 1898 with a major in music. Making music a secondary career, Ives went to work in the insurance business. He was soon active in his own firm, the partnership of Ives and Myrick, an organization that became one of the largest and most respected in the country. While he was making his fortune in the insurance world, he continued to compose. Ives's most musically creative years were also his most hectic ones in the business world. It is a source of amazement that an enormous number of major works were produced at night or on weekends. Yet the strain of a double life impaired Ives's health. In 1918, he had a heart attack, and his health was never secure after that time. World War I had also had an adverse effect on Ives. He was interested in national and international affairs and even dreamed of a world democracy, a logical outgrowth of his transcendental philosophy. Ives could see little hope for a world that had just gone through such turmoil.

He also had a distrust of technology and a visionary fear of its side effects, among them pollution. The text of one of Ives's songs (entitled *The New River* or *The Ruined River* as the composer first called it) is revealing, for it describes what Ives called "human beings gone machine" in less than enthusiastic terms. Ives's transcendental concepts and general approach to life placed him firmly in the nineteenth century, and he was not ultimately at home with the twentieth century.

The last thirty years of his life saw Ives withdraw first from composing, then from his business. His life was spent with his wife, Harmony, for the most part on their place in West Redding, Connecticut. Ives's existence was a secluded one, and during these years the Ives legend began to emerge. His music had not been understood or performed during his creative years; however, during these later years a belated recognition slowly began to emerge. Ives was elected to the National Institute of Arts and Letters in 1945, and he won the Pulitzer Prize in 1947 for his *Symphony No. 3*, a composition that he had begun around 1901 and finished in 1911. To the world he presented the picture of a grand and sometimes cranky old man. He publicly scoffed at the fact that he had won the Pulitzer Prize and gave the prize money away.

For years Ives had quietly promoted his music. He had the *114 Songs* and the *"Concord" Sonata* printed privately, sending copies to those who asked for them. If someone decided to perform Ives's music, he could receive help from the composer, sometimes in the form of written answers to questions concerning problematic aspects of a work. So a few performances took place when brave musicians were willing to try some difficult music. But even when Ives died there was little public indication that he was a great composer. John Kirkpatrick, the American pianist who had played the first complete performance of the *"Concord" Sonata*, felt differently, and in a letter to Carl and Charlotte Ruggles after Ives's funeral in May 1954 he wrote some prophetic words:

In retrospect . . . it seemed clearer to me than ever before that Charlie was probably here for a purpose, that the complacent patterns had to be upset, and that [he] . . . had necessarily to have all kinds of corresponding disadvantages, for instance the tragic enforced seclusion . . . or the dogged continuance of rebellion long after the complacent conventions had been overthrown. . . . Anyway, it will be fascinating to see what develops in the way of regard for Charlie's music (inherently it so invites any and all kinds of reaction, both to and from). . . . But let us thank God for its core of unshakable reality, so warmly human, so sure in form, so high in impulse. What a great example![27]

There are two points that are of particular importance in the preceding chronology. It has been noted that Ives's composition teachers represent the two widely divergent American "methods" of writing music. Specifically, there has always been the "correct" approach to composition, represented in this instance by Parker, and the "incorrect" method employed by America's musical "carvers," in this case Ives's father (who, of course, actually knew the "rules" too). Earlier chapters have shown the basic differences in the music produced by the two methods, and in a sense every American composer has been influenced by one approach in particular, usually as a result of circumstances beyond the composer's control. Ives is the first composer to profit from a combination of the two "methods." His circumstances led him to a firm background in which the "rules" were absorbed, tempered by an association with a carver who saw music as an all-encompassing activity far more exalted and visionary than the application of rules within a conservative framework.

As a result, Ives created a new music, firmly rooted in the nineteenth century, yet visionary far beyond the confines of late nineteenth-century romanticism. To list characteristics of this unique style is to state an exhaustive series of opposites: tunes that are reminiscent of the sentimental nineteenth-century parlor song and melodies representative of quasi-twelve-tone writing; harmony of the simple, diatonic kind and of the most complex and dissonant variety; uncomplicated rhythms and polyrhythmic structures; simple homophonic passages and multi-layered polyphony; formal structures that are conventional and others that are free and rhapsodic; conventional, "romantic" orchestration and previously untried instrumental combinations.

These discrepancies, of course, relate to Ives's philosophy, which resulted from his New England background and from the George Ives-Horatio Parker synthesis. Like Emerson, Ives set out along

Platonic lines to reconcile various aspects of philosophy and poetics. Ives did not believe music was only for pleasure. He felt that it had a purpose, and the purpose that Ives envisioned drew his ideas into line not only with Plato but with his own quasi-Puritanism and the Protestant ethic as well. Ives knew Henry Sturt's *Art and Personality* and had quoted it in the *Essays Before a Sonata*.[28] Sturt wrote that "selfish pleasure is the death of art."[29] In bringing art into conjunction with the human condition, Sturt found the reflection of an ". . . affectionate admiration for human persons."[30] When something is to be thought of as art, it is in terms of the personal element outside the self, found in nature or in humanity, which is to be enjoyed. Since art is seen in relationship to man's "higher life," pleasure is less important than a concept such as truth.

Ives, in thinking along these lines, envisioned music in terms of what he called "substance" and "manner," two words that may be found throughout his writings. Substance, which Ives admitted is difficult to define, concerns musical truths that constitute a substantial musical experience. Manner was less admirable: the conventional gesture, the common solution, the technical. Thus, Ives's aesthetic approach, with its relationship to philosophical concepts and ideals, differs considerably from that of his musical contemporaries, the American-Europeans who thought little about the philosophical aspects of music.

Ralph Waldo Emerson was Charles Ives's hero, and Ives's comments on the Concord philosopher are revealing: "We see him— standing on a summit at the door of the infinite, where many men do not care to climb, peering into the mysteries of life, contemplating the eternities, hurling back whatever he discovers there—now thunderbolts for us to grasp, if we can, and translate—now placing quietly, even tenderly, in our hands things that we may see without effort; if we won't see them, so much the worse for us."[31] Emerson's concepts were important to Ives's compositional process.

Ives's reverence for Thoreau also had an influence on his music. Ives states that "Thoreau was a great musician, not because he played the flute but because he did not have to go to Boston to hear 'the Symphony.'"[32] Ives comments that studying the life of Thoreau reveals the real fundamentals of transcendentalism: "It was the soul of Nature, not natural history, that Thoreau was after."[33] The poetic allusion to the faint sound of a bell that ". . . at a distance over the woods . . . acquires a certain vibratory hum, as if the pine needles in the horizon were the strings of a harp which it swept. . . ,"[34] a reference to the *Thoreau* movement of the *"Concord" Sonata*, brings again the concepts of music and nature into harmony. Ives felt that "the rhythm of his prose, were there nothing else, would determine his value as a composer."[35] From Emerson, Ives learned the importance of pondering truths; from Thoreau, he gained the knowledge that anything, even silence, can be music.

If, in fact, anything can be music, then the old "rules" are full of problems. In the *Memos*, Ives's recollections, the composer talks of fugue: "It is, to a great extent, a rule-made thing. So, if the first statement of the theme is in a certain key, and the second statement is in a key a 5th higher, why can't (musically speaking) the third entrance sometimes go another 5th higher, and the fourth statement another 5th higher?"[36] Harmonic rules, like those of counterpoint, are also stifling. George Ives once told his son that a composer normally started and ended a composition in the same key. The younger Ives had replied that this was as ridiculous as saying a person had to die in the same house in which he was born.[37] In his essay *Some Quarter-Tone Impressions*, Ives writes: "But quarter-tones or no quarter-tones, why tonality as such should be thrown out for good, I can't see. Why it should be always present, I can't see. It depends, it seems to me, a good deal—as clothes depend on the thermometer—on what one is trying to do, and on the state of mind, the time of day or other accidents of life."[38] To Ives there was no logical reason why a passage of atonality shouldn't "resolve" itself on a consonant chord. These thoughts help explain Ives's musical language: anything is a possibility.

Because Ives drew from many methods and numerous sources in his all-encompassing approach to composition, his music is a kaleidoscope of events, an entire world of relationships that can be approached from many directions. Several specific areas of Ives's musical thought reveal some of the transcendental qualities of his work. The first of these is Ives's use of quotation, one of the most important aspects of his style. The relationship to the composer's general philosophy is obvious. The works Ives knew and respected he considered part of a musical Over-Soul, part of the common property of mankind, to be used and transformed. Actually, the material for Ives's quotations is from many sources: "classical" works, popular melodies, hymns, or patriotic tunes that blend into the overall texture of a work, weaving in and out and around the music, becoming a vital and necessary part of its construction. One of Ives's favorite hymn tunes is *Beulah Land:*

Example 35a: J. R. Sweney: Beulah Land *(verses 2-4 omitted), from* John J. Hood: Goodly Pearls; *adapted from Ira D. Sankey and others:* Gospel Hymns Nos. 1 to 6 *(New York and Chicago: The Biglow and* Main Co., 1895). Original copyright: Hope Publishing Co., Carol Stream, Illinois.

In the *Symphony No. 2*, a fragment of *Beulah Land* is a part of the music:

Example 35b: Charles Ives: Symphony No. 2, *third [second] movement, violin I part, measures 7-18. Copyright 1951 by Southern Music Publishing Co., Inc. Used by permission.*

In the *String Quartet No. 1* a similar process takes place, this time employing the beginning of the chorus of *Beulah Land*; both of

Example 35c: Charles Ives: String Quartet No. 1, *second movement, violin I part, measures 5-13.* © *Copyright 1961 and 1963 by Peer International Corporation. Used by permission.*

these quotations are literal in the sense that the original melodic outline is clearly discernible.

Sometimes Ives creates an allusion to a piece. The following example, from the *Symphony No. 3*, is a reference to *What a Friend*, but one in which the hymn is blurred, as if being thought of only generally:

Example 36a: Charles C. Converse: What a Friend, *adapted from Ira D. Sankey and others:* Gospel Hymns Nos. 1 to 6, *measures 1-4 (melodic line only).*

Example 36b: Charles Ives: Symphony No. 3, *first movement, oboe part, measures 75-77.* © *Copyright 1947, 1964 by Associated Music Publishers, Inc. Used by permission.*

Yet a further extension of the idea of quotation is a tune that has a vague resemblance to a preexisting melody, but in reality is not a quotation. Example 37, from *Symphony No. 2,* is a case in point. It is not, as has been suggested, a reference to Stephen Foster's *Old Black Joe,*[39] but merely a tune that resembles that piece:

Example 37a: Stephen Foster: Old Black Joe *(New York: Firth, Pond & Co., 1860), measures 5 and 6; original a half-tone lower. Note values have been augmented to facilitate comparison with Example 37b.*

Example 37b: Charles Ives. Symphony No. 2, *fifth [third] movement, horn I part, measures 58-61.*

Sometimes Ives combines quotations in counterpoint (in the tradition of Gottschalk and William Mason). *Symphony No. 2*

Plate 6: Charles Edward Ives: ending of In the Inn *from* First Sonata
for piano (manuscript). Reproduced with the permission of the John

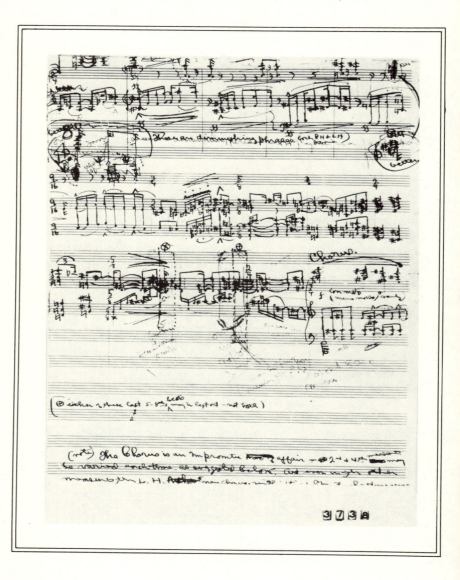

contains the following passage, in which *Camptown Races* and *Turkey in the Straw* are joined contrapuntally:

Example 38: Charles Ives: Symphony No. 2, *fifth [third] movement, violins I and II, cello and bass parts, measures 37-38 and 139-140.*

In the first movement of *Three Places in New England*, fragments of *Old Black Joe, Battle Cry of Freedom*, and *Marching Through Georgia* are combined ingeniously. Ives finds characteristics common to the three works and achieves a thematic metamorphosis.[40] A related procedure may be found at the conclusion of *Religion*, where two hymn tunes with common melodic formulas are combined. The final moments of the vocal line are the opening gesture of *Azmon (O for a Thousand Tongues)*, which is then continued in the piano. For a time we hear both *Azmon* and *Bethany (Nearer My God to Thee)*, before a fragment of *Bethany* concludes the work.

Some critics have contended that Ives's music suffers from the many references to outside sources, yet these quotations are a vital part of the Ivesian philosophy. Quotations are essential, for they refer to places, ideas, people, and things that are important to Ives. But a transformation takes place within the process of quotation. The quoted material emerges in a new light, shed by the composer.

Another aspect of Ives's music involves the freedom given to the performer, a further outgrowth of his general philosophy. In the *First Sonata* for piano the composer has bracketed notes in one particular passage, giving the performer several possible solutions:

Example 39: Charles Ives: First Sonata *(Piano),* "In the Inn," *measures 122-123.*

Near the end of the same movement Ives gives three optional ways of playing a particular measure. In its original form there are three counts, but in the alternate versions, four or even five beats are permissible. In addition to the differences in time signature, the rhythm varies in each of the versions:

Example 40: Charles Ives: First Sonata (Piano), "In the Inn," *measures 125-128.*

The Chorus is an impromptu affair (as is also the rest to some extent)—and may be varied according to the tempo taken. The 2nd and 4th measures of Chorus may be changed each time, as suggested below, and also in the other measures the L.H. may change ten. "shifts" ad lib. The last measure may be extended in similar manner.

There are numerous examples of similar procedures, where the performer is brought into the creative process. To Ives there was no really "authoritative" performance of a work—that would be too limiting. The same performance time after time would not be living music to one with Ives's aesthetic sense. Compositions such as the *"Concord" Sonata* saw numerous revisions as Ives worked with passages over the years, first evolving one thing, then another. If a performer wishes to do the same, he would have Ives's approval. Ives, in fact, saw his music as a blueprint that should guide the performer to his own realization. John Kirkpatrick has discussed one of his recordings of the *"Concord" Sonata* in which details differ from the second (or so-called authoritative) edition in various ways. Some of the changes Kirkpatrick employs are from the first edition, some are from sketches for the sonata, from "patches" (small scraps of paper with ideas for the piece), and from recollections of how Ives played things himself, which usually deviated from the printed page. Kirkpatrick describes a particularly delightful variant: "The march in *Hawthorne* (p. 35) has some naturals instead of flats which I once thought Ives might have meant that way (knowing how inconsistent his accidentals could be)—and even though the later proofs contradicted me, I still think Ives would have liked those naturals, as he liked the engraver's mistake in *Thoreau* (5th chord in the bottom staff of p. 61). He loved to surprise people, and it often struck his funnybone to be surprised himself."[41]

In addition to his ideas concerning the performer as creator, Ives saw another important requirement for a meaningful performance: a vitality of utterance. This vitality was evident in all aspects of his music, and he criticized music that he thought lacked it. In the *Essays* he wrote: "We might offer the suggestion that Debussy's content would have been worthier his manner if he had hoed corn [the original version was 'dug potatoes'] or sold newspapers for a living, for in this way he might have gained a deeper vitality and a truer theme to sing at night and of a Sunday."[42] Music was life to Ives, and both music and life were vital experiences.

The fact that many different melodic, harmonic, and rhythmic elements are admissible in numerous juxtapositions, that any piece may become a part of Ives's music, and that freedom and vitality are more important than order has led some critics to complain that in Ives's music there is too little attention to detail, a lack of unity bordering on chaos, and a bothersome, unreconciled quality. Ives would have scoffed at such ideas. If life is unreconciled, why shouldn't a piece of music be the same way? Why, in fact, should the un-unanswerable questions of existence not be attacked? *The Unanswered Question*, Ives's "cosmic landscape" for four flutes, trumpet, and strings, deals with these problems:

> The strings . . . are to represent—"The Silences of the Druids—Who Know, See and Hear Nothing." The trumpet intones "The Perennial Question of Existence," and states it in the same tone of voice each time. But the hunt for the "Invisible Answer" undertaken by the flutes and other human beings, becomes gradually more active, faster and louder. . . . The "Fighting Answers," as the time goes on, and after a "secret conference," seem to realize a futility, and begin to mock "the Question"—the strife is over for the moment. After they disappear, "The Question" is asked for the last time, and the "Silences" are heard beyond in "Undisturbed Solitude."[43]

Ives's musical solution to this program is to give each of the "characters" a separate music: the strings play consonant chords, heard as if from a distance; the trumpet intones an abstract, chromatic figure that asks the same, unanswerable question throughout the piece; and the flutes and "other human beings" perform agitated and unthinking material, far removed from the serious music of the Druids and the question. Despite the different character of the three sets of material, Ives achieves a continuity of expression.

A problem any composer must confront, in fact, concerns continuity and unity, and Ives's views on these important aspects of music are just as extraordinary as his other ideas. Musical unity is not merely related to form, for Ives thought that form had a more universal quality. In discussing Emerson in *Essays Before a Sonata*, Ives writes: "It must be remembered that truth was what Emerson was after—not strength of outline or even beauty, except insofar as they might reveal themselves naturally in his explorations toward the infinite." Ives continues: "His [Emerson's] underlying plan of work seems based on the large unity of a series of particular aspects of a subject rather than on the continuity of its expression."[44] Thus, form to Ives is related to the Emersonian concept of unity in the various aspects of a subject. Ives felt that "musical truth" could be produced if many simultaneous happenings and many different musical "styles" occurred within the same composition. In the orchestral piece *Central Park in the Dark,* the composer supplies a program:

This piece purports to be a picture in sounds of the sounds of nature and of happenings that men would hear some thirty or so years ago (before the combustion engine and radio monopolized the earth and air) when sitting on a bench in Central Park on a hot summer night. The strings represent the night sounds and silent darkness—interrupted by sounds from the Casino over the pond—of street singers coming up from the Circle, singing—in spots—the tunes of those days—of some "night owls" from Healy's whistling the latest or the Freshman March—the "occasional elevated," a street parade or a "breakdown" in the distance—of newsboys crying "uxtries," of pianolas having a rag-time war in the apartment house "over the garden wall," a street car and a street band join in the chorus—a fire engine, a cab horse runs away, lands "over the fence and out," the way-farers shout—again the darkness is heard—an echo over the pond—and we walk home.[45]

Most composers would be content to depict one isolated aspect of nocturnal Central Park, or to describe one happening at a time. But Ives will not accept anything but the "activity of truth." Here the aspects concerning Central Park are the sounds from a casino, the street singers, the pianolas, the cries of the newsboys, and the street players. Ives's desire to depict *all* of these aspects is what brings about the Emersonian concept of truth and the simultaneous happenings representative of Ives's musical language.

An analogy to language may be extended if the stylistic elements of Ives's "program" for *Central Park in the Dark* are examined. This is a singularly revealing passage, for the way Ives's mind works in prose reflects to an astonishing degree a listener's overriding responses to his music. Despite the whirlwind of specific sights and sounds impressed upon Ives's imaginary observer, it must not be forgotten that the general effect of the passage as a whole is passive, a receiving of assorted impressions. The relationship between these impressions, regardless of their individual enumeration, is as yet quite indistinct. This "blurring" of effect is created by Ives's prose itself. There is no sense here of a casual or sequential structure working within the paragraph. Rather, Ives's mind works associatively, almost poetically, even down to his punctuation, which consists of dashes and commas and contains hardly a full stop. In other words, Ives's writing style becomes, here, a kind of two-way mirror reflecting, in one direction, the mental impressions of an imaginary resident of Central Park, while it simultaneously serves as a window through which we see our own responses to the finished composition, even before they are articulated consciously. Ives's own work, the mirror, is the finished composition as well; he is responsible for actively reincorporating the imaginary impression of a fictional listener into the newly synthesized structure that an audience perceives. Thus, the passivity of impression is translated into the "activity of truth," and the listener is the beneficiary.

Lou Harrison's comparison of Ives and James Joyce is related to these concepts and presents another useful method of viewing the music:

Joyce begins composition often with very simple, banal narrative sentences. By associative accumulation, pun, scrambling, and rational as well as emotional suggestion he engages the mind in a progressive penetration of the subject, leading from the common locale, through myth and paradox, to the total (and personal) world, where meaning is provoked in many layers and the mind's eye sees both close and distant. In a certain sense Ives and Joyce decompose, rather than compose their subject.[46]

Many of Ives's subjects, quite obviously, result in program music, and in this respect Ives is part of the nineteenth-century tradition. Stravinsky has written: "Do we not, in truth, ask the impossible of music when we expect it to express feelings, to translate dramatic situations, even to imitate nature?"[47] Ives himself was aware of the problem when he wrote at the beginning of the *Essays Before a Sonata:* "How far is anyone justified, be he an authority or a layman, in expressing or trying to express in terms of music (in sounds, if you like) the value of anything, material, moral, intellectual, or spiritual, which is usually expressed in terms other than music?"[48] The view of Stravinsky is that of a classicist. Ives, in attempting to justify his depictions of "extramusical" elements, demonstrates an aspect of romanticism, but a transcendental romanticism that takes the concept of program music into areas of "musical truth," resulting in unanswered questions and elaborate philosophical programs. The concept that many musical happenings may occur simultaneously, creating layers of sounds that combine to create a musical Over-Soul, an essential part of the Ives "program," is one of Ives's greatest achievements. "Time to show the unnecessariness of necessities which clog up time," Ives wrote in the *Essays Before a Sonata*,[49] and the kind of "necessities" that Ives perceived were of a new and transcendental variety.

The central question concerning all of these ideas is how well they "work" in the music itself. Some critics think that Ives hides behind these elaborate philosophical "programs" to justify works that are either hopelessly repetitious or chaotic collections of unrelated elements. Virgil Thomson, one of Ives's harshest critics, mentions Ives's "musical materials . . . [which] seem to be only casually felt," and the extensive repetition in sequences, which presents problems because "real spontaneity does not repeat itself."[50] Thomson also cannot resolve Ives's musical and business existence, deploring the ". . . fatal scars left on virtually all his music by a divided allegiance." Additionally, Thomson refers to the "haste" and "limited reflection" in Ives's music.[51] Another critic has found that Ives's music sometimes "lacks what is most vital of all, a main rhythmic backbone."[52] These complaints cover the entire gamut of the composer's art, and like criticisms of the music of Griffes, indicate that Ives's music is not for everyone.

However, some of the complaints are difficult to substantiate. To deplore a sequence because ". . . real spontaneity does not repeat itself" is ludicrous and would mean the elimination of most of the "great" composers from the ranks of "spontaneous" and significant artists. Upon careful examination, there is also not a limited reflection on Ives's part. The composer, in fact, spent years revising and improving many of his most important works. The rhythmic backbone is there, too, although rhythmic complexities sometimes obscure it for the casual listener.

Ives was a careful artist who considered the implications of every note of his music. Nicholas Slonimsky, one of Ives's earliest champions, remembers discussing a minute detail in *Three Places in New*

England with the composer, a place in the viola part where A-sharp changes enharmonically to B-flat. Slonimsky wondered why a performer should be confused with the A-sharp, mentioning to Ives that the music would be easier to read if the notation were B-flat. But Ives refused to delete the note, saying that the A-sharp was a kind of unfinished chromatic—it should have gone to B but just didn't.[53] John Kirkpatrick recalls a similar situation when he was working on the song *Maple Leaves*. Ives's response to Kirkpatrick's suggestion of an enharmonic change was met with an emphatic "I'd rather *die* than change a note of that!"[54]

Ives in reality knew exactly what he was doing, and his music is the work of a well-trained and calculating mind. Even the most "chaotic" passages are planned carefully. In the large orchestral works, *Three Places in New England, Orchestral Set No. 2, Symphony No. 4, Browning Overture*, and *Symphony, Holidays*, there are instances of full orchestral sound where many different elements are stated simultaneously. Because of the haphazard and almost untutored way these sections appear on the page, some critics have thought that the composer was writing almost *anything*.[55] When examined carefully, however, these "chaotic" passages are too calculated to be the arbitrary jottings of someone not worried about specifics. Indeed, it is the *sameness* of these sections in the works that leads to the conclusion that Ives did plan carefully. To write anything on the page would produce results with a great amount of variance, although the variables would be notated fully and not left to the discretion of the performer. If Ives had in fact sat down in each particular case and written just anything, the results would never have been so similar and the passages in question would not be one of the familiar aspects of the Ives style. In each case the composer sought a specific orchestral texture and went about achieving it as a craftsman might—through organized compositional procedures.

An examination of some of the more "traditional" pieces is also revealing. The *Symphony No. 2* is an example of a work composed according to principles of the late nineteenth century. It is really in three movements, each of the outer ones containing a long introduction; it is cyclic in a manner reminiscent of César Franck; and its content is logical, well-stated, and expertly orchestrated. But the dual aspects of Ives's personality may also be seen in the work. The last "chord" of the symphony, a crashing dissonance, is foreign to the rest of the piece. This cluster was not a part of Ives's original version. The composer added it many years later to replace the conventional ending he had originally provided, and the result is a strange conclusion to a work so conservative in other respects. Many of Ives's compositions underwent similar changes. Elliott Carter remembers visiting Ives around 1929. Carter thinks that Ives was working on *Three Places in New England,* preparing the score for Nicholas Slonimsky's Boston Chamber Orchestra performance of 1931. Ives was changing octaves into sevenths and ninths and adding numerous dissonances. Carter speculates that much of Ives's "progressive" music underwent this kind of change.[56] It is a dichotomy, the conflict of consonance and dissonance. Ives was caught between the nineteenth and twentieth centuries. A work such as the *Symphony No. 3* displays the romantic warmth of a period long gone from America. Other pieces compel because of an urgency that is contemporary far beyond the time in which they were written.

These fascinating crosscurrents alone make Ives's music a literature filled with unanswered and unresolved questions. Among these are the composer's late works, among them a 1919 setting of a poem of his wife's, written for their daughter Edith's birthday, and a *Cradle Song,* works which return to the nursery, much as Stravinsky's *The Owl and the Pussy-Cat* presents a similarly curious conclusion to a composer's life. There are a few other works from the 1920s, an occasional outburst (such as *The One Way*), but Ives's "last period" itself trails off into an unanswered question, and finally into silence.

Another issue concerns Ives's reaction to the indifference that surrounded his music for so long. In public, of course, he presented the picture of a man who did not care about the lack of understanding with which his music was received during his lifetime. Yet his memos are filled with the comments of a man who was irritated by the problems he faced when he showed his music to musicans. In public he implied that the Pulitzer Prize was of little importance, yet the citation for the award was framed and hung in the study of Ives's West Redding home along with the framed certificate of the

National Institute of Arts and Letters. Ives was, quite obviously, thrilled with the recognition, despite the impression he gave in public of not caring. But these discrepancies are part of Ives's background, personality, training, professions, and philosophy.

There is a new aesthetic here because of the discrepancies. The result is a unique and monumental literature. At the conclusion of the *Essays Before a Sonata*, Ives wrote: "The strains of one man may fall far below the course of those Phaetons of Concord, . . . but the greater the distance his music falls away, the more reason that some greater man shall bring his nearer those higher spheres."[57] Ives himself reached those higher spheres with music that is as American and as lyrical as a Kansas wheat field—or a Connecticut landscape. It is a microcosm of America at the turn of the century— a music that is timeless and quite likely to emerge as one of the brightest pages in Western music.

chapter 6 _____

QUINCY PORTER: COMPOSER-PROFESSOR

> In the day-to-day sketches of my students I have been brought
> face to face with far more musical problems, of far more
> varieties, than I should have encountered in a lifetime
> of composition.
> —Halsey Stevens, "The Composer in Academia:
> Reflections on a Theme of Stravinsky"

When John Knowles Paine was hired by Harvard University to
become university organist and to teach a noncredit course in music
in 1862, an important aspect of American musical life began. During the 1875-1876 academic year, music was added to the Harvard
curriculum as a course of study, and Paine became America's first
professor of music.

The teaching of music in schools is a positive element in itself.
Much of the growth of music in America, in fact, can be traced to
what has taken place in the educational institutions. From the standpoint of the composer, however, there are some important questions concerning the viability of artistic creation in a scholarly context. One is the question of what the academic environment does to
the composer's creativity. Not only is teaching a time-consuming
activity, but the "academic" atmosphere, with its emphasis on continuous verbalization, may affect the composer-professor's creative
life. There is also the problem of composing "academic" music,
which composers who becomes teachers supposedly write. Finally,
there is the question of whether or not a composer-professor can

teach someone else to become a composer. To teach the facts of music history is one thing, but to relate the secrets of creativity is a more complicated, nebulous endeavor. The essential question is really whether the college or university is a positive or a negative force in the development of the composer's aesthetic.[1]

In the best of circumstances, there should be no debate about these matters. Jacques Barzun, writing in 1956, saw the university as the ideal environment for the development of a democratic culture and said that, in effect, such a culture already existed.[2] The university is where independent forces gather. The great university is a place of freedom, and this freedom should extend to the realm of musical composition. This atmosphere, in fact, should be perfect for a composer to work and think about his discipline. Yet there are potential problems. Elliott Carter notes that public apathy may drive a composer into the protective atmosphere of a university. Consequently, music is placed with other academic disciplines, and its value as a "public artistic communication"[3] may be destroyed. If the direction of musical enterprise is altered in such a way, the central position of the composer is in peril.

The composer can also be compromised if the "democratic" atmosphere of the university hinders his musical expression. In speaking of experimental music in the universities, Virgil Thomson notes that "possibly a certain scholastic timidity may be causing these composers to shun radical expressive aims."[4] Aaron Copland, on the other hand, speaks of the universities as former "hotbeds of conservatism," where "education and art were divorced." Copland notes that this changed suddenly in the 1960s, when schools became havens where the avant-garde could flourish. The most experimental composers were now given excellent faculty positions.[5] One reason for this phenomenon was the increasing acceptance of public relations' success as a criterion for faculty appointments. The tradition launched by the premiere performance of Stravinsky's *Le Sacre du Printemps* in 1913, in which the scandalous nature of the event was responsible in part for the notoriety of the work and its composer, became institutional by the 1960s. Novelty equaled media attention, and media attention became important to administrators seeking to attract the "best" students to their schools. The place of creativity in the academic context is obviously a controversial sub-

ject, and the numerous questions involved have an important relationship to the composer-professor and his music.

With the association of the composer and the university, the
label *academic* became a common term for describing both the
composer and the nature of his work. But what is academic music,
and what does the critic mean when he accuses a composer of being
academic? The term is generally used in a derogatory sense, synonymous with such adjectives as *dry* and *uninspired*. But is a composer's
music academic because he teaches at a university? Is a composer-
professor's counterpoint academic just because he "teaches" counterpoint? In *America's Music* Gilbert Chase writes of John Knowles
Paine: "Fortunately for his reputation as our leading academic composer, Paine seldom succumbed to the temptation of writing catchy
tunes." Horatio Parker's *Mona* is described by Chase in these words:
"That it contains some well-written academic music is undeniable,
but this does not establish it as a viable dramatic work for the lyric
theater."[6] Why is the music academic? This is the crux of the matter.

Charles Villiers Stanford wrote in 1902 that academic had "been
worked to death as a kind of term of reproach for everyone who
takes the trouble to know his technique before he foists his work on
the world. . . ."[7] Counterpoint, as an example, is an aspect of music
that requires study, if one decides to begin with a firm knowledge
of accepted practice rather than by carving out his own contrapuntal
method. To become fluent in the use of counterpoint is a process
that requires practical experience. Professors are supposed to be sure
in their handling of counterpoint. Yet a professor who composes a
piece employing counterpoint is more likely to be accused of being
"academic" than one who is not an academician. Daniel Gregory
Mason's *Prelude and Fugue for Piano and Orchestra* (1921) is a
contrapuntal work written by a professor. The critics had a field
day in reviewing the piece, using such words as *learned, erudite,
academic,* and *austere in emotional expression* to describe the composition.[8] Admittedly this work, as well as many of the efforts of
the composer-professors, is some of the things these words imply.
But all professors do not write dry counterpoint, although most of
them are accused of doing so.

In a sense, John Knowles Paine, in beginning the academic tradition in the United States, helped to foster these attitudes. As a teacher

he assisted a future generation of composers, but in a manner that some believed was anything but exciting. Frederick S. Converse remembers Paine's "sleepy lectures in musical history, in which he [Paine] frequently bent forward over the desk until his nose almost touched it."[9] John Tasker Howard writes that probably "if he [Paine] had not been academic, even to the point of dryness, he would never have been tolerated in a nineteenth-century university."[10]

Paine's music, it has been noted in a previous chapter, was also dry. This is the origin of the "academic" label in America, and by 1900 Rupert Hughes was referring to Paine and his followers as academics.[11] A general idea, in fact, existed for many years: a composer-professor was an inferior creator. And, this opinion was at least partially accurate. Then, in the 1920s, 1930s, and 1940s, a number of important composers who were not at all inferior creators became associated with American colleges and universities. Such names as Ross Lee Finney, Howard Hanson, Douglas Moore, Walter Piston, Quincy Porter, William Schuman, and Roger Sessions are as important to the growth of music in American higher education as their music is to the refinement of American music. As students of these composer-professors reached maturity, another larger generation became involved in creating and teaching in the universities. By examining the work of Quincy Porter, one of the distinguished members of the group of so-called academicians, the situation of a composer in the university becomes clearer.

Quincy Porter was born in 1897 in New Haven, Connecticut, a direct descendant of Jonathan Edwards, and the son and grandson of Yale University professors. Porter attended the Hill School in Pottstown, Pennsylvania, then went to Yale, where he was a composition student of Horatio Parker. After graduation from Yale in 1920, Porter went to Paris to study with Vincent d'Indy. Returning to the United States in 1921, he studied with Ernest Bloch in New York. When Bloch went to Cleveland to teach at the Cleveland Institute in 1922, Porter went with him to commence a career of teaching. During his years at the Institute, Porter was the violist of the Ribaupierre Quartet. In 1928, Porter returned to Paris on a Guggenheim Fellowship, where he remained for three years, spending much of his time composing. After his fellowship expired, he taught for one more year at the Cleveland Institute. In 1932, Porter joined the faculty of Vassar College where he remained until he became the dean of the New England Conservatory in 1938. Three years later he was named director of that institution, a position he held until he joined the faculty of Yale University in 1946. Porter taught at Yale until his retirement in 1965. He died in New Haven in 1966.

This brief account of Porter's life points to his academic affiliations. It also demonstrates a background typical of many American composers of Porter's generation. There is still a period of European study, but this might be prefaced by preparatory work at an American university. Composers often lived in Europe (which in the 1920s meant Paris) and composed in this atmosphere. Future generations of American composers were to find Europe an unnecessary experience. But for Porter and such contemporaries as Piston, Thomson, and Copland, the Paris years were invaluable. Porter had the opportunity to work uninterruptedly on his compositions during this period, and the results are numerous and positive.

Porter's music is distinguished by a number of notable characteristics. Perhaps the greatest compliment to his writing is the fact that it is intensely *musical*. In an age when composers were doing their best to write the latest sound, to explore the newest harmonic system, or to deal with formless constructions, Porter wrote conservative music. Yet his conservatism was simply an outgrowth of his philosophy of music, which was founded upon a reverence for the past and a faith in the present. In one of his scrapbooks, Porter documented some of his thoughts:

To my mind the two most important possessions of a composer are his imagination and his skill. The former is mostly a gift of the gods, but the latter is something which has to be acquired by labor and experience. The composers of the past that have survived are obviously those who had something to say, and who said it in their own way. Every composer of the present would like to have his music survive for the very same reasons, but in striving for originality he often loses his sense of direction. This is due in no small measure to what seems to me a deplorable confusion on the part of critics, students, mathematicians, and even the general public, as to what really makes music new.

Porter contended that an easy way to write music was simply to borrow ready-made formulas. One might also try to think of what has not been done, although this would be "pure fake" if the composer lacked imagination and skill. Porter continued:

If the cart can be put before the horse, as so often happens nowadays, and if the mathematical formulas and processes dictate the ideas, then we are very near the point where the computers will take over. Figure out the formulas, feed them to the machine, let it chew them up, and in less than nine seconds we shall reap the grim rewards.

As far as I, myself, am concerned, I have come to feel that the music I have written which has been the most successful (and this is from my own point of view) is that of which I would have the hardest time trying to explain its origin, its system, and the like. Thus my own experience strengthens my conviction that the chief source of musical materials is the strange workings of the musical imagination, untrammeled by the influences of conscious formulization or by a cold and calculated move on the part of the brain to do something new or different.[12]

Porter's style is reflective of such ideas. His works demonstrate solid architectural forms, always molded in tight, yet imaginative ways.

Porter's work is melodic, and the composer had little tolerance for compositions that were not. In a letter to Sidney Brudick dated November 24, 1958, Porter criticized a composition he had been asked to examine by saying that it was "successful in some ways, but [it had] almost no melody."[13] In Porter's work there is always a logic of melodic evolution. An early, unpublished composition, the *Andante for String Quartet* (1917), displays characteristics of Porter's mature melodic style. Examples 41a and b show the melodic line in two sections of the work. The dynamic markings as well as the melody itself indicate that Porter's intent is an expressive line.

Example 41a-b: Quincy Porter: Andante for String Quartet *(from the manuscript, Porter Collection, Yale University); measures 2-9 and 14-16 (violin I part only). Reproduced with the permission of Mrs. Quincy Porter and the John Herrick Jackson Music Library, Yale University.*

The chromaticism is representative of Porter's melodies, as are the asymmetrical rhythmic constructions. The auxiliary that characterizes the opening gesture of Example 41a was employed over and over in Porter's music, usually in conjunction with subsidiary motives. The *Symphony No. 1* contains examples of Porter's use of this figure as an important constructional element (Example 42a). Example 42b, from Porter's *Sonata No. 2 for Violin and Piano,* is a similar construction. In Porter's last work, the *Quintet for Oboe and Strings,* he uses the auxiliary at the beginning of each of the four movements of the work:

Example 42a: Quincy Porter: Symphony No. 1 *(adapted from the two-piano reduction by the composer, Porter Collection, Yale University); first movement, measures 28-32.* © *1938 by Quincy Porter, All Rights Reserved. Reprinted by permission of the American Composers Alliance, N.Y.*

Example 42b: Quincy Porter: Sonata No. 2 for Violin and Piano, *first movement, measures 1-5. Copyright* © *1933 by C. F. Peters Corporation, 373 Park Avenue South, New York 10016. Reprint permission granted by the publisher.*

Example 42c-f: *Quincy Porter:* Quintet for Oboe and Strings, *beginnings of the four movements. Copyright © 1967 by Highgate Press. All rights reserved. Used by permission.*

C

D

In each case, the three-note figure leads to extensive development. A simple instance occurs in Example 43a. Here the motive is stated, then immediately elaborated upon:

Example 43a: Quincy Porter: Dance in Three-Time, oboe part, measures 191-192. © 1937 by Quincy Porter, All Rights Reserved. Reprinted by Permission of American Composers Alliance, N.Y.

The *Quintet for Harpsichord and Strings* is yet another indication of Porter's proclivity for the auxiliary figure and its ensuing development. Example 43b shows the melodic material at the beginning of the work. In just these three measures, there are two instances of the figure, offset by the exact center of the phrase, which creates variety by deviating from the auxiliary. Porter develops the figure in countless ways. Example 43c shows one treatment:

Example 43b-c: Quincy Porter: Quintet for Harpsichord and Strings, *first movement, violin I part, measures 1-4; measures 45-48.* © *1961 by Quincy Porter, All Rights Reserved. Reprinted by permission of American Composers Alliance, N.Y.*

B

C

Porter's development of motives is unmistakable, whether he is writing a symphony or a simple teaching piece. Example 44a is the beginning of a two-page work, *Day Dreams,* dedicated to his son and written with a piano student in mind. The opening figure consists of some familiar Porter material, for there are upper and lower auxiliaries; there is also a descending third, and all of these elements are developed in numerous ways. The opening measures are only a sample of the transformation that takes place within the piece. Example 44b, taken from the last measures of *Day Dreams,* is a further demonstration of this development, involving a subtle use of counterpoint:

Example 44a-b: Quincy Porter: Day Dreams, *measures 1-16 and 45-51.*
© *1958, Merion Music, Inc. Used by permission.*

The work, although slight, is typical Porter: it is an expressive piece, written with care.

The auxiliary figure, which is exemplified in *Day Dreams* and in so many other works, is reminiscent of Baroque musical material. (The mordent comes to mind immediately.) Much of Porter's compositional style is of a similar nature: derived from the past, yet synthesized into the present. The previous musical examples point to an important aspect of his style: he is a motivic composer, and this quality is seldom absent from his music. It is the tightness of Porter's motivic construction that gives his compositions unity. In the preface to his *Symphony No. 2* Porter writes: "*Symphony No. 2* is in four movements which do not, in any conscious way, relate themselves to one another thematically."[14] Yet the composer's subconscious technique brings about a tight unity in the work that gives the thematic material of the various movements an associative relationship, although the associations are of a general nature.

Porter's skill as a contrapuntalist was as fine as his ability as a melodist. Example 43c is an illustration of Porter's counterpoint. His early training, especially his work with Ernest Bloch, gave him a sound contrapuntal technique. Porter's study of some of the great sixteenth-century masters of polyphony led to a short book on Orlando di Lasso's counterpoint, and Porter also wrote a textbook on fugue.[15]

Although there is usually an independence of lines in Porter's writing, his later compositions show a particular mastery of counterpoint. The *Concerto Concertante* of 1952-1953 is an example of a work in which imitation is important. The second *lento* section contains examples of conventional imitation, although at unusual intervals. The entry of the third voice in Example 45 is an inversion of the first statement of the material:

Example 45: Quincy Porter: Concerto Concertante *(from the composer's manuscript, Porter Collection, Yale University); measures 112-115.*
© 1956 by Quincy Porter, All Rights Reserved. Reprinted by permission of American Composers Alliance, N.Y.

Another contrapuntal passage from a work of Porter's later years is found at the beginning of the *Concerto for Wind Orchestra.* Porter establishes a richness of texture in which the voices imitate each other, forming numerous relationships. In the opening measures of the work the oboe and horn work in quasi-canonic fashion, the two bassoons stating another melodic element that is treated imitatively:

Example 46: Quincy Porter: Concerto for Wind Orchestra, *measures 1-9 (trumpet and trombone parts omitted from measure 9). Copyright* © *1959 by C. F. Peters Corporation, 373 Park Avenue South, New York 10016. Reprint permission granted by the publisher.*

These measures demonstrate yet another aspect of Porter's style. There is always a clarity of texture in his music, a quality that enabled him to achieve a particular distinction in his chamber works. His nine string quartets, a very large number for a twentieth-century composer, as well as his numerous other efforts in the field of chamber music, have, in fact, labeled him as a master in that field.

It was Porter's ability as a performer that enabled him to write particularly effective music for strings. The composition notebooks from his youth contain numerous pieces for strings, and his graduation piece for the Yale School of Music (which won honorable mention in competition for the *Prix de Rome*), was a *Concerto for Violin and Orchestra*. Porter played the solo part when the work was performed at Yale. This affinity for string writing continued with Porter's first published work, the *Ukrainian Suite* for string orchestra (1925). Another early example, and one of Porter's finest compositions, is the *Sonata No. 2 for Violin and Piano* (1929). Yet Porter was not content to write solo music only for the violin. As a violist, he was aware of the lack of a substantial viola literature. The *Suite for Viola Alone*, the *Poem* for viola and piano, and the *Speed Etude* for viola and piano are examples of his music for that instrument. The contrabass literature was also enriched by the *Lyric Piece* of 1949.

Porter's expertise extends to orchestral writing where he handles instruments in a manner that achieves the transparency and intimacy of chamber music. Sometimes the employment of solo instruments, such as the solo violin, viola, and cello passages in the *Symphony No. 2*, creates the effect of a concerto grosso (another instance of Baroque influence in Porter's work). The use of solo winds gives further evidence of a chamber music approach. A more surprising aspect of many of the orchestral pieces is Porter's handling of percussion. In particular, the tendency to use these instruments in unusual and imaginative ways gives his music an individual quality. In the first movement of his *Symphony No. 2*, Porter employs gourds as an important element in a musical texture, again reminiscent of chamber music. In other movements of the symphony, snare drum and woodblock function in a similar manner. Another unique combination of sounds is the swish of sandpaper combined with the dry staccato of bassoons in a section of *New England Episodes*.

Irrepressible expressiveness within a solid architectural unit is at the core of Porter's writing. Fluidity of motion may be noted not only in the manner in which Porter treats a transition but in the way his ideas evolve. Even Porter's most dissonant passages create this impression of smoothness. Howard Taubman, reviewing Porter's *New England Episodes,* summarized these qualities when he stated that "Mr. Porter writes with disarming modesty that does not conceal his feeling for form and style. He is somewhat sentimental in his feeling for old New England. Even when there is a suggestion of the harshness that inhabited that world, a warm glow takes the edge off it."[16] These aspects are common not only to *New England Episodes* but to Porter's music in general.

Porter was recognized as a composer with potential as early as 1926 by Aaron Copland, who noted that Porter had ". . . an especially fine mastery of contrapuntal technique and an easy handling of the problems of form."[17] Nathan Broder, writing on "The Evolution of the American Composer," summarized Porter's style effectively: "Of the Harris-Copland-Sessions-Piston generation, he has gone quietly along, avoiding isms of any kind, working out his own style, which features long, curved lines and harmony spiced with dissonance."[18] H. Wiley Hitchcock's opinion that Porter's is an "international style" is also an accurate and fitting description.[19] Porter did not worry about his style; he simply expressed his ideas, and the resulting style was an individual one.

Yet it will be remembered that Porter was not only a composer but a teacher as well. The questions concerning the relationship of his teaching to his creativity revive the problem of the composer in a university. Is the counterpoint in Porter's music "academic," for instance? Did his working with students on the subject, his writing of books dealing with counterpoint, and his association with counterpoint in an academic atmosphere hinder his freedom to write imaginative counterpoint in his own compositions? It is obvious that the answer to this question is an emphatic *no.* Porter's teaching of counterpoint did not hinder his composing of counterpoint. His use of contrapuntal texture is fresh, interesting, and not the kind associated with the term *academic.* During the years when Porter was teaching, his composing, or at least the creative part of it, took place mainly during the summer. Near the Porter summer home on Squam Lake, New Hampshire, the composer worked in a little hut on a hill in the woods, about four miles from the main house. The Porters summered in New Hampshire for many years, and early each morning the composer would go to his retreat to work for several hours. He once wrote: "I am very selfish with my summer time, and save as much of it as I can for composition. . . ."[20] By leaving for New Hampshire as soon as possible in the late spring, Porter was assured of three months of work. During his years at Yale, with this composing schedule, Porter produced a number of significant compositions. There were two periods in Porter's life, however, when he was not teaching. The first was his stay in Paris from 1928 to 1931; the second was his sabbatical leave from Yale during the 1952-1953 academic year.

Porter's Guggenheim Fellowship of 1928 made it possible for him to go to Paris, where he was able to devote much of his time to composing. He did not worry about the fact that he was an American in Paris, writing that "a change of horizons, a new set of forces to react against, will never harm a composer who has anything interesting to say." Porter believed that if one went to Europe an American, he would return an American. "A composer is not a sponge,"[21] he wrote upon his return to the United States, and at least for Porter the statement was true.

Porter composed some of his finest music during the Paris years. In addition to the *Sonata No. 2 for Violin and Piano*, there was the piano *Sonata, Quintet for Clarinet and Strings, Little Trio* for flute, violin, and viola, *Suite for Viola Alone, Blues Lointains* for flute and piano, two *String Quartets* (numbers 3 and 4), and twelve songs. This is a large body of music, and it is an indication of what a composer can do when his attention is focused on composing.

Porter's letters to his family give clues concerning the way he worked. On October 31, 1928, he wrote that the *Little Trio* for flute, violin, and viola had been written in three days. Although Porter said that he made no attempt to be original, this was the piece that was encored when most of Porter's Paris compositions were performed at the Salle Chopin on February 18, 1931. Other compositions required more effort. On January 6, 1929, Porter wrote: "My composing is going fairly well. I am working on a sonata for violin and piano, and have a good many ideas for the 1st and 3rd movements and have finished the 2nd." By January 19, the last movement was almost completed, and by January 25, the first movement was well under way. On February 5, Porter reported that the first movement was going along well: "I have got most of the ideas, & when that is done it sometimes doesn't take so very long to finish." Porter's letter of March 8 indicates that he had completed the work. The composer's appraisal of the sonata was positive and accurate: "I think it by a good deal the best thing I have written. The 1st and last movements are quite brilliant, more so than anything I've written before. The first movement is more or less solemn, the second quite bright and sunshiny, with a little light scherzo like part in the middle. The last movement has quite a lot of go to it."[22]

On January 27, 1930, Arthur Shepherd reported in the *Cleveland Press* that in the *Sonata No. 2* "one discovers . . . both sound craftsmanship and expressive appeal. It discloses a clearly achieved organism and a finely woven texture. It is replete with well-balanced sonorities, pungent and adroit rhythms and persuasive lyrical passages for the violin. It amply fulfills the Mozartean dictum that 'Music must first of all "sound."'' It is an effective 'sound' piece."[23] There are numerous reasons for such a positive reaction. Porter's description of the work in a 1949 letter points to some of them. In mentioning the use of 3/8 and 2/8 measures, which often combine to give the feeling of five, Porter describes one of the strengths of the work. The barlines of the violin and the piano parts do not always coincide:

I was interested at the time in the effect of strong, lop-sided rhythms, which may give the feeling of physical motion which is . . . eccentric, uneven in speed, hence implying the extra energy necessary to carry out such motion. I have always felt that a strong rhythmic feeling makes its impression through muscular reactions. I did not want to make the complication of frequent bar changes, but it [was] only in this way that I felt it possible to notate the rhythmic ideas I had.[24]

The rhythmic strengths of the work are considerable, and the rhythmic vitality and asymmetry help identify the work as American. There are other American qualities, including the subtle infusion of blues elements in the outer sections of the second movement.[25] One of the most engaging aspects of the work is the tightness of its construction. There are three melodic "cells" in the first move-

ment that are also used in the last movement. Other ideas are introduced against the three motives, which lend variety to the manipulation of the basic elements of the composition. Yet, despite this
tightness, Porter's employment of form is flexible: the first movement is not a strict sonata form, and the *scherzando* section of the
second movement takes the place of a scherzo movement. When
material is repeated, as in the last section of the second movement,
there is always considerable modification. The sonata is an exciting
work, not only because of its sturdy architecture but also because
the structures assist the composer in achieving a considerable expressiveness.

Although they were written abroad, the Paris compositions are
those of an American who has synthesized his musical language into
a personal style. Porter as a composer was learning to look inward,
reflecting and synthesizing. His Paris compositions are the beginning
of that synthesis.

By the time Porter was awarded a sabbatical from his teaching,
almost a quarter of a century had passed since his years in Paris.
His leave of absence from Yale during the 1952-1953 school year
was spent in Italy, and once again the opportunity to work uninterruptedly on composition produced positive results. Among the
compositions he wrote during this period is the *Concerto Concertante*
or *Concerto for Two Pianos and Orchestra,* as the piece was called
when it was first composed. The work, the result of a commission
from the Louisville Orchestra, was created between November
1952 and May 1953, while Porter was living in Florence.

At this point in his career, Porter had achieved a considerable
distinction as an American musician, and the years of experience
coupled with the opportunity to reflect on them resulted in an important composition. In the *Concerto* there is the usual careful
workmanship, an ingenious manipulation of motives, and a concern
for the total unity of the piece. The latter led Porter to integrate the
piano writing with the other elements of the piece rather than to
treat it as a vehicle for virtuosity. Ultimately he changed the title of
the piece to *Concerto Concertante* to signify a concerto in a general
sense of the word, rather than a display piece in the romantic tradition. A comparison of Porter's orchestration in this composition to
that of his earlier works finds that a significant refinement has taken

Plate 7: *Quincy Porter: sketch for a section of* Concerto Concertante
(from one of the composer's notebooks). © *1956 by Quincy Porter, All*
Rights Reserved. Reproduced by permission of American Composers
Alliance, N.Y., and the John Herrick Jackson Music Library, Yale
University.

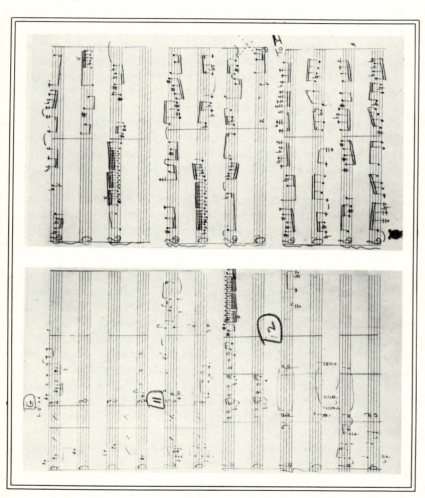

place. The motivic development itself, always a positive factor in Porter's writing, is especially masterful in the *Concerto Concertante*, and the emotional level is particularly intense. The work, which was first performed in March 1954, won the 1954 Pulitzer Prize for music.

It is obvious that the time away from the university was a positive one for Porter. Yet his experiences at the university undoubtedly contributed to his general development as a composer and helped him to write a piece of the stature of a *Concerto Concertante*. Students sometimes make a professor think, and the students' interaction with their professor contributes to his own development. One is reminded of Charles Ives's reasoning that his music helped his insurance business and that his insurance business helped his music. A composer-professor usually will try to make the two aspects of his career react positively on each other, since the necessity of earning a living makes the luxury of composing on a full-time basis impossible for most musicians.

There is, further, the thought that the best composers are able to participate in many musical activities besides composing. In a sense, the supreme ideal is to be a *musician*—performer, composer, and teacher. The American university has helped to bring about many of these "total musicians," who, in turn, have contributed to the development of American music.

Porter's comments on education show that teaching was almost as important to him as composing. His goal was for a student to become a good all-around musician. To accomplish this, Porter believed that a child should be given a solid knowledge of musical notation and as much ear and rhythmic training as possible. At the beginning of his career, Porter had realized that students were insufficiently prepared in matters of rhythm, and that their technique was developed far in advance of their musical understanding.[26] He also advocated the study of an instrument to gain performance proficiency at an early age.[27]

Porter had definite ideas concerning music students who attend a college or university, especially those who wish to study composition. It has been stated that teaching someone to compose presents difficulties, and a comment by Roger Sessions is an appropriate appraisal of one of the results of these difficulties: ". . . the traditional basis of the university is the training of critics rather than composers."²⁸ A reason for this situation is the fact that composition is in many ways the most difficult of the musical disciplines to "teach." Porter recognized this fact in an article he wrote in 1932. He also noted the composition teacher's need for the gift of what Porter termed "second sight"—the ability to see into the personality of a student. The composition teacher may "draw certain general musical conclusions," but the student must do the rest.²⁹

Porter's theories are elaborated upon in a set of answers to questions concerning various aspects of the composer's art. These comments were written during his years as master of Yale's Pierson College (September 1958-June 1965) and are contained among his unpublished papers.³⁰ To the question of what constitutes a good education for a composer of the mid-twentieth century, Porter's response was detailed:

Composition is not an easy thing to teach, and there are not too many prescriptions that can be laid down that will work in the case of every student. I will tell you a few of my beliefs.

1. The chief thing which a teacher can do is to help a given student to save time in arriving at his goal, whatever that may be.

2. A student without a real gift, without a real musical imagination, will remain that way the rest of his life, regardless of patient hours spent in the endeavor of trying to make a composer out of him.

3. As before implied, a composer must have a wide, practical, working knowledge of the music of the past. I follow the belief that a composer may be greatly benefited by a study of 16th century counterpoint, and a very intensive one; by a good solid training in the harmony which was used by Bach, Haydn, Mozart[,] Beethoven and Brahms, because this is quite essential in order to understand and derive principles from the great music of the past.

4. He must also study the music of the present, especially that which he comes to be particularly intrigued with.

5. He must have as much knowledge as possible of the principles of performance, since he will be writing music which is going to be performed as a necessary step in the presentation of his music to the listener, and he must understand the points of view and the problems of performance—and best of all, be a good performer himself.

To the question, "Aren't there a number of ready-made, modern methods of writing music which make it possible for a student to write contemporary music without going through all this previous study of music of the past?" Porter responded:

> It seems to me that music is the art which is the most vulnerable to formulas without the guidance of the musical imagination, and music which does not come from the inner ear of the composer is most likely to be doomed. Music is something to be listened to, and it really implies that it must be heard somehow or other by the composer as he is writing it.
>
> There are various ways in which mathematical formulas may be imposed on music. It is possible to formulate melodic systems, rhythmic systems, and even harmonic systems. When such mathematical formulas are used by some one who didn't invent them for his own purposes, the resulting music is liable to turn out meaningless and unsuccessful. Music written by computing machines is very similar. It lacks a human equation—it lacks the motivation of a human being.
>
> The great danger nowadays is that a student will be carried away by a desire to write music which seems to him to be new and modern, and that he will accept ready-made formulas which have been handed out to him as the accepted means of writing music for the present. In most cases the person that originally used these formulas was a composer with a solid knowledge of the con[s]tructive principles of the proven masterpieces of the past. The composer may have groped for several years to find some new system which seemed to make for him a plausible point of departure in some new direction. Sometimes these formulas can be stated in all too convenient form for use by other people, and they are avidly seized on by students who themselves have no such broad knowledge of the music of the past. The result is that they are using a means which may be a very limiting one, and that they will write less original music than they might have if they had started with an extensive study of the music of the past.

This last comment led to a question concerning whether or not students should be taught to write music in the styles of the past. Porter replied in the affirmative:

> Yes, I do believe that there is much to be learned in attempting to write motets, and fugues and minuets and sonata movements in the well-known and successful idioms of the past, because in that way one gets to have a more first-hand knowledge of the principles which underlie the music. If the styles are really familiar ones, there is little danger that the student will write later on using these familiar formulas—or he may find some interesting point of departure which will add new freshness to a familiar style. It is

much more dangerous to imitate formulas of the present. I have seen these act as a poison on students, who have come to think of these formulas as the rules of composition. Sometimes they never recover, and are always writing second-hand music which may have a lot less originality than they think. In order to be original one has to have a wide knowledge of a great many styles. How otherwise can one be sure that what one is writing is not pretty stale stuff [?]

Porter's observation that Haydn's harmony could be studied with profit elicited a question concerning whether Haydn's harmonic formulas were still usable in contemporary music. Porter's answer was as follows:

I'm glad you brought up the name of Haydn. I have felt that a present day composer could still learn an enormous amount from that gentleman, and many of the things one can learn from him, may be applied at least in principle to contemporary music—and many of his extraordinary discoveries in the art of composition are being lost sight of by many contemporary composers. As far as Haydn's harmony is concerned, there is not likely to be much that can be used as such in contemporary music— though it is quite astonishing what can be done by giving a slightly new twist to a very familiar procedure. In order to get the most out of a study of Haydn, it is essential to know about his use of harmony, and to understand it in relation to his predecessors, as well. But as far as I am concerned what Haydn has particularly to offer to the contemporary scene, is a wide comprehension of rhythmic principles. He was certainly a rhythmic genius, and he tried a great variety of rhythmic tricks, and he suggests a great many which could still be used in new ways. Some people have even tried to make formulas which cover a rhythmic management of a piece of music. I think it would be a very good field for research to see if one could put in a reliable set of formulas, the rhythmic devices which Haydn used in a given piece. It would be pretty hard to figure out a set of mathematical formulas which would cover all of the unexpected turns; all the manipulations which Haydn carries out in order to surprise the listener and keep his attention. And if one could do it for one piece, it would be impossible to fit these formulas to another piece. Haydn was always trying something new. Haydn would have thrown up his hands in horror at some of the mathematical means that are being used at the present time, which are based on the working out of mathematical formulas. I have heard music written on a computing machine. I have also heard music written according to mathematical formulas—both of them more or less equally sterile.

Porter's ideas epitomize a conservative approach to a musician's preparation as a composer. A very different opinion was expressed by Roy Harris: "This teaching of definite rules about harmony, counterpoint, and form, this academic emphasis on rules that have been culled from the most obvious formulas of obsolete styles is of course so much dead wood which must be burned out of your students' minds before they can have any intelligent understanding of the nature of American music."[31] These words were written about the time Harris and Porter were studying in Paris. Harris' ideas are a reflection of the radical tendencies that were a part of some American thinking during the 1920s when an American musical identity was of great importance to composers and when ways of achieving it were being pondered. Unlike Porter, Harris was not enthralled with his Paris experiences, and he ultimately gave up his studies and returned to the United States.

Yet there cannot be an effective music without the technique to produce it, and Harris' method would understate or minimize much of the development of this technique. Porter's attitude is different: one acquires a firm knowledge of the past and then uses it to his advantage. When asked if he was in favor of an academic institution, Porter replied in a manner that would further substantiate his belief in the development of a compositional technique founded on principles of the past:

I think the word Academic in relation to music is usually used in a derogatory way. It is not art which flourishes under dry pedantry. The process of giving a composer the proper background is, indeed, a very complicated one, which has to be very much varied according to the particular talents of the individual student. I think it is quite possible to say with a good deal of certainty that there has been no composer of any stature who has not had wide acquaintance with the music of the past.[32]

Porter's faith in the past did not stop him from attempting to use it in a manner that was free from the "dry pedantry" he condemned. Porter's works attest to this fact as does his attitude concerning the musician in the university. His comment on Schönberg's treatise on harmony, "It never teaches by rules, but rather by reasons,"[33] could apply to his own approach to teaching and composing. Reasons are important, for they provide an explanation for what a composer is doing. Condemning rules *as rules* is an aspect of Porter's logical thinking.

Other considerations shed light on Porter's philosophy. To the question, "Can you describe any common qualities shared by music which has survived, and which is going to survive?" Porter gave this revealing answer:

If it were only possible to be sure what these qualities are, it might be easier to aim for them oneself, and to insure the future of one's own music. It is a very difficult question to answer, but there are a few things which one might say without too much danger of being entirely off the track.

As we all know, music consists of certain chosen sounds which are organized in time. This organization in time seems to me very like the organization in space of objects of art which we see with the eye. I think it is something which is much more important than some present day students of composition realize. Regardless of the complications of harmony or counterpoint, or instrumentation, if a piece of music is not written in such a way that it has rhythmic shape it is not likely to survive. So I feel that is one thing that one can say about music which is likely to survive—it needs to have rhythmic interest. There must be something which propels it, something which holds it together and makes you feel that the sounds are held together and belong together as they occur successively. I heard of an experiment in which the various parts of Beethoven's 5th symphony were transposed so that 12 different keys were represented at once—obviously causing a tremendous change in the amount of dissonance. Nevertheless, the music still made sense, because it was held together by the rhythmic drive which it had been given originally by Beethoven. I have noticed that when one listens to the new *musique concrète* which is all the rage, it is very possible to judge that which has a sense of rhythm, and which gives a sense of having shape, as it goes along in time, and that which seems quite hit-or-miss, and consequently disorganized. In this case the sounds themselves are secondary in importance. They are often the sounds of everyday life which have been taken down in tape and manipulated around by the composer so that they are arranged in time the way he wants to have them. Here, for instance, is an example of sounds which are made by a saucer dropping on a table, by a train engine gaining speed, and by a great many other similar sounds which are gathered in a sort of classified tape library by a composer, and subsequently arranged. The principle of arrangement has to do with this basic organization of sounds in time. They may be well arranged, or badly arranged, and this is at least one factor which can be judged in deciding on the validity of a new composition. The rhythm must be somehow contrived so that the music will seem to hang together. The originality and the vitality of a piece of music depend more than a great many people seem to think on the shape that the music is given by its rhythmic treatment. All sorts of new harmonic devices are invented, but regardless of the vocabulary of sounds, if the music lacks a sense of rhythm it is not likely to survive. And this is why I said that Haydn was a very good person for a present day person to study. He knew so much about rhythm. He knew how to organize his music in time so that the listener's attention is maintained, and directed at the very points in the music which he wants stressed.[34]

Porter refers to the listener and to the composer's concern for his audience in reply to yet another question: "Music has often been called the 'Universal Language.' If this is the case, why is it that this language may often seem unintelligible to a person untrained in music?" Porter's answer is typical of the composer's logic:

I think there are two parts to the answer of this question: First, there is a great deal of bad music—there always has been and there is surely plenty being written in the present. If the music is badly written, its meaning simply doesn't come across, and the listener who makes nothing of it may be perfectly justified. Secondly: there is no doubt that music has a better chance if it is played often enough so that a listener at least has a chance to get acquainted with it. It so often happens that a piece of new music gets played once, and then is not heard again for some time. I have heard as fine a musician as Paul Hindemith say that he can not make up his mind about a new piece of music right away. He has to hear it several times, and live with it before he can judge whether it is good or bad or just mediocre.

This all adds up to the fact that one of the great battles of the composer is to somehow succeed in intriguing the ear of the listener, so that even on first hearing that person will want to hear the piece again.[35]

The last statement of Porter's answer points to the real problem concerning his own music, at least as it affects the general listener. The composer's compositional style, an inordinately "intellectual" one, is a kind of writing that on first hearing appeals much more to a musician than to a layman. One reason for this is Porter's by now familiar method of working with motives that he begins to develop immediately rather than simply spinning out an appealing tune.

Music composed in this manner is difficult music from the standpoint of a general audience. Porter's writing takes time to assimilate, but the study of his works is both an important and a rewarding one for the listener and for the performer.

On the manuscript of one of his earliest compositions, a childhood piano piece entitled *Grief*, Porter wrote the following notation: "Toward the end of this lamenting it will be noticed that the chords change to dischords. This is due to the fact that the grief becomes distracting, and the composer has endeavoured to make the audience in sympathy, which end has, I believe, been accomplished."[36] Porter thought about his audience, just as he was concerned with his students and the many other aspects of his musical life. This concern helped him, in his own quiet way, to achieve a significant career. That he was one of a number of distinguished composers who thrived within the framework of the university should prove that, for the right person, there is a validity to the situation of a composer in an academic institution.

Porter wrote that he was hopeful about the future of American music: ". . . I am sure that we have no business to feel any sense of inferiority to other nations in the field of musical composition. Much music has been written by Americans which has proven its value. The Americans have a great deal of ingenuity, and when this is coupled with a musical sense, the result is something of great value, and often of great significance to our own scene—as an expression of our life which seems right to fellow Americans that hear the music."[37] Porter's own musical output demonstrates that American composers were at last producing fine works as a matter of course— works that were an indisputably distinguished American music.

chapter 7

VIRGIL THOMSON

Since the Whisky Rebellion and the Harvard butter riots there
has never been anything like it, and until the heavens fall or
Miss Stein makes sense there will never be anything like it
again. By Rolls-Royce, by airplane, by Pullman compartment,
and, for all we know, by specially designed Cartier pogo
sticks, the smart art enthusiasts of the countryside converged
on Hartford for the dress rehearsal [of *Four Saints in Three
Acts*].

—Lucius Beebe, *Snoot If You Must*

I just try to make sounds.

—Virgil Thomson, in an interview with the author

It has been said that Virgil Thomson "moves . . . across the musical
skyline like a baroque covered-wagon. More unexpectedly," the
writer continues, "there's a pioneer inside."[1] Thomson is certainly
one of the important American musical personalities of the twentieth century. It is perhaps questionable if his "baroque covered-
wagon" carries a pioneer or a hopeless and unadventurous conservative. Yet the significance of Thomson's work as a composer,
as a critic, and as a champion of American music cannot be ques-
tioned. History may well remember him chiefly as a critic and as a
promoter of American music. His decade and a half at the *New
York Herald Tribune* established new levels of, and approaches to,
musical criticism. Thomson's work from an early date demonstrated
his belief in the importance of an *American* music, and many of his

early writings, in the periodical *Modern Music* and elsewhere, offer
important statements on American composers.

His music does pose problems, for it is in many ways a strange
utterance for a composer living in the twentieth century. Some
musicians even wonder if Thomson is a very good composer, argu-
ing that his connections and powerful position as a music critic
helped his second-rate music reach the concert hall, publishing
house, and recording studio.[2] But Thomson's music is a reflection
of the man who wrote it, a personality who is contradictory in many
ways, but whose importance derives from these very contradictions.

Thomson's life has been discussed in his effectively written autobiography, *Virgil Thomson* (1966). He was born in Kansas City,
Missouri, in 1896 and graduated from Harvard twenty-six years
later. He went to Europe, taught at Harvard, and was an organist
in the Boston area before settling in Paris in 1925. Thomson lived
in Paris until 1940, absorbing the French civilization: studying,
composing, meeting "the" people of the time, and enjoying ele-
gant French cuisine and great French wines. A *soirée* at Thomson's
Left Bank apartment in the 1930s would likely have been a memorable one, with important people performing new music, reading
poetry, and taking part in sophisticated conversations. A typical
evening might find Christian Bérard, the Duchess of Clermont-
Tonnerre, Jean Cocteau, Christian Dior, F. Scott Fitzgerald, André
Gide, Ernest Hemingway, Henri Sauguet, Gertrude Stein, and Alice
B. Toklas engaged in the art of being witty and cosmopolitan.[3] In
addition to his social life, Thomson was composing witty, cosmopolitan music, and many of his works date from these Paris years.

His return to the United States in 1940 found Thomson in New
York City with his newspaper job at the *Herald Tribune,* a position
he held until 1954. After Thomson left the newspaper he continued
his musical life, "traipsing and trouping" as he put it. His composing, of course, had never stopped, and even in 1975, at the age of
seventy-nine, he continues to produce new works. Thomson's
American years have also seen much activity outside of the newspaper and composing worlds. He has lectured and conducted; he
has written extensively, including a book on American music;[4]
and he has been honored with degrees and citations in recognition
of a long and varied career.

Eva Goldbeck's description of the violin *Sonata* of 1930 gives an initial impression of the Thomson style: "It has the relaxed mood of a well-carpeted cocktail hour, fundamentally sanguine, with a few well-timed sighs."[5] Thomson's music is not emotional; it moves along coolly. It is, in fact, a detached writing. Yet Thomson's "cocktail hour" is his alone—it is hard to miss the Thomson trademarks that are reflected in so much of his work.

Concerning one of the most important of these trademarks, the composer's famous simplicity, Aaron Copland has noted Thomson's feeling "that so-called modern music is much too involved and pretentious in every way."[6] Thomson has sought an aesthetic of simplicity to counter the twentieth-century characteristic of all-encompassing complexity. This aesthetic explains the simple writing—the uncomplicated tunes and the "plain-as-Dick's-hatband" harmony, as Thomson calls it, which is an important characteristic of his music. Thomson, in justifying this approach, notes that ". . . there is no law against the common chord. It usually creates a scandal when music is supposed to be bumpy. The press is beginning to discover that I am a conservative composer because my music is quite often grammatical."[7]

Sometimes the Thomson simplicity is for a practical reason. The *Piano Sonata No. 3*, for example, was composed for Gertrude Stein, who was not a very good pianist. On the other hand, his simplicity can be puzzling. In the last movement of *Piano Sonata No. 4*, the short, page-long piece recalls final movements of Haydn's piano sonatas, but Thomson's content, with its lack of harmonic direction and wandering scales, is merely curious and really rather dull. Here is an example of the central problem that Thomson's aesthetic creates: how does one keep plainness from becoming dullness, or a lack of pretention from becoming pretentious by its lack of pretention?

Returning to the characteristics of Thomson's style will help us in our consideration of this question. The Thomson melodic structures are outwardly simple. The harmony is usually diatonic, although some of Thomson's works contain high levels of dissonance. There is an abundance of music that demonstrates only the simplest kind of homophonic writing, and there are works that are predominantly contrapuntal. The rhythmic structures may range from the simplest "oom-pah" or "oom-pah-pah" to rhythms that are subtle and more interesting. Thomson's orchestration can be conventional, or it may employ unusual and innovative combinations. The music may be judiciously conceived, with numerous relationships suggesting a carefully constructed organic whole, or it may give the impression of being spun out with complete abandon. Thomson's music, in fact, often has elements that seem incompatible with each other. Such widely divergent aspects of musical style and musical approaches, when presented in the same composition, often produce a bewildering effect. But this is the Thomson style, and the dichotomy is an American quality. It even helps the music achieve a certain level of effectiveness.

Although Thomson has written numerous abstract works—sonatas and quartets that are purely musical commodities—he is most famous for pieces that add a further dimension to the music. His operas are an important part of his output, and he has written successful film scores. Other pieces are "musical portraits," a novel concept derived from Gertrude Stein in which a "subject" sits, as for a painting. Thomson composes music inspired by the subject, and the sitting results in a musical composition. Some pieces are programmatic in the more old-fashioned meaning of the word with titles and contents representative of the composer's numerous and far-flung influences. Typical of these is *Filling Station*, a ballet that tells the story of a gas station attendant (Mac) and the various adventures that occur at his place of business one day. Among the characters are Ray and Roy, truck drivers who are chased by a state trooper. A motorist loses his way and stops, burdened by a wife and child experiencing various frustrations induced by a long automobile trip. A rich couple motors in and dances a tango, and a gangster brings about the climactic moment of the ballet. Thomson achieves local color not only by the setting and by the characters but also by the simple music itself, which presents such quaint dances as the Big Apple, which was all the rage when Thomson wrote the ballet in the late 1930s.

Wheat Field at Noon, a work evoking a Midwestern setting, reflects Thomson's lifelong reverence for his Missouri boyhood. Another glimpse of a nostalgic America, this time a seaside concert of many years ago, is suggested by *At the Beach*, a composition for trumpet and wind band. Many times, too, Thomson's musical recollections are in the form of quotations of American folk and hymn tunes.

Although the French side of Thomson has been thought by some to be excessive, the composer's Missouri background actually always manages to come through. *The Seine at Night* is an evocative tone poem, obviously the work of an American who is much involved with the Paris he is depicting. Sometimes Thomson's compositions compel because of the bizarre synthesis of quasi-programmatic elements, both American and European. The chorale that begins the *Sonata da Chiesa* of 1926 recalls a black church service in Kansas City, a far cry from the cultivated Paris of the 1920s where the piece was first heard. The central tango, which later became the music of the rich couple in *Filling Station*, is anything but ecclesiastical. In the fugue that concludes the work, the subject is unusual, being derived from the previous tango. The concept of a *Sonata da Chiesa* is European, but Thomson transforms it into an American hodgepodge. In an attempt to summarize the feeling Thomson's music creates, the critic John Rosenfeld has stated: ". . . he has invented something that might be called our 'Middle Western Sound.'"[8] And Thomson is always Thomson, whether in Kansas City, New York, Paris, or even Boston.

Thomson's first two operas present a particularly unique assortment of people and places, and here Thomson is helped by the librettos of his friend Gertrude Stein. *Four Saints in Three Acts*, first produced in 1934 under the sponsorship of "The Friends and Enemies of Modern Music," is not about just four saints, but about many saints, and it is not even in three acts. It is a delightful and illogical piece, and much of Thomson's reputation resulted from the success of this opera. *The Mother of Us All* (1947) is mainly about Susan B. Anthony, but it contains a variety of other people from several corners of the nineteenth and twentieth centuries. The costumes, which are specified carefully in the cast of characters, are from various years between 1825 and the present. The composer comments: "The variety of these against a more generalized historical background should offer a spectacle no more anachronistic than that suggested to the mind by the perusal of a volume of old photographs."[9]

Plate 8: Virgil Thomson: opening of Jour de Chalear aux Bains de Mer *(manuscript).* © *Copyright 1963 by Virgil Thomson. Reprinted by permission of Virgil Thomson, Copyright Owner, and Boosey & Hawkes, Inc., Sole Licensees.*

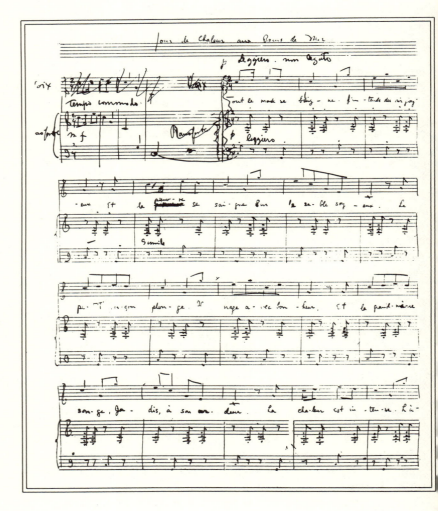

All of these works, as well as many others, verify the Thomson musical simplicity. Many times, in fact, this simplicity is almost maddening, at least until the composer's intention becomes clear. The vocal line of *Jour de Chaleur aux Bains de Mer*, which is typical Thomson, is an example:

Example 47: Virgil Thomson: Jour de Chaleur aux Bains de Mer, *measures 5-20 (vocal line only). © Copyright 1963 by Virgil Thomson. Reprinted by permission of Virgil Thomson, Copyright Owner, and Boosey & Hawkes, Inc., Sole Licensees.* *

The unceasing repetition and singsong characteristics are offset by an "oom-pah-pah" accompaniment that is really in a meter of 3/8 against the 2/4 of the tune. The composer's deadpan setting of the words (which were written by the Duchesse de Rohan, "a naïve writer often unconsciously comical," Thomson comments in his autobiography[10]) and the deadpan accompaniment that should not

---

*The text for *Jour de Chaleur aux Bains de Mer* (Hot Day at the Seashore), as translated by Sherry Mangan, is included in the Boosey & Hawkes publication. The opening lines give an indication of the Duchesse de Rohan's poetic abilities:

The water's full of swimmers.
I hear a tuneful band.
An octopus still shimmers
Upon the silken sand.

A little boy is diving
And swimming to and fro,
While grandma sits reviving
Her loves of long ago.

really fit with the vocal line create the Thomson trademark. This is, in fact, a very effective setting of the text.

There are numerous examples of this pure and simple music. Another song, *John Peel*, begins with the following vocal line, supported by simple triadic wanderings in the piano:

Example 48: Virgil Thomson: John Peel, *measures 3-10 (vocal line only). Copyright 1962 by Southern Music Publishing Co. Inc. Used by permission.*

Yet Thomson's writing is not always quite this melodically or harmonically elementary. Example 49 demonstrates a highly chromatic figure in the upper voices, offset by a chromatic chord progression. *A Solemn Music*, from which this excerpt is drawn, has been analyzed by John Cage in his study of Thomson's music. Cage

Example 49: Virgil Thomson: A Solemn Music *(condensed score), measures 17-25. Copyright © 1949, 1965 G. Schirmer, Inc. Used by permission.*

views the work as a masterpiece and even finds twelve-tone writing
in the composition.[11] But, despite some highly chromatic lines here
and elsewhere in his music, Thomson's approach to harmonic matters is not based on twelve-tone or serial procedures. Thomson
prefers to use the twelve available pitches in other ways. The following triads, for example, state the twelve pitches of the chromatic
scale:

Example 50a: Four triads.

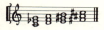

The result is chromatic, certainly, but the associations of the pitches
in combination—the major and minor triads—present a consonant
impression. Thomson employs the twelve pitches in these kinds of
combinations, "arranged conveniently and systematically," as he
puts it,[12] in works such as *The Seine at Night, Wheat Field at Noon,*
Sea Piece with Birds, Concerto for flute, strings, harp, and percussion, and *Missa Pro Defunctis.* Example 50b demonstrates one of
these systematizations:

Example 50b: Virgil Thomson: Wheat Field At Noon, *horn parts,*
measures 61-65. Copyright © 1954 G. Schirmer, Inc. Used by permission.

For Thomson, these "multiple chord relations" are more effective
than twelve-tone arrangements, which he thinks sound "muddy."
    Thomson's ideas concerning chord movement in general relate to
the above example. The composer believes that if every voice moves
with each chord change, "each chord is a first chord." Example 51a
is a conventional chord progression as a tonal composer would
usually write it. Example 51b shows Thomson's idea for an "updated"

harmonization. The parallel fifths between the bottom two voices, rather than the retention of the common tones (as in Example 51a),

Example 51a-b: A "Standard" and an "Updated" Harmonization.

help achieve direction and even motion. Thomson's music contains many examples of this harmonic approach. Examples 51c and 51d are but two of many passages constructed from this premise:

Example 51c: Virgil Thomson: Pange Lingua, *measures 1-4. Copyright © 1962 G. Schirmer, Inc. Used by permission.*

Example 51d: Virgil Thomson : Jerusalem, My Happy Home *from* Praises and Prayers, *measures 1-5. Copyright © 1963 G. Schirmer, Inc. Used by permission.*

Thomson considers the only "real" chords to be major, minor, augmented, the dominant seventh, and the diminished seventh. The rest, according to the composer, are derivations. Serial composers, Schenkerian theorists, and other writers who approach harmonic matters from a different premise will disagree. But Thomson's opinion is a result of a firm belief in tonality and clarity. Example 52, from *Pange Lingua,* shows a concern for clarity within a tonal framework. The three-note combinations here are dissonant, but the organ registration, stressing the top pitch, helps achieve the usual Thomson neatness. The composer believes that the sonority is improved in such cases if one "hangs from the top." The same thinking is evident in his orchestral writing. If Thomson were orchestrating this passage, he would divide the cellos on the bottom two pitches and give the top pitch to the violas. This would make

Example 52: Virgil Thomson: Pange Lingua, *measures 27-28.*

the sound "top-heavy" and achieve the clarity that Thomson finds so important.

The composer's contrapuntal passages show the same basic procedure. Example 53, another section of *Pange Lingua,* is a canon, and the familiar "common chord," arranged and spaced carefully (for distance is always a factor in matters such as these) combined with another meticulously specified organ registration, creates a passage that minimizes the dissonances produced by the counterpoint. *Lamentations* for accordian contains a passage of three-note combinations, similar to those in Example 52, treated canonically, this time creating what might best be described as counterpoint between the accordion keyboard and the accordion buttons. As in Example 53, there are six pitches sounding simultaneously, producing, in this case, a denseness of texture.

Thomson's harmonic structures have been much criticized, but

Example 53: Virgil Thomson: Pange Lingua, *measures 104-111.*

his treatment of words has been universally admired. Victor Yellin writes that ". . . only Thomson's music provides a consistent, uniform, and therefore classic model of American musical speech unencumbered by stylistic mannerisms or personal eccentricities."[13] Thomson strives for an ideal union of text and music so that neither suffers. Like the composers of Tudor England, he has the ability to catch rhythmic cadences of language and to compose music whose pitches and rhythms reflect the inflections of the words, forging a suitable union between them. Sometimes the "tunes" are rather bland, as *John Peel* has demonstrated, but the composer tries at all times to keep the music from getting in the way of the text. The settings of words by Gertrude Stein show the Thomson philosophy in a particularly strong light. *Capital, Capitals,* for example, is best described as a study in recitative, so subservient is the music to the text. There is the question of how much the music suffers when it retires so completely into the background, and indeed sometimes the words themselves cannot alone sustain interest in what is supposed to be a musical experience. But words and their musical setting will always pose problems for composers, in particular the common tendency to let one element overshadow the other. Thomson's attempt to give the music an effective union with the text is admirable.

Thomson's rhythmic structures, in general, relate by their simplicity to his rhythmic treatment of words. The best that might be said of Thomson's rhythm is that it is natural. The music flows easily along, helped by a rhythmic life that does not hinder its evolution. Sometimes the straightness of this evolution tends toward boredom, so uncomplicated is its statement. Certain works have such unvarying rhythms and so little rhythmic conflict that the simplicity becomes tedious. An examination of any of the examples in this chapter confirms the existence of plain rhythms in Thomson's music. And, of course, Thomson would assert that there is nothing wrong with common rhythms.

Another aspect of Thomson's style is his use of quotations from various sources in his music. Thomson's approach differs from that of Charles Ives, whose transformation of musical materials during the process of quotation was discussed in Chapter 5. Unlike Ives, Thomson states music by others as a more or less literal transcription. In the second movement of his *Suite from "The River,"* the section entitled *Industrial Expansion in the Mississippi Valley,* there is the following quotation of *Hot Time in the Old Town Tonight,* which for all practical purposes is a direct transcription:

Example 54a-b: Virgil Thomson: Suite from "The River," *second movement:* Industrial Expansion in the Mississippi Valley, *measures 17-24 and 43-46 (trumpet part only), and measures 39-41.* © *Copyright 1958 by Virgil Thomson. All Rights for the World Exclusively Controlled by Southern Music Publishing Co. Inc. Used by permission.*

When Thomson does alter a quotation, the change usually is not extensive. Example 54b shows two simple transformations:

Many of Thomson's works use transcription or quotation. In the last movement of the *Concerto for Violoncello and Orchestra*, quotations of "Yes, Jesus Loves Me" and a passage from Beethoven's *Sonata in F Major* op. 10 for piano find their way into the music. In *Four Saints in Three Acts* there are the unmistakable strains of "My country, 'tis of thee." *Lord Byron* contains, among other things, a passage set to a tune that is normally sung to the words, "Believe me if all those endearing young charms," a reference to the German drinking song, *Ach du lieber Augustin,* and a choir singing an unaltered version of the famous hymn *Jubilate, Amen.*

Thomson's quotations sometimes present the familiar practice of two tunes combined contrapuntally. *Pastorale on a Christmas Plainsong* for organ contains a passage in which *Divinum Mysterium* and *God Rest You Merry* are presented against each other in conjunction with a third element, a countermelody that complements the two.

Thomson has been criticized for his quotations, and Lou Harrison's contention that Thomson ". . . rather too timidly restricts the play of his punning facilities so that his productions in the style resemble newsreels more than fluid montages"[14] summarizes a valid opinion that sometimes the Thomson process of quotation is a rather superficial one. A quotation must be more than a literal rerun; the material must undergo a transformation in the new work that places it in the context of its new setting. In Ives this process is successful, for that composer's quotations emerge as fluid montages. In Thomson's work this is seldom the case.

Part of an explanation for Thomson's music is found in an examination of his compositional methods. In his autobiography, Thomson tells of writing three piano sonatas that "had poured right off,"[15] and one gets the impression from the music itself that much of it is composed easily and quickly. Two of Thomas's etudes (*For the Weaker Fingers* and *Ragtime Bass*) were composed on August 12, 1943. *English Usage* and *My Crow Pluto,* songs set to poems of Marianne Moore, both bear the following inscription: "Peterborough, N.H., August 8, 1963." Thomson, in fact, can write a short piece (an etude or one of his "portraits," for example) in an hour or so. If, for some reason, the piece isn't completed in that amount of time, fifteen minutes of work the next day will usually finish the composition.

The composer is not certain how he actually receives the inspiration for a work. John Cage relates that the initial measures of the *Quartet No. 2* came to Thomson while he was half-dozing before dinner. The composer ate, then wrote down the ideas.[16] Thomson's own analysis of the beginning moments of the creative process is picturesque. In stating that one gets started in whatever way one can, the composer comments, "How you get pregnant, God knows. But once you're pregnant, you know what to do." Knowing what to do in Thomson's case means composing quickly ("let it come," he says), and then "stopping to breathe." Before commencing again, Thomson reads the work from the beginning to help achieve continuity. This process works much better for Thomson than what he calls a "known layout," or a predetermined plan of attack. "You just do it," he comments. Once the work is completed, Thomson puts it away for a time before looking at it again. This is the time for changing, revising, and deleting to bring the piece to its final form. Thomson feels that a person can view the work objectively, as if he hadn't written it after "putting it in the ice box for awhile." This rather uncomplicated approach to composition, though one suspects that it is not Thomson's only method, explains much in the music. Certainly the music's spontaneity and even simplicity can be traced to the method of "just doing it."

Thomson's music does pose problems for some critics which can be related to the very method of composition and the musical results he advocates. Thomson's *Stabat Mater,* for example, has been likened to a "Ouija board production" by Theodore Chanler: "The vocal phrases, ranging from the sentimental to the trite or merely inept, and the accompaniment, with its purposeless meandering, its loose counterpoint whose strands begin at no particular point and break off for no particular reason, and the haphazard sequence of tonalities, all combine to give the air of a piece of 'automatic writing.'"[17] This is the problem with "just doing it," and Chanler's complaints stem from Thomson's method, which is thought of in some circles as a process of "churning it out."

Yet many of the pieces could not possibly have been composed in such a manner. The two string quartets are examples. *Quartet No. 1* (1931, revised in 1957) is based on the following compositional premise: "The structure of the first three movements is based on the constant transformation of motivic materials without any thematic or melodic repetition. The forward motion thus produced comes to rest only at the end of the last movement, a running rondo in which the energy generated earlier achieves its expansion."[18] In the *Quartet No. 2* the method is different, for the entire work is drawn from the opening measures in which two motives are stated, and then elaborated upon. This quartet is so tightly organized that there are relationships everywhere. "Thus," writes John Cage, "the greatest difficulty this work presents to the understanding is that it presents none."[19] A further example of structural tightness may be seen in the piano introduction to *Jour de Chaleur aux Bains de Mer:*

Example 55: Virgil Thomson: Jour de Chaleur aux Bains de Mer, *measures 1-4.*

If these measures are compared to Example 47, the relationship becomes apparent. The piano introduction, in fact, is a microcosm of the entire song.

An understanding of Thomson's music is not just in these relationships, nor in the matters discussed with reference to the music itself. Thomson claims that "all good composers write in a great many manners. Style—communicating power—you have it or you don't."[20] Another important aspect of Thomson's music is the humor that many listeners and critics have found in it. The composer is philosophical about the whole question: "I don't think music's ever very funny, you know. One can have lots of ideas for musical jokes, but the funniness soon disappears. Beethoven was full of musical jokes—he called them scherzos, but they're not funny anymore. Any joke, literary ones included, is likely to get tired as the years wear on. Shakespeare's comedies are not exactly laying 'em in the aisles, as you may have noticed."[21] One could argue about Beethoven's intention in his scherzos and about Shakespeare's power of communicating with a twentieth-century audience, but the real point concerns Thomson's idea that music is not funny. It is striking, especially, when one thinks of the composer's music, with so many passages that are surely attempts at musical humor.

Thomson gives further evidence of his singular musical philosophy when he speaks of nonsense in music. Thomson's opinion is that "music *is* nonsense!" And what of unintelligibility in music—works that do not really make sense, musical or otherwise? "The flaw in unintelligible music . . . is that it becomes intelligible. It's the same for unintelligible poetry or painting. It's really very difficult to make anything that won't, inside of five or ten years, become perfectly clear. To make a true abstraction, or a true piece of nonsense, is the most difficult problem in art."

If music is nonsense, and if even the unintelligible becomes meaningful, is it possible for a charlatan to become a great artist? "Everybody's a bit of a charlatan, and some of the great geniuses are the greatest charlatans." How does one recognize the charlatans? "You don't have to. If you've seen through someone's work, fine, you've seen through it. But there's no such thing as a real charlatan anyway. Certain works are just more obviously dishonest than others, that's all!" In the last scene of *The Mother of Us All*, Susan B. says, "I am not puzzled but it is very puzzling." How appropriate a statement, when one views the singular and contradictory world of Virgil Thomson!

Perhaps these various inconsistencies are simply part of the Thomsonian condition. He is, in many ways, the American Satie. Peggy Granville-Hicks sees a relationship between Thomson and the Dada movement in art, with its debunking of dated forms, stuffiness, sham, and pomposity,[22] and some of Thomson's comments suggest that Granville-Hicks has a valid point of comparison. Certainly the outward simplicity of much of his work results in a plain speech far removed from the musical language of the "far outs," as Thomson calls a number of his more adventurous contemporaries. Thomson's music can even be said to bridge a gap between the simple music of America's folk tradition and cultivated music. The second movement of the *Concerto for Violoncello and Orchestra* is a set of uncomplicated variations on *Tribulation*, a Southern hymn found in such tunebooks as Carden's *Missouri Harmony*, Walker's *Southern Harmony*, and the *Sacred Harp*.

The old idea that simple speech wears well might possibly apply to Thomson and may endear his music to a future generation less interested in the complexities of life and art. And there is the possibility that the music is not quite as simple as it seems. Lawrence Gilman's description of *Four Saints in Three Acts* as "deceptively simple"[23] is an intriguing thought.

For the present, Thomson the critic and champion of American music will have the respect of a large number of his countrymen. *The Mother of Us All* contains a character, Virgil T., who is described as "a pleasant and efficient master of ceremonies, in modern morning dress (top hat, cutaway coat, striped trousers, gardenia)."[24] It does not say whether the man is a charlatan or whether he is pretentious in his pleasantness and efficiency (and probably, in his simplicity). But the description as it stands is fitting and appropriate to the man who has created a pleasant and efficient musical existence, puzzling in its lack of puzzlement and simple even in its sometime complexity. Few composers, certainly, have managed such a feat.

chapter **8** _____

THE
NEW ECLECTICISM

The beautiful idea has no relation to size, and may be as
perfectly developed in a space too minute for any but
microscopic investigation as within the ample verge that is
measured by the arc of the rainbow.
  —Nathaniel Hawthorne, "The Artist of the Beautiful"

Every age must confront a series of problems that need to be solved
successfully before a vital and important music can emerge. Twentieth-
century music encountered difficulties that for some years seemed
almost insurmountable. Of the various choices open to American
composers in the first parts of the century, there was the traditional
approach—the way of the Porters and the Thomsons. A second
method, the "scientific," became an important aspect of American
musical composition in the 1940s and in the years that followed,
and was nurtured by composers such as Milton Babbitt and by the
development of electronic music and computer synthesis. The experimental way was another possibility, exemplified at first by
Charles Ives and later by others. Each approach produced some
excellent music, but each was filled with problems that could only
partially be solved.[1]

  The more traditional composers faced the problems of falling too
much into patterns of the past or into what were rapidly becoming
the stereotypical procedures of the twentieth century, and of emerging
from these attempts with unimaginative and even sterile results.

Neoclassicism and serialism were especially susceptible to such pitfalls. On the other hand, the more adventurous composers were faced with a dilemma of another kind: how to make music of substance that communicated despite its difficult and many times extramusical qualities. Until about 1950 most American composers were conservative by European standards, and even after that time much conservative music continued to be produced. However, the worldwide enthusiasm for new kinds of music, which began after World War II, finally had a profound influence in the United States, where some composers began to bring about a new American music—ultimately picking up the train of thought that Ives had left unfinished forty years earlier.

Some of the attitudes of midcentury American composers are summarized by Elliott Carter: "I want to invent something I haven't heard before."[2] It can be argued that the greatest geniuses of Western music did not think this way, and that *their* new sounds developed not because they wanted them to be new, but because the new music happened as a matter of course. But for a time many post-World War II American composers did strive for the new. Composers began to think of the old-fashioned ways of development—manipulation of motives, sequential treatments, and the like—as stifling. As with Debussy earlier in the century, they wondered what other procedures could be used to organize sounds. These alternate methods led to music whose compositional premises, far different from the majority of previous compositional plans, produced sometimes vital, sometimes perplexing results.

John Cage was one of the artists who moved the furthest away from "tradition." Cage himself says that he was trying to accomplish what Ives wanted many years before: to be able to sit on the back doorstep at sundown, listening to the music.[3] In continuing and expanding the Ivesian tradition, Cage shattered the old notions of music as organized sound consisting of melody, harmony, and rhythm. He wondered why music had to be these things. His questioning led to new concepts of how musical elements could be freed from the restraints imposed on them by conventional thinking. Most music contains only a few of the available pitches. Melody in its most elementary sense draws attention to a single line, which is a rather primitive way of perceiving music. Rhythm in which events occur "in time" is also limiting. Why, within a particular space of time, can an event not happen at any point, its rhythmic aspects thus being freed from time in the more traditional sense? As Cage puts it: "In a painting an image can go anywhere on the canvas. Why can't a rhythm do the same thing within the framework of a piece of music?"[4]

Cage's revolutionary ideas have led to many innovations. He is usually credited with having invented "chance music," music created under conditions that leave certain of its parts to the vagaries of the moment. Virgil Thomson notes that chance in composition is rather like a kaleidoscope, and "what kaleidoscopes and arabesques lack is urgency."[5] The music may not always have this quality, a condition that can ultimately hinder its expression in purely musical terms. But there is a new kind of musical awareness, a vitality of thought and of imagination.

Cage has redefined the entire concept of direction in music, since he has not been particularly interested in where events are going. Rather, he is more intrigued with the moment and with the possibilities of what can happen during that moment. Cage has also thought about music's purpose, deciding that actually there does not have to be any intent, that sounds alone can be the purpose. He says that "a sound accomplishes nothing; without it life would not last out the instant."[6] His aesthetic that *everything is music* is important, for it opens countless possibilities. And, it is not nearly as haphazard as one might think:

Question: That is, there are neither divisions of the "canvas" nor "frame" to be observed?

Answer: On the contrary you must give the closest attention to everything.[7]

Cage's ideas have made a generation of composers rethink concepts that were taken too much for granted or were ruled out of musical consideration by previous generations. These concepts have, in fact, furthered music beyond its old boundaries.

Many of Cage's works are famous because of the revolutionary concepts that formed them. The composition for piano that consists of four minutes, thirty-three seconds of silence, *4'33"*, is a case in point. To dismiss the work as a gimmick or as insignificant because it really is not music is to miss the point. Composers have pondered the silences in music in previous ages, but it took Cage to realize that silence itself was an opportunity for a complete work and a complete experience. According to Cage, silence is deciding in favor of sounds that are not intended. And Cage feels that silence has philosophical overtones, for it strikes the foundations of the ego. *4'33"* is a difficult work, for there is so much to hear—nothing—and it is a memorable experience, for it shows a world of multiplicity, something that interests Cage far more than aspects of unity within a particular work.

Because anything is possible in Cage's compositional process, some works are highly organized, while others give an outward impression of random and unrelated orderings. Most of his early pieces, among them the *5 Songs for Contralto* (1938) and the *Quartet for Twelve Tom-Toms* (1943), are carefully conceived and conventionally notated. *Music of Changes* (1951) was created with the aid of the Chinese book of changes, *I Ching,* one of Cage's favorite aids in the evolution of a work. The tempo changes in the piece are highly controlled. For example, one might move from ♩ = 69 to ♩ = 176 after accelerating for three measures; retard for five measures to ♩ = 100; remain at that speed for 13½ measures before retarding for five measures to ♩ = 58. Note durations are measured horizontally with 2½ centimeters equaling a quarter note. Measurements are made from note stem to note stem, and constantly changing dynamic levels such as PPPP to FFFF occur within the space of an eighth note. Among Cage's works that appear to be less structured are his various "imaginary landscapes" that have been composed for anything from forty-two phonograph recordings to twelve radios to landscapes for more conventional instruments. *Imaginary Landscape No. 4* for twelve radios (another work that involves the *I Ching* in certain aspects of its creation and performance) is a demonstration of the kinds of sounds that Cage appreciates. It also exemplifies how he employs events of the moment to produce musical results. Two people are at each of the radios, one to control dynamic levels, the other to select the stations. The addition of a conductor to oversee the performance brings the total number of performers to twenty-five. The work is an attempt to create fascinating textures with a common appliance, employing Ivesian textural levels and chance combinations of sounds to achieve the final results. The legendary performance in the early 1950s took place so late in the evening that many radio stations had gone off the air. The result was not as interesting as it might have been had there been more activity coming from the radios. But this is an aspect of the element of chance. And there is always a certain amount of interest simply because there is only a general awareness of what is going to actually take place when the performance occurs.

In the *Concert* for piano and orchestra (1957-1958) the pianist is given a sixty-three page piano part with eighty-four different "sound aggregates" that can be played in whole, in part, in any order, or in no order at all. In other words, we might conceivably hear a piano concerto in which the pianist was silent. The work gives the orchestra a great amount of freedom and even contains an optional aria for voice that can add another dimension to the work. There is no master score, although the individual parts are carefully written. Certainly the *result* of this treatment of the concept of soloist and orchestra, with no "final" performance a possibility, is a composition different from most of the other concertos in the repertory.

If a result cannot be predicted, the excitement of the moment can. Cage's *Musicircus* (1968) is a work in which everyone in the community is invited to perform. The piece has been done at the University of Illinois, in Minneapolis, and in Paris. High school bands, church choirs, boys' choirs, string quartets, folk dancers with phonographs, Scottish dancers in costume, and even a clavichordist have descended on one location, performed "like trains coming and going," Cage says, and by doing so have reaffirmed the idea of a music of the people, of a musical experience where everyone is the creator. In addition, these happenings have also drawn large audiences who have enjoyed other benefits of the experience. Food, for example, is a necessity in *Musicircus* ("rather like a church social" in the opinion of the composer[8]) for music is not the sole purpose. The event, as an experience in living, is a reaffirmation of Cage's belief that art should be an introduction to life.[9]

In addition to his novel approaches to the general aspects of composition, Cage utilizes fascinating "instruments" in some of his pieces. He has written compositions containing parts for brake drums. He has composed music for toy piano. Cage, in fact, has not rejected any possibility if that possibility has an intriguing sound. Thus, the amplified sound of water being swallowed, of a glass breaking or clinking, and of a balloon bursting are excellent sources, as good in their way as a piano or a trombone.

Cage's love of both conventional and unconventional sounds has made him reconsider the various traditional instruments and how they can be changed to produce a new result. One of these investigations resulted in the "prepared piano," which consists of objects such as nails, bolts, pins, and other materials placed between the strings of a piano, creating a diversity of different timbres. Henry Cowell had experimented with various possibilities of piano sonorities earlier in the century, including playing on the inside of the instrument, and Cage was undoubtedly influenced by some of Cowell's discoveries. But in most respects, Cage's is an original concept. As a result of his pioneering efforts, the prepared piano is for all practical purposes a new instrument, reminiscent of a Balinese gamelan orchestra. (As if anticipating this quasi-Eastern timbre, *Sonatas and Interludes*, Cage's largest set of compositions for the prepared piano, employs *rāgas* and *tālas* as a part of the compositional process.) Another unusual effect occurs in *The Wonderful Widow of Eighteen Springs*, a song for voice and piano in which the pianist plays on the piano lid and on various other wooden parts of the instrument rather than on the keys. The piano, in other words, has many sound possibilities from which Cage has realized a diversity of new and unusual timbres.

Cage has been accused of being narrow-minded, of only working with novelties and current avant-garde fashions.[10] This is untrue. Cage actually is an important figure whose mind is an open one and whose "novelty-fashions" in their total implications are significant and even visionary. They are not fraudulent, nor are they aimed at the destruction of Western musical civilization, although Cage has been accused of that and of just about everything else by his critics. The problem is simply that to the casual observer Cage's music is undisciplined. But this is also false. In some of his works chance itself is the discipline, a "method" that is used to bring about that which is not necessarily intended.

Plate 9: John Cage: sketch for Etudes Australes (No. 1). Copyright ©
1975 by Henmar Press Inc., 373 Park Avenue South, New York, N.Y.
10016. Reprint permission granted by the publisher.

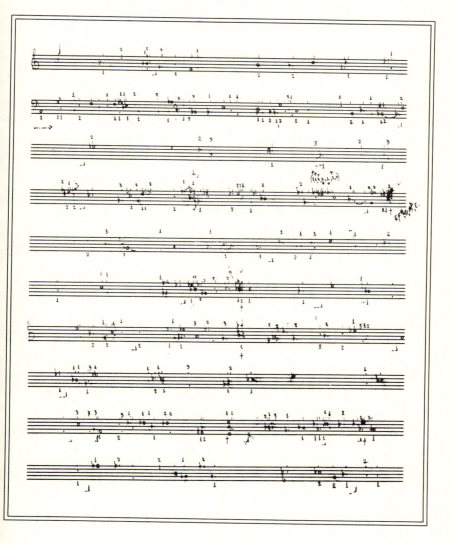

The compositional premises behind one of Cage's latest works, the *Etudes Australes,* is proof that there is a definite method behind chance procedures and that the results can present as unified a whole as if more conventional methods of organization had been employed. Cage says, concerning the piece:

The title of these etudes comes from *Atlas Australis,* a book of star maps printed in six colors (blue, green, orange, red, yellow, violet), published in Czecho-Slovakia. In order to write one of the thirty-two two-page pieces, I began by placing transparent grid over a particular one of the twenty-four maps. The width of the grid (approximately 9 and 1/2 inches) corresponds to the width of the music paper designed in collaboration with Carlo Carnevali. The vertical distance apart of the parallel lines (11/16ths of an inch) was settled upon after experimentation. Smaller spaces did not seem to give sufficient room for distinguishing between the twelve tones of the octave, while greater spaces permitted the tracing of such a large number of stars that the resulting music, it seemed to me, would be consistently dense and possibly unplayable. In addition to the narrow grid, I decided to distinguish between the six colors, so that though at times all stars might be traced, at other times only certain of them would be.

I also made use of the *I Ching* as a means of answering questions through chance operations in relation to the number 64. Thus, having placed the transparent grid over the star map (eight of its sixteen spaces for the right hand, eight for the left), I asked which stars I was to trace and how many. Numbers 1-9 give blue and green; 10-18 orange and red; 19-27 yellow and violet; 28-37 blue, green, orange and red; 38-46 blue, green, yellow and violet; 47-55, orange, red, yellow and violet; 56-64 all stars. When this tracing was finished for both hands, I translated the points in space into musical notation (the twelve tones), and then distributed these tones into the available octaves by means of chance operations.

As this distribution into different octaves took place, I kept track of which tones of the three lower octaves are utilized, and, if all of them are, which was the last to be introduced. I then changed the octave of this last tone so that for each single etude at least one tone remains unplayed. This unplayed tone is held down (by wedge, or tape) throughout a single etude, producing a tonal drone of harmonics that arise as the other tones are played.

I then ask whether a given note is a single tone or whether it is to give rise to an interval, triad, quatrad, or quintad. In Etude I only the number 64 brings the intervals, triads, etc. into operation. For Etude II both 63 and 64 yield intervals, etc. For the thirty-second etude 32 numbers (33-64) yield tone-aggregates.

It was when it was not clear to me how to write this music that I decided to begin again from the beginning, that is to go back to Grete Sultan herself [the pianist for whom the etudes were written, and who played three of them in New York on January 25, 1975]. Sitting beside her at the piano, I asked her to place her hands on the keys. I began to imagine duets for her two hands, each doing its own work unassisted by the other. I then went home and made tables, as exhaustively as I could, of what a single hand unassisted by the other can do. I was surprised to find 546 quintads, 520 quatrads, 81 triads, and 28 intervals (all within the interval of a ninth). Thus, by means of chance operations I am able to introduce harmonies into a music which is not based on harmony but rather on the uniqueness of each sound, of each combination of sounds.[11]

Cage reports that the pieces created the impression of serial music to some listeners,[12] and indeed the uncompromising aspects of the method of creation and the resulting combinations of pitches from that procedure would undoubtedly give an audience an impression of "twelve-tone" writing. Strictly speaking, of course, it is usually impossible to tell if a work is serial simply by listening to it. Yet this association proves a point, for to mistake the chance operations of Cage for serial procedures is to demonstrate that two different "methods" can produce similar aural results. For a serial composer, serial procedures provide the answers to most of the compositional questions and to the continuity within a particular piece. For Cage, chance operations answer the compositional questions, and from these procedures a continuity of musical expression develops.

One of Cage's literary methods is a further example of the logical use of chance operations. In trying to find a title for a book of writings that in a typical Cage manner contains a liberal sprinkling of absurdities. Cage subjected the twenty-six letters of the alphabet to a chance operation with the help of the *I Ching*. The letter "m" was the winner, and the book was subsequently entitled *M*. Although any letter would have worked as well, Cage noted that "m" was a good choice and particularly appropriate because it begins the names of many of his favorite people and things, among them music, mushrooms, *Modern Music,* and Mao Tse-tung.[13] It was an absurd method for choosing an absurd title for a book of absurdities! (In literary criticism, this would be called the "imitative fallacy.")

Another aspect of Cage's writing demonstrates more positive and visionary qualities of his music. *Prelude for Meditation for Prepared Piano Solo* (1944) is early Cage, and the preparation of the piano involves stove bolts and wood screws. The work itself follows:

Example 56: John Cage: Prelude for Meditation for Prepared Piano Solo.
Copyright © 1960 by Henmar Press Inc., 373 Park Avenue South,
New York, New York 10016. Reprint permission granted by the
publisher.

This piece, like *4'33"*, can be viewed initially and superficially as one event—a monolith. Within this monolithic experience is an inner world of relationships, of sounds and events that reach far beyond the two pitch classes that Cage employs. The philosophical concept behind a work such as this is simple: why should a piece of music begin, develop itself in intricate ways, and prove itself by an infinite variety that keeps an interest going in the work itself? Why should the variety not be of a different kind? A piece of music can simply suspend itself in time, although time itself is usually conceived as a terribly limiting artistic commodity. Pieces begin and pieces end. What about what is before the beginning and after the ending? Time, itself a measured fragment of eternity, is always there on either side of an experience of any kind, and, in effect, what happens within the time of a work need not always make the time pass but rather might make it exist within a vacuum, within a world of monolithic yet many-faceted events.

Cage's work is an early example of what has become a new aspect of musical experience. Other composers began thinking about the possibilities of the monolith, and numerous examples have been written in the last quarter of a century. La Monte Young's *Composition 1960 #7* is a case in point. The work consists of two pitch classes, a B and an F-sharp (the relationship to Cage's *Prelude for Meditation* is obvious), which the composer says should be held "for a long time." In 1961 the work was played in New York by a string trio, and the forty-five minute duration of that particular reading resulted in "a whole world of fluctuating overtones" for those who were willing to listen.[14] An even more famous example of the same basic premise from the early 1960s is Terry Riley's *In C*, a work for any ensemble of instruments. The score, which is merely a "launching pad," consists of fifty-three musical fragments. The performers themselves govern the progression of events. A player performs the first fragment until he decides to move on to the second. Since each player is "on his own," can start at any time and end either quickly (by playing the fifty-three fragments one after another) or after a great amount of time has passed (by doing the fragments many times each), a constant interplay results. The work emerges as a monolith because the material itself is squarely and unashamedly concerned with the pitch class C. And as if to stress the supremacy of that entity in each performance, a piano, the "pulse," plays the two highest Cs on the instrument repeatedly.

This "pulse" begins the work, and then any performer is welcome to commence his playing of the fifty-three fragments. The piano continues to sound the "pulse" for a time after the other players have stopped, and this gesture concludes the piece. The work is an excursion into a world of timelessness and of immobility. Yet within the strange universe of this one event are many smaller worlds and relationships, fascinating simply because they are instances of time suspended, and yet examples of intense activity within that suspension. In fact, the concept of the monolith is such that the experience becomes many things, not one. There are numerous other "monolithic" works, among them sections of Elliott Carter's *Eight Etudes and a Fantasy,* Mel Powell's *Immobiles,* and from rock music, Frank Zappa's *Weasels Ripped My Flesh.*

Experimental composers are not nearly as outrageous as their critics might think. Even a work that attempts by its chance procedures or other random methods of construction to be formless still achieves a form, which, in turn, expands our conception of "form." For example, if a composer writes some musical fragments on notecards, shuffles the cards, and then plays the music in the order in which it appears, there will be many different orderings but always the same music, rearranged each time. If one writes a chance piece for ten players with ten instruments, there is a limitation in the fact that the performers are ten, that the instruments are ten, and that the efforts are taking place within an inescapable time span. A composer cannot, in other words, achieve complete freedom, complete formlessness, for that is an impossibility. What a composer can do is achieve a new musical result.

Others have joined Cage in the search for a music free from convention, among them Earle Brown, who has attempted to give a spontaneity to the formal aspects of music. Brown was inspired by mobiles of Alexander Calder: ". . . basic units subject to innumerable different relationships or forms." Brown wondered why musical components could not be put together spontaneously.[15] The concept of mobility or immobility in composition relates to the search for a format that will prove to be a meaningful experience. Brown's works, like those of Cage, achieve this meaning. Harry Partch, another visionary, has divided the octave into forty-three tones. He has also invented an assortment of original instruments to play his music, for his imagination for sound was too great to be content with what he found in a conventional orchestra. But for all of these experimentations, the composers have been interested primarily in the creation of a vital experience. Many have succeeded, and if a listener thinks creatively, he too can experience the new and the exciting in music. Music is not a limited activity, but an all-encompassing one. Here is the experimentalists' most important contribution to music, for their ideas have widened concepts concerning music's possibilities.

While the experimentalists worked for the extension of the human experience from one standpoint, a group of other thinkers, emerging from the more traditional composers of the twentieth century, were in the process of writing music that treated traditional concepts and formulas of music in a quasi-scientific manner. A music was emerging inspired by Schönberg and Webern, whose general concepts concerning music have reshaped a great deal of twentieth-century musical thinking. The music produced by the "scientific" composers is extremely complicated but at times is capable of extraordinary expression. Milton Babbitt is representative, a writer who took Schönberg's concept of serialization of pitch and widened it considerably. Babbitt and many of his followers are convinced that their music is more *efficient* music than that which was composed previously. They avoid such stock procedures and redundancies as sequential treatment. Thus, pitch-class, dynamics, registers, durations, and timbres find themselves subjected to complex schemes that amount to an enormous amount of sheer virtuosity from the standpoint of the drawing board.

To Babbitt, texture is an important element, as evidenced by the elaborate polyphonic webs that comprise much of his music. So, too, is the complete control that total serialization makes possible. The 1950s saw a tremendous amount of composition based on the premise of serialization and its many side effects. The music communicated to a very few, and despite its marvelous virtues from an analytical standpoint, the impression to a general listener and to many musicians was a chaotic one. Babbitt answered complaints about the all-encompassing complexity of his works in an article, "Who Cares If You Listen?"[16] Despite the shocking fact that the title implied a disdain for the public, Babbitt's arguments were sound. Progressive composers and general audiences found themselves more and more at odds in the mid-twentieth century—more than they had ever been. Like their scientific counterparts, composers had advanced quickly in their thinking. The general public moves more slowly; and the vacuum that existed between the two became a frightening one. A composer might suggest that he did not care about whether or not his audience listened, but an artist wishing to communicate could not help but brood about the fact, at least privately.

The electronic medium and the development of the computer in its relationship to music and to musical creation added further complications, at least for a time. The older composers sneered, claiming a lack of communication when listening to an evening of music produced primarily by loudspeakers, and audiences found themselves even more befuddled. The 1950s and 1960s represent an age when tonality and other "old" procedures were strictly *out* as the second and the seventh became the most common intervals employed in a composition, often written and performed by machines rather than by human beings. The important question was really whether or not the new methods of pitch and formal organizations were capable of making an imprint on the human sensibility. To a small number of auditors, the impact was considerable. To others, the vast majority, it was not.

Andrew Imbrie's statement "The rules of music keep changing, because they are based not on convention but on human sensibility,"[17] is an appropriate prelude for an analysis of what has ultimately evolved from these various twentieth-century "factions." For from the experimentalists, the "scientists," and even from the traditionalists, who usually provide a backbone for new events, has emerged a new music—a music that combines and refines aspects of previous Western music and even music of various other cultures.

Of course, this new music has its precedents. Charles Ives and his use of various kinds of music often in juxtaposition, and Charles T. Griffes and his early cultivation of Oriental scales come to mind as composers who considered the possibility of new sources, as does Cage with his later reliance on elements both Eastern and Western. The boundaries between cultures began to disintegrate as more and more composers realized that having the whole world rather than only Western civilization as a source offered more positive and varied possibilities for a composer's inspiration.

Just as the boundaries between musical cultures were being broken, so was the philosophical approach to the past. Composers in the mid-twentieth century began to question whether "progress" was a common or a natural occurrence and whether the progression of time always brought an improvement in the musical condition. The realization that there is no final truth and no ultimate answer to compositional problems made writers think differently about the music of the past. Leonard B. Meyer says it this way: "The present is no longer seen as the glorious culmination from the primitive and misguided to the refined and the enlightened. The past has once again become a relevant source of insight and, like both the present and the future, of provisional truth."[18] If music of another culture provides a valuable source of inspiration, why should the music of a previous century not function in a similar manner? Why, in fact, should not an infinite variety of presents and pasts make an ultimately more diversified, more universal music? One is reminded of Ives's thought that a piece should be able to mix tonality and lack of tonality together. In the old way of thinking this was a lack of consistency; more recently we feel it to be part of a work's variety.

Composers began to think that music's ultimate purpose is communication. And were composers really communicating if they employed aspects of chance or total serialization as the major premise of a work? The answer of the majority of composers and listeners was a simple "no." These could be tools, but not the most important consideration in the compositional process. The early American composer Andrew Law wrote in 1814 that "music is the language of the heart; and almost every passion of the human breast may be excited by this art."[19] Composers of the mid-1960s revived this premise with enthusiasm. The artist, once again, sought to make his music speak from the heart, a possibility that many earlier twentieth-century composers had ignored. The idea that communication is of paramount importance brought about a different approach to music. Some composers even began to think seriously about music much as Lowell Mason did when he wrote in the mid-nineteenth century that "music's highest and best influence is its moral influence."[20] Broken boundaries, uses of the past, new compositional procedures, expression, and communication are elements and considerations that, when combined or synthesized, produce a new music. And it is this music that is being written today and that promises a bright future for the art. George Rochberg summarizes the importance of the new approach: "The '20th century' started about 1914-1918, ended about 1965-1970; and we are now metaphorically in the 21st century."[21] This thought is logical, for this new music is far removed both in purpose and in sound from that of the fifty-year twentieth century that Rochberg mentions.

The characteristics of what I shall call the "New Eclecticism" are evident in the work of four representative composers: George Crumb, James Drew, Robert Morris, and Rochberg. All have written significant music that has evinced positive audience reaction. These writers do care whether or not people listen, yet they have not sacrificed standards or written only music that is immediately appealing in order to communicate with an audience.

George Crumb, who teaches at the University of Pennsylvania, has received critical acclaim for his exciting and impeccably written works. Crumb writes from fundamental and strong philosophical presuppositions: in composing *Makrokosmos I*, for example, "the 'larger world' of concepts and ideas" influenced the evolution of his music:

While composing *Makrokosmos*, I was aware of certain recurrent haunting images. At times quite vivid, at times vague and almost subliminal, these images seemed to coalesce around the following several ideas. . .: the "magical properties" of music; the problem of the origin of evil; the "timelessness" of time; a sense of the profound ironies of life. . .; the haunting words of Pascal: "Le silence éternel des espaces infinis m'effraie" ("The eternal silence of infinite space terrifies me"); and these few lines of Rilke (Das Buch der Bilder): "Und in den Nächten fällt die schwere Erde aus allen Sternen in die Einsamkeit. Wir alle fallen. Und doch ist Einer, welcher dieses Fallen unendlich sanft in seinen Händen hält" ("And in the nights the heavy earth is falling from all the stars down into loneliness. We all aré falling. And yet there is one who holds this falling endlessly gently in his hands").[22]

Crumb's fascination with sounds has led him to employ numerous unusual instruments in his music. The use of musical saw, stone jug, banjo, Jew's harp, and electric guitar played "bottle-neck style," by sliding a glass rod over the frets, brings Appalachia and the timbres associated with mountain musicians to some of his music. Other oddities include a metal thunder-sheet, an African log drum, Tibetan prayer stones, a *quijada del asino* (jawbone of an ass),

Japanese Kabuki blocks, and an alto African thumb piano. In certain of his works violinists are asked to draw their bows over five water-tuned crystal glasses or to slacken the hairs on their bows to create an unusual sound effect. In *Makrokosmos I* the pianist is requested to play the strings on the inside of the piano "with thimble-capped fingers," using the kind of thimbles found in a sewing box. A chain placed on the piano strings produces an unusual timbre in another movement of the same work. In order to achieve special harmonics or glissandi on the piano strings, a "5 /8-inch chisel with a smooth cutting edge" is called into service; or, in another work, a percussionist is asked to raise and lower a gong in a bucket of water. These aspects of the compositions are not experiments or superficial excursions into the world of the bizarre; they are an important part of the work's ultimate meaning, its total impression, just as Crumb's instruction for the players to wear masks in sections of his orchestral composition *Echoes of Time and the River* is an attempt to create a more total experience, both aural and visual.

Like so many of his American predecessors and contemporaries, Crumb delights in employing musical quotations. Part of Bach's *Fugue in D-sharp Minor* (from the *Well-Tempered Clavier,* second book), Beethoven's *Hammerklavier,* Chopin's *Fantasie-Impromptu,* or Ravel's *Bolero* can be found in various works, each quotation interacting successfully with other parts of the composition. From the vernacular tradition, the Appalachian hymn tune, *Will There Be Any Stars in My Crown?* adds a further dimension to the texture of *Nightspell I* from *Makrokosmos I,* just as allusions to Mahler and Haydn present an impression of another continent's musical past in Crumb's *Night of the Four Moons.* The quotations or reminiscences are combined in various ways: Bach with a hint of flamenco; Mahler with a feeling of the Orient.

Crumb's music is elaborately conceived, and his appreciation of logical procedures was developed in part by going the route of serialism for a time. As with his Baroque predecessors there are numerous symbols in his music, both visual and numerological. In *Makrokosmos I* every fourth piece is notated symbolically. *Crucifixus* is written on the page to form a cross. Crumb's symbols may be expressed in formal terms that are amazing in their simplicity. The structures themselves sometimes are of the most elementary kind, and the textures are often simple, which led a student leaving the

Plate 10: George Crumb: Makrokosmos I *(No. 8) (manuscript). Copy-right © 1974 by C. F. Peters Corporation, 373 Park Avenue South, New York 10016. Reprint permission granted by the publisher.*

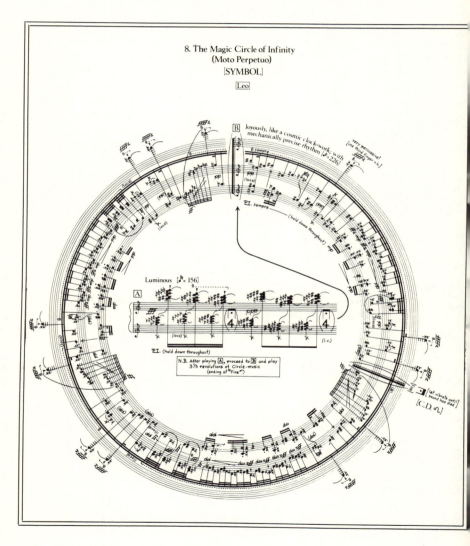

performance of a Crumb piece to say: "Imagine, 35 minutes and not a note of counterpoint."[23] But the composer is not interested in counterpoint for the sake of counterpoint. The decisions concerning its inclusion or exclusion rest solely on the ultimate *expression* the composer is seeking. Above all, and more important than the numbers and other peripheral elements, is Crumb's intuition. If a simple form will achieve the desired result, an ABA for example, Crumb uses that form. If, for proper musical effect, wordy instructions to a performer are necessary, such as those in the *Makrokosmos I* that ask a pianist to play "Musingly, like the gentle caress of a faintly remembered music," "Joyously, like a cosmic clockwork," or "Eerily, with a sense of malignant evil," Crumb writes elaborate instructions. If the music will be performed more effectively from an unorthodox presentation on the page, Crumb uses the unusual notation. Nothing is left to chance, and the results attest to the fact that this care has produced some significant works. Crumb, quite simply, communicates with his audience.

Another composer who has approached composition from the communicative aspect is James Drew. Drew's music may best be described by his statement, "Diversity is the American characteristic in Art."[24] There is a great deal of variety in Drew's works, brought about by the combinations of numerous events and different kinds of music and by the superimposition of these various elements upon each other. An example of Drew's music is the piano piece *primero libro de referencia laberinto*, about which the composer writes the following:

> The work was . . . composed in 1969, and was one of my first encounters with thinking in various degrees of tonality within a single frame of reference. I consider everything "tonal"—it is only the degree of consonance or dissonance that shapes the projected impressions. So, I composed a kind of stream of consciousness work in which a relatively consonant music is interrupted, and commented on, by a more dissonant kind of music, or the other way around. The most important aspect of the work is the relationships between these diverse musics—in other words the unifying features that bring the relationships into being.[25]

There are some references in the work to the music of others which Drew prefers to call "recomposed" rather than quoted. Among them is the following passage:

Example 57a-b: James Drew: primero libro de referencia laberinto.
© *1974, Theodore Presser Co. Used by permission.*

A

Drew says that "it is ultimately Ives [from the *Largo* for violin, clarinet and piano], but I extracted it and comment on it (through its context-development) with reference to where I found it—and that was in George Rochberg's *Contra Mortem et Tempus.*" Of another section of the *primero libro de referencia laberinto* Drew writes: "[It is] a fragment, reharmonized, with the popular show-song 'Tea for Two' as the 'echo' from the past referencia. Shortly after that particular point, the reference comes through a new setting of 'Bringing in the Sheaves' with a definite nod to my 'ancestor' Charles Ives."[26]

B

Plate 11: James Drew: sketch for primero libro de referencia laberinto.
© *1974, Theodore Presser Co. Used by permission.*

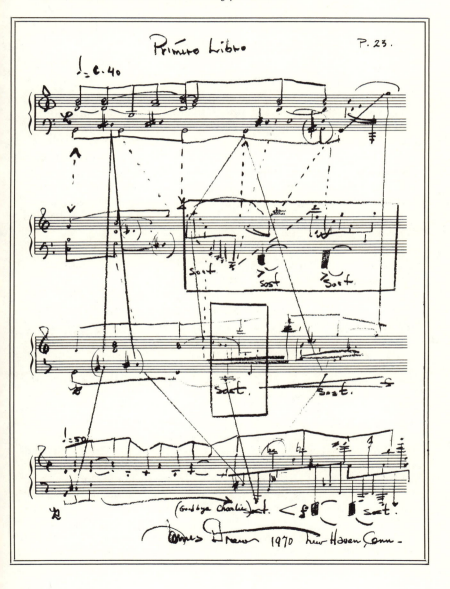

As a guide to reading the examples, the following explanation is helpful, for like many of his contemporaries, Drew does not rely strictly on conventional notations. The symbols █ △, and ▽ indicate, respectively, a cluster of chromatic pitches, highest (approximate) pitch, and lowest approximate pitch. As for the music on the small staff lines: "[It] should be played by making room for it in between the principal material. Accurate rhythm is not the principal goal, but rather the energies resulting from the intrusions of the 'other material' into the general time framework."[27] Two different entities interacting upon each other produce the effect Drew desires, and in this case a mixture of different concepts of tonality, rhythmic structures, and even musical traditions gives an overwhelming impression of vitality. The result is a virtuoso piano work, a collection of varied musical gestures, and yet a unified composition despite the various kinds of music and multi-leveled activities that are found in the piece.

Drew's orchestral work *West Indian Lights,* which Gunther Schuller conducted at Tanglewood in 1973, won the Panamericana Prize in 1974. The composer writes:

The initial notion behind my *West Indian Lights* was, and has remained, an abstract one. If there is a narrative at all in the work it might be glimpsed in the following lines:
Man symbolizes his highest aspirations in his creation of the fantastic. By such means he can attempt to rise to a bizarre, but understandable, place in the universe. In such a world his fantastic beings, impenetrable mysteries, and Gods are necessary.

I have tried to translate as clearly as possible a series of essentially abstract images into a musical language with which I am the most familiar. Since these images have to do with the subject of ancient religious rites and mankind's continuing quest for universal truths, within the constantly changing allusion of his existence, I have perhaps sought to glimpse within the work the human experience as an awesome adventure that is equally understood by all human beings—but in a setting that remains abstract.
The geographical reference of the title not only has musical implications, but is significant in the sense that it is particularly in the Caribbean region that the fusion of two of the most ancient celebrations of life and death, the

Roman Catholic and African rites, continue to exist in a fundamentally innocent manner. In such a context all destinies are still possible; the mysterious rites bells can signify either the Halls of Heaven or the Gates of Erebus.[28]

The work contains many references to tonality that would have made it unsuitable as "contemporary" music a decade ago. The *New York Times* noted that Drew's work "thumbed its nose at most of the dogmas of contemporary music." The review continued: "Lushly scored with the obvious intent of pleasing the ear, Drew's music flirted with exoticism and invoked traditional tonality. . . ."[29] But in this piece, tonality is the most appropriate expression for Drew's particular intention and is an expression of what the composer calls the "reality" of the 1970s. He writes: ". . . I am convinced of one thing in particular, and that is that tonality, in the very basic sense, is far from dead. It is . . . a means to extend expression another step or two."[30] The extension, however, is not at the price of the music's emotional effect and its expressive power.

For the music must, above all, communicate: Drew is interested in his performers, his audience, and in music's effect as a valuable part of all human experience:

My current musical thinking continues to pursue ways to better construct the complexities that have become synonymous with our particular century. The idea of making the interpretation of music possible within such complexities rather than the performers having heart attacks constantly while attempting just getting the "notes" is absolutely necessary. Only then will the performer be able to feel secure enough that he or she can go on to the deeper dramatic aspects of the music.[31]

From these deeper aspects comes the final step in the communicative process: the meaning that the composer wishes to impart to his audience.

Robert Morris is yet another composer whose music reflects the philosophies of the New Eclecticism. Morris teaches at Yale, and his background includes work at the Eastman School of Music and at the University of Michigan. Many different kinds of music have fascinated him and have been a part of his experience. As an undergraduate at Eastman, Morris developed an interest in the possibility of combining Western music with the music of India. Later, he became an expert in serialism, and Webern's influence is noticeable in some of his music. Work with the improvisatory aspects of music and with the electronic medium followed, and while he was at Michigan, Morris received an advanced degree in composition and in ethnomusicology. Morris' experiences have resulted in a number of works in which the composer seeks to unite supposedly uncombinable entities. Morris calls his adaptation of music to new cultural patterns "acculturation:"

> . . . I am attempting literally to manifest the way in which musical cultures change and influence one another as an intrinsic aspect of a composition's *raison d'être*. The fact that music can usually be described as a "cool medium" (i.e. needing the listener (performer) to interpret or "complete" the message) is the primary reason why such an undertaking is possible or valuable. The problem is finding the appropriate compositional tools that will allow the interaction of styles to occur in a natural and democratic manner.[32]

Morris is conceptually indebted to McLuhan. His "acculturation" results in general allusions to various works, both familiar and unfamiliar. Yet to say that Morris always employs simple quotation in these instances is not entirely accurate, as he works his material in ways that assure a transformation of what had previously existed. The process is a difficult one, as Morris notes:

> Composing with pre-existing or preformed material and/or working within traditional styles is rather subtle. Combining musical entitles immediately becomes problematical since the sources usually have a tendency to obscure, cancel out, or dominate one another. A fresh compositional strategy that is highly responsive to the musics to be combined must be discovered for each piece. Starting with a particular compositional situation can also be fruitful if it gives rise to a family of different musics.[33]

An example of a work that demonstrates Morris' process of acculturation is the *Motet on Doo-dah* (1973), a composition for alto flute, double bass, and piano that sets Stephen Foster's *Camptown Races* in the form of an isorhythmic motet. Foster's tune becomes the basis for a quasi-twelve-tone pitch structure. The gestures of the piece and the general character of the instrumental parts are based on Korean and Japanese court music. Morris writes: "The irony of this particular collection of elements is intended to comment on the more negative aspects of cultural interactions."[34] The work itself, although it is constructed elaborately with numerous relationships typical of serial writing, and although it concerns itself with the Far East, Medieval Europe, and the Old South, nonetheless achieves a unity within this wide diversity of elements. There is also a feeling of spontaneity about the piece, despite the fact that the notes and rhythms can be analyzed elaborately, uncovering numerous relationships based on numbers.

At times, Morris' thinking results in combinations of music that are not quite so outwardly antithetical as in *Motet on Doo-dah.* *Thunders of Spring Over Distant Mountains* (1973) is an electronic work that deals entirely with musical sources from Southeast Asia. The title shows the influence of T. S. Eliot's *The Wasteland* and gives a subtle impression that Western culture alone is a dead end. *Thunders of Spring Over Distant Mountains* contains Chinese/Taiwanese music, part of a Buddhist cremation service, Japanese Court Music, an Indonesian ballad, a Japanese *Nō* dance, sections of a Tibetan Buddhist service, and the Korean *Ah-ak* (wine ceremony), which are transformed first into electronic sounds and then into each other.

Another composition that combines different elements is the work for two pianos entitled *Variations on the Variation of the Quadran Pavan and the Quadran Pavan by Bull and Byrd* (1974), based on three pieces from the *Fitzwilliam Virginal Book.* John Bull's *The Quadran Pavan* is the "theme" of the work, and the same composer's *Variation of the Quadran* and William Byrd's *Quadran Paven* provide the source material for the rest. In attempting to reconcile the music of Byrd and Bull, Morris writes that he has tried "to connote the friendly bickering between the . . . pieces (and by implication, the composers) by producing events wherein corresponding parts of each piece are presented simultaneously so that the basically melodic and harmonic deviations are allowed to clash in a heterophonic manner."[35]

Morris' juxtaposition of the works is only the beginning of a compositional process that reconciles them. The composer notes

that numerous compositional operations, among them re-registra-
tion, multiple doublings, inversions and retrogressions, sampling,
fragmentation, canonic writing, and dynamic alterations make the
work run the gamut from quotation to complete alteration:

The purpose for all of the above was to establish the relationships between
the activities of transcription, arranging, editing, orchestration, making
variations and composing. It can be easily shown that any of these activities
have resulted in the acculturation of one style on another in the history of
Western art or popular music. Indeed, the source material itself is the result
of such activities. The aural result of these operative procedures on a source
subject in this piece involve the evocation of other musics beside Eliza-
bethan keyboard music; there are references to the piano style of late Beethoven, the neo-classic Stravinsky, post-Webern pointallism, French rococo
and impressionistic styles, the recent modal/rhythmic style, etc.

I hope I have been able to convey musically the extremely rich, complex
and subtle relationships between musics of different periods, genres, functions, and styles, as it seems obvious in this particularly pluralistic cultural
environment, this is the primary aim of a composer (among others).[36]

Another of Morris' reconciliations is *Not Lilacs!* (1974) for jazz
quartet, a bebop tune complete with instrumental solos, which is at
the same time an intricate serial compositon. *Not Lilacs!* is in some
ways reminiscent of the concepts of Hall Overton and Francis Thorne
and of the Third-Stream music of Gunther Schuller. Example 58 is a
section of the work, demonstrating Morris' approach to this particular "acculturation:"

Example 58: Robert Morris: Not Lilacs!, *piano part, measures 157-160.
Reproduced by permission of the composer.*

Plate 12: Robert Morris: sketch for Not Lilacs! *Reproduced by permission of the composer.*

In Different Voices (1975) for wind ensemble divided into five groups (with five conductors) attempts to reconcile even more divergent musical styles. All of the writing is original Morris, composed in imitation of these various styles and juxtaposed in various ways. Passages are reminiscent of Bach, of Praetorius chorales, and of eighteenth-century Bohemian music. There is South Indian music, 1940 jazz, and sections in the style of Mendelssohn and Schubert. Bartók and Japanese *Nō* music are synthesized. There is 1955 jazz of the Errol Garner variety, percussion music à la Varèse, a saxophone solo reminiscent of the style of Thelonius Monk, and passages of fife and drum music. This is only a small indication of what is actually in the work. The "acculturation" of these various elements results in the music's total experience. (The work is to be performed so that the audience can move about from group to group, and even so that food will be available during the hour-long performance.) The final moment is typical, for it is the simultaneous reconciliation of Dixieland jazz, Tibetan instrumental music, an eighteenth-century Viennese piano concerto, a seventeenth-century Venetian brass work, and African rain forest drumming, all cadencing on a chord that for the most part is B-flat major.

Morris' ideas concerning the creative process are revealing, for they show an organized approach that undoubtedly helps the composer achieve unity in his music. The composer says that the first stage of the process, or really the pre-first stage, is the evolution of ideas. After a composer has ideas he must decide how to give them coherence. Next comes what Morris calls "interpretation," which is the process of reification, of realizing the concepts that have gone before. The final notation of the piece, the actual writing down of the notes is the most intuitive place, where refinement over and above all of the previous work takes place. Although some composers would say that all of these stages intermingle as a work takes shape, for Morris they are separate divisions.[37] An awareness of what is happening during the creative process is typical of a composer such as Morris, for his music demonstrates a balance of concern for the construction of the piece (he is a fine mathematician in addition to his musical activities) as well as for the expressive intent and effect that his music will have on its listeners. Composers of the past have worked with these premises, of course. But Morris' approach, typical of the composers of the New Eclecticism, extends concepts and divergent elements into a new kind of expression. And, despite the seeming conglomeration of unrelated events, the music emerges as a logical synthesis, where music from many parts of the world has been "acculturized."

A fourth composer who demonstrates some of the same approaches to music is George Rochberg. Rochberg is also a composer-professor and for a number of years has been on the faculty of the University of Pennsylvania. Like Crumb and Morris, Rochberg wrote serial music and found himself influenced by Webern's work. Around 1960, Rochberg became interested in the simultaneous musical happenings that Ives had employed many years before. Ives, in fact, was an important influence on Rochberg:

To me the "20th century" is a wasteland littered with the bones of lost prospectors because either they followed wrong maps or perverted intuitions. Ives, whom I consider great though flawed, was the only one who saw that the life of music lay not with methodology or theoretical constructs but with the enlargement of expressive devices. He, more than any other composer, gave me the courage to break with the false limitations of serialism.[38]

One of the results of Rochberg's "break" with serialism was an attempt to rediscover the music of previous ages and to make use of it: "I came to realize that the music of the 'old masters' was a living presence, that its spiritual values had not been displaced or destroyed by new music. The shock wave of this enlargement of vision was to alter my whole attitude toward what was musically possible today."[39] One possibility for Rochberg was the technique of quotation, and several of his works from the mid-1960s relied on this procedure. Later came the wholehearted reembracement of tonality as a probable new means of expression. Like Ives, Rochberg decided that tonality and lack of tonality could work side by side or in juxtaposition with each other and not suffer as a result. *Carnival Music* (1971) is a five-movement piano work with tonal passages as well as sections of atonality. The titles of the movements: "Fanfares and March," "Blues," "Largo doloroso," "Sfumato" (a style of Renaissance painting in which figures, objects, and shapes emerge out of veiled, dreamy backgrounds), and "Toccata-Rag" demonstrate a multitude of influences and musical sources. Similar approaches may be found in several of Rochberg's other works, among them the *String Quartet No. 3* (1971-72), a composition that succeeds in achieving Rochberg's goal. Here he employs melodic and harmonic language of the nineteenth century, in particular the "styles" of Beethoven and Mahler. The variation movement is almost classical in its approach, a scherzo is a fugatto, and other sections contain approaches that are reminiscent of the music of previous generations. Numerous relationships bind the various movements together into a tightly organized entity. But the piece is something more. As Rochberg says: "The essential, absolutely basic thing is that music remains an expressive act. . . . The major question is . . . to probe the meaning of the word 'expression' not in technical, musical terms but in human terms." In determining what actually brings this about, Rochberg says that it is "certainly not the notes, not the devices of music but something which imprints itself as design, structure on musical means, or something which in purely human terms wants to, needs to complete itself. The struggle is a spiritual one, for the single individual as for the race."

The question of expressivity leads Rochberg one step further: "In the end the question must take us to see art again as *moral* in the Kantian sense. Survival or renewal is not possible without morality; not the morality of religious orthodoxies although they certainly possess the seeds but a humanistic morality that understands that *all* human behavior must be integrated into, identified with the processes which sustain the life of the cosmos." Many works have short lives because they "tend away from the search for collective human wisdom which is not *simple* but varied and diverse because it starts from individual minds who seek to connect with the wisdom of the past."[40] This, then, is Rochberg's answer for an age that has had to redefine many things, among them musical values. The past has become an important source in preparation for a meaningful present and future. Rochberg's "morality" is shared by many of his contemporaries who have also come to feel that music has a lofty purpose in the life of the cosmos.

The New Eclecticism is for the most part an American idea, for few composers outside of the United States have employed similar concepts. The four composers who have been mentioned represent what is becoming a common practice on the part of American composers, as seen in the work of Salvatore Martirano, Jacob Druckmann, and Stanley Silvermann. And one of the most telling examples of the New Eclecticism's acceptance can be discovered in a work that the composer Donald Martino is in the process of composing. Martino, one of Roger Sessions' and Milton Babbitt's most important students, is a master of serial procedures and of the whole spectrum of complexities of twentieth-century writing. Like Babbitt, his works are impeccably constructed and fiendishly difficult. Martino's music compromises nothing, and his flawless workmanship has already produced important works, among them the *Notturno,* which won the 1974 Pulitzer Prize in music. Martino's idea of writing an opera based on Dante's *Inferno* grew out of a commission from the Paderewski Fund to write a choral piece. The composer's setting of the *Paradiso* from the *Commedia* calls for two live choruses, ten small choruses heard antiphonally on tape from various parts of the hall, a live orchestra and a taped orchestra, and a large number of soloists. The writing of this work has led Martino to the prospect of composing a three-act opera based on the *Commedia.* Martino's plan is an *Inferno* composed serially, a *Purgatorio* written in a transitional style, and a *Paradiso* that is tonal with "ghosts of Brahms and Berlioz" lurking in the background.[41] A few years ago Martino would never have written music that moved from serial procedures to the tonal world of a previous century. Yet even some of the composers who were the most "difficult" a decade ago are readjusting their thinking. The change is striking.

None of the composers discussed in this chapter has spent a great amount of time writing and worrying about being "American." And, by being true to themselves, they have produced an American music of high quality and of great individuality. The idea that to write American music a person need only be an American and then write anything he wishes is certainly true. But in the 1970s the nationalistic worries are over. Composers are writing American music that is a culmination, not only because they have learned to deal with the present but because they have also learned to accept the past. The many "systems" of earlier parts of the century have been synthesized, with positive results.

The most encouraging thought for the future lies in composer Jon Appleton's idea concerning "systems." Appleton's belief that "we have hardly begun to discover the possibilities"[42] is shared by many composers, and it speaks well for the future of music. Today is the New Eclecticism. For tomorrow, for the future, one can only speculate, and speculate positively.

EPILOGUE

> . . . Music, like life . . . is a becoming. It rests, not in what it
> is, but in what it would be; it seeks expression, not in terms of
> fact, but in terms of hope.
> —Reverend C. Robbins, at a memorial service
> for Horatio Parker

We could, of course, cite a number of problems: conditions that
explain past and current hindrances to the evolution of American
art. There is the American musical inferiority complex that has
affected some composers; the American tendency to treat every
activity, even music, according to the canons of business; and the
widespread and unfortunate anti-intellectual approach to life that
has dominated the American experience. These are only a few of
the serious problems confronting the American musician.

Yet there is hope for America's music. This hope lies in the fact
that there are currently composers at work who are creating a vital
and exciting new music based on the experiences of former generations. With these composers, only a few of whom have been mentioned in the previous chapter, rests the possibility of a profound
American musical maturity. Roger Sessions' mid-1950s comment
that "the 'great line of western tradition' provides the most fertile
source of nourishment . . . for American music"[1] has proved to be
only partly accurate, for although America is linked to European
culture in countless ways, American individuality has finally as-

serted itself, making such concepts as "acculturation" a distinct possibility—and a non-European one at that. This is a philosophical elaboration of the ethnological fact of the development of America from many nationalities.

The beginnings of an American maturity may be seen in the way current composers apply common techniques of composition. Americans still use the age-old practice of musical quotation, for example, a device that has established itself as an important characteristic of American music. Now, however, the quotations are not just folk songs or hymns pasted on a musical framework that cannot accommodate them. They are unmistakably a part of the compositional whole. Some of the composers discussed in the previous chapter are masters of the art of musical quotation. Donal Henahan writes of George Crumb's quotations: ". . . Crumb uses the technique so deftly and with such sure instinct for dramatic impact that one can experience not only a twinge of nostalgia but something like the sense of irretrievable loss that arises when one leafs through an album of family pictures or yellowing snapshots of half-forgotten friends in half-forgotten wars."[2] This is but one example: American music in general is reaching a refinement known as maturity. If all goes well, a large number of major works will be written as a result of this maturity.

An article in *Newsweek* in May 1975 discussing the exciting possibilities for the arts begins with the positive statement: "An explosion of young talent is bringing change and vitality to American arts as rarely before in the nation's history."[3] The title of the article, "Young Genius on the Rise in U.S.," is a reminder of what John Hubbard wrote in 1808: ". . . genius only can give force and energy to music."[4] Today there are a number of geniuses in American arts, and the vital and forceful results are beginning to show. America seems to be on the verge of an artistic maturity that can take place if false boundaries are broken and if art becomes a way of life for more than the few. Then we will have the state of affairs that men such as Charles Ives dreamed of: a great musical unity, a "musical Over-Soul," as it were.

Some of the older composers are not so optimistic. Virgil Thomson contends that the arts are in a dreadful state and says that nothing new has happened in music for at least a quarter of a century.[5] This, of course, is untrue, although it demonstrates a pessimism that is felt by many. Aaron Copland discusses the boundaries that exist between the cultivated and vernacular traditions of music as permanent entities. "Everyone is *not* on the same wave length," Copland says, and he sees no hope for change.[6] A further note of pessimism may be found in Tui St. George Tucker's observation that "John [Cage] labors to build beauty, the Tao with star-map and Chinese oracle as our civilization collapses around us."[7] These words are also a demonstration of the pessimism that has accompanied so many of the enormous changes and struggles of the twentieth century and are reflective of the opinion that the United States and even the Western world is in a state of decline. Only the events of the next decades will show how civilization fares in an ever-changing concept of world culture and in an ever-shifting balance of world authority. It is to be hoped that as changes occur musical boundaries will be broken, creating a world in which music means, simply, music. At best, civilization's enormous potential will somehow triumph, and music itself will be a part of this new and visionary experience.

Concerning American music there is room for optimism. Henry Gilbert wrote in 1915 that out of all of the various sources available to American composers would come "an art of music, which, . . . shall yet be superior in expressive power to any of the single elements from which it has been built."[8] Sixty years later, Michael Tilson Thomas says that "Americans have no roots, no culture. They're just a jumble of people from all over the place.

"Well, exactly so. We have absorbed all those cultures, and created a magnificent new one of our own. There has never been a country before that has been in such a position."[9] James Drew calls it "that American boiling cross-sectional pot—all kinds of music but still uniquely one's own."[10] What an enviable way for George Rochberg's twenty-first century to begin! And what a promise for the possibility of a great American music, which, with the help of other music, might someday develop beyond that limitation into a synthesis—a world music that transcends all national boundaries. Should that possibility ever occur on a worldwide scale, the work of the Charles Iveses, the John Cages, and other visionary pioneers will not have been in vain.

NOTES

PROLOGUE

1. Thomas A. Bailey, "The Mythmakers of American History," *Journal of American History* 55 (June 1968): 5. Bailey's essay has been reprinted in Nicholas Cords and Patrick Gerster, eds., *Myth and the American Experience* I (New York: Glencoe Press, 1973), pp. 2-17.

2. Arthur Mendel, "Source Book of American Music," *Modern Music* 9 (November-December 1931): 35-36.

3. George Hood, *A History of Music in New England* (Boston: Wilkins, Carter, and Co., 1846), p. 1.

4. Virgil Thomson, *American Music Since 1910* (New York: Holt, Rinehart, and Winston, 1971), p. 15.

5. This quotation is from an interview with Gregg Smith. See *New York Times*, July 27, 1975.

6. Olin Downes, "An American Composer," *The Musical Quarterly* 4 (January 1918): 35.

7. Gilbert Chase, ed., *The American Composer Speaks* (Baton Rouge: Louisiana State University Press, 1966), p. 91.

8. Virgil Thomson, *Music Reviewed* (New York: Random House, 1967), pp. 232-233.

9. *Dwight's Journal of Music*, October 9, 1852.

10. *New York Musical Review*, February 16, 1854.

11. Louis Moreau Gottschalk, *Notes of a Pianist*, ed. Jeanne Behrend (New York: Alfred A. Knopf, 1964), p. 233.

12. *Ibid.*, p. 291.

13. Nathaniel Hawthorne, Preface to *The Marble Faun* (Boston: Houghton Mifflin Company, 1900), p. xxiv.

14. *The Musical Times*, October 1, 1893.

15. Henry Bellamann, "Charles Ives: The Man and His Music," *The Musical Quarterly* 19 (January 1933): 51.

16. Aaron Copland, *The New Music: 1900-1960* (New York: W. W. Norton & Company, 1968), p. 17.

17. Andrew Law, *Essays on Music* (Philadelphia: The Author, 1814), p. 6.

18. Aaron Copland, *Music and Imagination* (Cambridge: Harvard University Press, 1972), p. 84.

19. Henry Cowell, ed., *American Composers on American Music: A Symposium* (New York: Frederick Ungar Publishing Co., 1962), p. 151.

20. Paul Henry Lang, ed., *One Hundred Years of Music in America* (New York: G. Schirmer, Inc., 1961), p. 163.

21. Thomson, *Music Reviewed*, p. 232. The same concept may be found in Thomson's *American Music Since 1910*, pp. 18-19.

22. Winthrop Sargeant, *Jazz: Hot and Hybrid* (New York: E. P. Dutton & Co., 1946), p. 71.

23. Copland, *Music and Imagination*, p. 79.

24. Daniel Gregory Mason, *Tune In, America* (New York: Alfred A. Knopf, 1931), p. xiii.

25. Chase, *The American Composer Speaks*, p. 148.

26. Constance Rourke, *Charles Sheeler: Artist in the American Tradition* (New York: Harcourt Brace Jovanovich, 1938), p. 78.

27. George Kubler, *The Shape of Time: Remarks on the History of Things* (New Haven: Yale University Press, 1962), p. 129.

CHAPTER 1

1. H. Wiley Hitchcock, *Music in the United States: A Historical Introduction* (Englewood Cliffs: Prentice-Hall, 1974), pp. 9-22. See also Hitchcock's "William Billings and the Yankee Tunesmiths," *HiFi Stereo Review* 16 (February 1966): 55-65. Hitchcock defines the "Second New England School" as a group of composers that included John Knowles Paine, George Whitefield Chadwick, and Horatio Parker.

2. Percy A. Scholes, *The Oxford Companion to Music* (London: Oxford University Press, 1970), p. 501.

3. The Harvard Library contains an order to pay Billings' salary for teaching singing at the Old South Society, dated 9 March, 1779, and such instances of payment were common.

4. Alice Morse Earle, *The Sabbath in Puritan New England* (New York: Charles Scribner's Sons, 1891), p. 229.

5. Francis Gould Butler, *A History of Farmington, Franklin County,*

Maine: 1776-1885 (Farmington: Press of Knowlton, McLeary, and Co., 1885), pp. 92, 329, 331, 335, and 378-379.

6. William Billings, *New-England Psalm-Singer* (Boston: Edes and Gill, 1770), p. 11. Billings also discusses the same matter in *Continental Harmony* (Boston: Isaiah Thomas and Ebenezer T. Andrews, 1794), p. xv.

7. One of the most widely circulated recordings of Billings' music, Columbia MS 7277, uses the SATB concept rather than what the composer had intended.

8. Billings, *Continental Harmony*, p. xxxi.

9. E. Webster, "Timothy Swan" (Unpublished memoir: 1842): [6]. Swan Papers, American Antiquarian Society.

10. John G. McCurry, *Social Harp* (Philadelphia: T. K. Collins, Jr., 1855), p. 14.

11. These conclusions were reached for the most part after studying and performing the music. "Goodness, Renaissance music!," a comment made by one of the members of my church choir after reading a work by Belcher, is a typical feeling that results when music of the Yankee tunesmiths is performed. Two sources examined after this chapter was written offer similar conclusions: cf. David P. McKay and Richard Crawford, *William Billings of Boston: Eighteenth-Century Composer* (Princeton: Princeton University Press, 1975), pp. 174-175. See also an interview with Gregg Smith: "Europe, of course, passed through the Baroque and Classical periods—but not Billings and the Revolutionary composers, who were isolated from European culture. So if you view them in Renaissance terms, especially regarding such matters as modality and word-painting, you get a much different, more useful, fairer perspective. Suddenly their music doesn't seem so primitive." *New York Times*, July 27, 1975.

12. *The Tocsin* [Hallowell, Me.], May 10, 1796.

13. The influence of English composers is discussed in Ralph T. Daniel, "English Models for the First American Anthems," *Journal of the American Musicological Society* 12 (Spring 1959): 49-58. The article is drawn from Daniel's Harvard Ph.D. dissertation, which has been published: *The Anthem in New England Before 1800* (Evanston: Northwestern University Press, 1966). See, in particular, pp. 18-96.

14. The numerous misconceptions concerning this subject are discussed in Irving Lowens, "The Origins of the American Fuging-Tune" in *Music and Musicians in Early America* (New York: W. W. Norton & Company, 1964), pp. 237-248.

15. William Billings, *Singing Master's Assistant* (Boston: Draper and Folsom, 1778), p. 25.

16. Billings, *New-England Psalm-Singer*, p. 21.

17. Billings, *Continental Harmony*, p. xxviii.

18. See Billings' setting of *Psalm 19*.

19. Roger Sessions, *Questions About Music* (New York: W.W. Norton & Company, 1970), p. 77.

20. Billings, *New-England Psalm-Singer*, pp. 19-20.

21. Francis Brown, *An Address on Music* (Hanover, N.H.: Charles and William S. Spear, 1810), p. 19.

22. Robert Stevenson, *Philosophies of American Music History* (Washington, D.C.: The Lewis Charles Elson Memorial Fund, 1970), p. 7. Stevenson is quoting *The Musical Cyclopedia* (Boston: James Loring, 1834), pp. 322-323.

23. Nathaniel D. Gould, *Church Music in America* (Boston: A. N. Johnson, 1853), p. 58.

24. Carl E. Lindstrom, "William Billings and His Times," *The Musical Quarterly* 25 (October 1939): 495.

25. Hamilton C. MacDougall, *Early New England Psalmody* (Brattleboro, Vt.: Stephen Daye Press, 1940), p. 61.

26. Oliver Holden, *Union Harmony* (Boston: Isaiah Thomas and Ebenezer T. Andrews, 1793), p. iii.

27. John Hubbard, *An Essay on Music* (Boston: Manning and Loring, 1808), pp. 15-19. Interestingly enough, Billings had once been compared favorably with Handel by an anonymous Philadelphia writer: "His style, upon the whole bears a strong resemblance to that of Handel, and nature seems to have made him just such a musician, as she made Shakespeare a poet." cf. *The Columbian Magazine or Monthly Miscellany* (April 1788): 212-213.

28. Thomas Hastings, *Dissertation on Musical Taste* (Albany: Webster and Skinner, 1822), p. 108. This concept persisted for many years. An 1886 biographical account of Billings notes: "Counterpoint was something he had no idea of, . . ." an indication that fuging was hardly considered to be a respectable form of counterpoint. cf. F. O. Jones, *A Handbook of American Music and Musicians* (Canaseraga, N.Y.: The Author, 1886), p. 13. A more recent example of Billings' alleged "primitivism" may be found in Wilfrid Mellers, *Music in a New Found Land* (New York: Alfred A. Knopf, 1965), p. 8. Virgil Thomson expressed the same opinion in an interview with the author on June 4, 1975.

29. Daniel, *The Anthem in New England*, pp. 136-137.

30. Supply Belcher, *Harmony of Maine* (Boston: Isaiah Thomas and Ebenezer T. Andrews, 1794); Oliver Holden, rev., *Worcester Collection of Sacred Harmony*, 6th ed. (Boston: Isaiah Thomas and Ebenezer T. Andrews,

1797); Samuel Tenney, comp., *Hallowell Collection of Sacred Music* (Hallowell, Me.: E. Goodale, 1817); *Ancient Harmony Revived,* 2nd ed. (Hallowell, Me.: Masters, Smith and Co., 1848).

31. Hubbard, *An Essay on Music,* p. 10.

32. Gould, *Church Music in America,* p. 46. A further aspect of Billings' legendary reputation is found in a Philadelphia publication of 1875, where he is listed as the composer of *Adeste Fideles!* cf. J. G. Schmauk, *Deutsche Harmonie, oder Mehrstimmige Gesänge für Deutsche Singschulen und Kirchen* (Philadelphia: Schaefer and Koradi, 1875), p. 205.

33. *Ibid.* (Gould)

34. Billings, *Singing Master's Assistant,* p. 13.

35. Billings, *New-England Psalm-Singer,* p. 18.

36. The only work that deviates significantly from the diatonic harmonic world is *Jargon,* a composition Billings wrote in response to critics who complained of his consonant writing. But this work, with its combinations of dissonant intervals, is obviously an experiment, the kind of procedure that Charles Ives would have appreciated. Yet the work is typical Billings, for from one standpoint the complete reversal from his usual diatonic language presents the same kind of aesthetic situation as his consonant writing: something completely consonant and something entirely dissonant negate each other. The fact that in this short piece there is no release from the dissonance creates a result not unlike that of Billings' other compositions that are almost exclusively consonant.

37. The problems concerning Billings and rhythm are discussed in J. Murray Barbour, *The Church Music of William Billings* (East Lansing: Michigan State University Press, 1960), pp. 14-42.

38. Belcher, *Harmony of Maine,* p. 15.

39. Ned Rorem, *Music and People* (New York: George Braziller, 1968), p. 142.

CHAPTER 2

1. H. Wiley Hitchcock, Editor's Foreword to *Earlier American Music Series* (New York: Da Capo Press).

2. Arthur Loesser, *Men, Women and Pianos: A Social History* (New York: Simon and Schuster, 1954), p. 492.

3. *Ibid.,* p. 511.

4. Richard Hoffman, *Some Musical Reflections of Fifty Years* (New York: Charles Scribner's Sons, 1910), p. 104.

5. Daniel Spillane, *History of the American Pianoforte: Its Technical Development, and the Trade* (New York: D. Spillane, 1890), pp. 258-260.

6. Henry Kmen, *Music in New Orleans* (Baton Rouge: Louisiana State University Press, 1966), p. 3.

7. H. D. probably refers to Henry Didimus, who published a biography of Gottschalk in 1853 (see note 8). He may have obtained his material from Paul Arpin's *Biographie de L. M. Gottschalk, Pianiste Américain*, some of which had been translated from the French by H. C. Watson in about 1852. cf. John Godfrey Doyle, "The Piano Music of Louis Moreau Gottschalk" (Ph.D. Dissertation, New York University, 1960), p. 5.

8. H. D. [Henry Didimus?], *Biography of Louis Moreau Gottschalk* (Philadelphia: Deacon and Peterson, 1853), p. 7.

9. Louis Moreau Gottschalk, *Notes of a Pianist*, ed. Jeanne Behrend (New York: Alfred A. Knopf, 1964), p. 42.

10. *Ibid.*, p. 309. The concert the Lincolns attended is mentioned in the *Notes*, pp. 170-171.

11. William F. Apthorp, *Musicians and Music-Lovers* (New York: Charles Scribner's Sons, 1894), pp. 280-281.

12. An example is the article, "The Intellectual Influence of Music," *Dwight's Journal of Music*, November 5 and 19, 1870. This essay also appeared in the *Atlantic Monthly* 26 (November 1870): 614-625.

13. *Dwight's Journal of Music*, October 22, 1853.

14. *Dwight's Journal of Music*, October 29, 1853.

15. William L. Hawes, "Gottschalk's Views Regarding Beethoven's Sonatas," *The Musician* 13 (October 1908): 440.

16. George P. Upton, *Musical Memories* (Chicago: A. C. McClurg and Co., 1908), pp. 76-77.

17. *Dwight's Journal of Music*, January 7, 1865.

18. Harold C. Schonberg, *The Great Pianists* (New York: Simon and Schuster, 1966), p. 211. Schonberg is quoting the *Philadelphia Music Journal*, January 28, 1857.

19. *Dwight's Journal of Music*, October 18, 1862.

20. *Dwight's Journal of Music*, December 12, 1863.

21. *Dwight's Journal of Music*, July 12, 1862.

22. Gottschalk, *Notes of a Pianist*, p. 217.

23. *Dwight's Journal of Music*, March 4, 1865.

24. William Arms Fisher, "Louis Moreau Gottschalk," *The Musician* 13 (October 1908): 438.

25. Roger Sessions, *Questions About Music* (New York: W. W. Norton & Company, 1970), p. 11.

26. William Mason, *Memories of a Musical Life* (New York: The Century Co., 1902), p. 25. A biography of Teresa Carreño expresses a similar opinion concerning the plight of the nineteenth-century artist: "Touring the United

States and Canada in the Seventies and Eighties must have been a doubtful pleasure for one who looked upon music as an art." cf. Marta Milinowski, *Teresa Carreño* (New Haven: Yale University Press, 1940), p. 129.

27. Gottschalk, *Notes of a Pianist*, p. 200.

28. *Ibid.*, p. 43.

29. *Ibid.*, p. 120.

30. *Ibid.*, pp. 26-27.

31. Fisher, "Louis Moreau Gottschalk," p. 466.

32. Gottschalk, *Notes of a Pianist*, p. 37.

33. Gustave Chouquet, preface to Louis Moreau Gottschalk, *The Last Hope* (Boston: Oliver Ditson Co., n.d.).

34. *Dwight's Journal of Music*, October 18, 1862.

35. Mason, *Memories*, p. 208.

36. For a listing of Gottschalk's uses of some of these rhythms, cf. Doyle, "The Piano Music of Louis Moreau Gottschalk," p. 147.

37. Gottschalk, *Notes of a Pianist*, pp. 118-119.

38. Mason, *Memories*, pp. 188-189.

39. Prefaces to *Suis Moi!* and *O, Ma Charmante, Epargnez Moi!* (New York: William Hall and Sons, 1862).

40. Robert Offergeld, "The Gottschalk Legend: Grand Fantasy for a Great Many Pianos," in *The Piano Works of Louis Moreau Gottschalk*, ed. Vera Brodsky Lawrence (New York: Arno Press and the New York Times, 1969), I, pp. xvii-xviii.

41. Carlo Gatti, Verdi: *The Man and His Music* (New York: G. P. Putnam's Sons, 1955), p. 246.

42. Mary Alice Ives Seymour, *Life and Letters of Louis Moreau Gottschalk* (Boston: Oliver Ditson Co., 1870), p. 31.

43. Frédéric Ritter, *Music in America* (New York: Charles Scribner's Sons, 1883), p. 353.

44. John Tasker Howard, *Our American Music*, 4th ed. (New York: Thomas Y. Crowell Company, 1965), p. 205. Irving Lowens calls Gottschalk America's first matinée idol in *Music and Musicians in Early America* (New York: W. W. Norton & Company, 1964), p. 223.

45. Norbert Wiener, *The Human Use of Human Beings* (Garden City, N.Y.: Doubleday Anchor Books, 1954), p. 21.

46. Sessions, *Questions*, p. 84.

47. Gottschalk, *Notes of a Pianist*, p. 120.

CHAPTER 3

1. Ralph Waldo Emerson, *Miscellanies* (Boston: James R. Osgood and Co., 1875), p. 151.

2. Howard Mumford Jones, *The Age of Energy: Varieties of American Experience, 1865-1915* (New York: The Viking Press, 1971), p. 239.

3. Amy Fay, *Music Study in Germany* (Chicago: Jansen, McClurg and Co., 1881), p. 348.

4. H. Wiley Hitchcock, *Music in the United States: A Historical Introduction* (Englewood Cliffs: Prentice-Hall, 1974), p. 132; Rupert Hughes, *Contemporary American Composers* (Boston: L. C. Page and Co., 1900), pp. 145-266 ("The Academics"); Gilbert Chase, *America's Music*, rev. 2nd ed. (New York: McGraw-Hill Book Co., 1966), pp. 365-382 ("The Boston Classicists").

5. *Boston Globe*, December 29, 1905.

6. David Stanley Smith, "A Study of Horatio Parker," *The Musical Quarterly* 16 (April 1930): 159.

7. *New Haven Journal and Courier*, March 15, 1895.

8. *New Haven Journal and Courier*, March 13, 1896.

9. Richard Aldrich, "John Knowles Paine," in Dumas Malone, ed., *Dictionary of American Biography* XIV (New York: Charles Scribner's Sons, 1934), p. 152.

10. Alexis de Tocqueville, *Democracy in America*, ed. J. P. Mayer and Max Lerner, trans. George Lawrence (New York: Harper & Row, Publishers, 1966), pp. 456-457.

11. John Tasker Howard, *Our American Music*, 4th ed. (New York: Thomas Y. Crowell Company, 1965), p. 299.

12. Identified by Hitchcock in *Music in the United States*, p. 134.

13. Isabel Parker Semler, *Horatio Parker* (New York: G. P. Putnam's Sons, 1942), p. xx.

14. Daniel Gregory Mason, *Music in My Time* (New York: Macmillan Publishing Co., 1938), pp. 292-293.

15. Daniel Gregory Mason, *The Dilemma of American Music and Other Essays* (New York: Macmillan Publishing Co., 1928), p. 1.

16. Mason, *Music in My Time*, pp. 374-375.

17. Daniel Gregory Mason, *Tune In, America* (New York: Alfred A. Knopf, 1931), p. 15.

18. Mason, *Music in My Time*, p. 300.

19. *Ibid.*, p. 323.

20. Henry T. Finck, *My Adventures in the Golden Age of Music* (New York: Funk and Wagnalls Company, 1926), p. 283.

21. Lawrence Gilman, *Edward MacDowell: A Study* (New York: John Lane Co., 1908), pp. 177-178. See also some comments of Henry T. Finck: "He is fond of fishing, hunting, riding, walking, which he calls 'living like a human being'; and here we have the key to his music, which is as healthy

and as free from any morbid taint as is his robust physique. On seeing him in his habitual golf suit, no one would fancy that his favorite companions are fairies, witches, nymphs, dryads, and other idyllic creatures of the romantic world." Henry T. Finck, "An American Composer: Edward A. MacDowell," *The Century Magazine* 53 (January 1897): 453.

22. Paul Rosenfeld, *An Hour with American Music* (Philadelphia: J. B. Lippincott Co., 1929), p. 46.

23. Gilman, *Edward MacDowell*, p. 59.

24. de Tocqueville, *Democracy in America*, p. 434.

CHAPTER 4

1. The French composer Jules Massenet realized this possibility when he told Louis C. Elson "And it must be no copy either . . .; the American School must be eclectic." cf. Louis C. Elson, *European Reminiscences, Musical and Otherwise* (Philadelphia: Theodore Presser, 1896), p. 218.

2. John Wilmerding, ed., *The Genius of American Painting* (New York: William Morrow & Co., 1973), p. 189.

3. Donna Kay Anderson, "The Works of Charles T. Griffes: A Descriptive Catalogue" (Ph.D. Dissertation, Indiana University, 1966). The biography of Griffes: Edward M. Maisel, *Charles T. Griffes* (New York: Alfred A. Knopf, 1943).

4. John Tasker Howard, *Charles Tomlinson Griffes* (New York: G. Schirmer, 1923), p. 11.

5. Maisel, *Charles T. Griffes*, p. 235.

6. Marian Bauer, "Charles T. Griffes As I Remember Him," *The Musical Quarterly* 29 (July 1943): 372.

7. *New York World*, December 5, 1919.

8. Maisel, *Charles T. Griffes*, p. 173. Maisel is quoting an entry in Griffes diary for March 26, 1916.

9. William Treat Upton, "The Songs of Charles T. Griffes," *The Musical Quarterly* 9 (July 1923): 328. Upton revised this article, which was included as a part of his book *Art-Song in America* (Boston: Oliver Ditson Co., 1930), pp. 249-268.

10. *Ibid.*, p. 324.

11. *Ibid.*, pp. 320 and 322. Upton here refers to Griffes' setting of the poem *Phantoms* by Arturo Giovannitti, not the composer's other *Phantoms*, which sets a poem of John Bannister Tabb.

12. *Ibid.*, p. 328.

13. Aaron Copland, *Music and Imagination* (Cambridge: Harvard University Press, 1972), p. 102.

14. Maisel, *Charles T. Griffes*, p. 97.

15. *Ibid.*, p. 272.

16. Wilfrid Mellers, *Music in a New Found Land* (New York: Alfred A. Knopf, 1965), p. 148.

17. H. Wiley Hitchcock, *Music in the United States: A Historical Introduction* (Englewood Cliffs: Prentice-Hall, 1974), p. 147.

18. Upton, "The Songs of Charles T. Griffes," p. 328.

19. Bauer, "Charles T. Griffes As I Remember Him," p. 356.

20. Howard, *Charles Tomlinson Griffes*, p. 8.

CHAPTER 5

1. Numerous opinions on Ives were given at the New York/New Haven Ives Festival, which took place as a part of the celebrations concerning Ives's one hundredth birthday in October 1974. Among the varied approaches were those of Frank Rossiter, whose ideas are found in *Charles Ives and His America* (New York: Liveright Publishing Corp., 1975). A review of the festival discusses some of its aspects: Victor Fell Yellin, "Current Chronicle: Charles Ives Festival-Conference," *The Musical Qurterly* 61 (April 1975): 295-299.

2. Virgil Thomson, *American Music Since 1910* (New York: Holt, Rinehart and Winston, 1971), p. 30.

3. Ralph Waldo Emerson, *Works* I (Boston: Houghton Mifflin Company, 1883), p. 214.

4. Perry Miller, *The American Transcendentalists* (Garden City, N.Y.: Doubleday Anchor books, 1957), p. ix.

5. Herbert W. Schneider, *A History of American Philosophy* (New York: Columbia University Press, 1946), p. 281.

6. Margaret Fuller Ossoli, *Memoirs*, II (Boston: Philips, Sampson and Co., 1852), p. 97.

7. Bronson Alcott, *Journals*, ed. Odell Shepard (Boston: Little, Brown and Company, 1938), pp. 127 and 174.

8. *Ibid.*, p. 219.

9. Henry David Thoreau, *Journal* II (Boston: Houghton Mifflin Company, 1906), p. 330.

10. Annie Russel Marble, *Thoreau: His Home, Friends and Books* (New York: Thomas Y. Crowell Company, 1902), p. 315.

11. Thoreau, *Journal* I, pp. 271-272.

12. Thoreau, *Journal* IV, p. 472.

13. Thoreau, *Journal*, I, p. 251.

14. Thoreau, *Journal* III, p. 288. Ives, too, was fascinated by sounds.

His nephew Brewster recalls a typical incident: "When I took an apartment on Third Avenue overlooking the El, Uncle Charlie, on his visits, would always lean out of the window. He loved the sound of the elevated train as it approached and left. . . ." Vivian Perlis, *Charles Ives Remembered: An Oral History* (New Haven: Yale University Press, 1974), p. 74.

15. William James, *Pragmatism* (New York: Longmans, Green, and Co., 1907), pp. 45-46.

16. Charles Ives, *Essays Before a Sonata and Other Writings*, ed. Howard Boatwright (New York: W. W. Norton & Company, 1962), p. 16.

17. Mary Baker Eddy, *Science and Health*, 1st ed. (Boston: Christian Scientist Publishing Co., 1875), pp. 10-11.

18. *Ibid.*, p. 456.

19. *Ibid.*, p. 21.

20. *Ibid.*, p. 181.

21. Ives, *Essays*, p. 71.

22. Charles Ives, *Memos*, ed. John Kirkpatrick (New York: W. W. Norton & Company, 1972), p. 132.

23. Perlis, *Charles Ives Remembered*, p. 16.

24. George W. Chadwick, *Commemorative Tribute to Horatio Parker* (New Haven: Yale University Press, 1921), p. 8.

25. Ives, *Memos*, p. 49.

26. David Wooldridge, *From the Steeples and Mountains: A Study of Charles Ives* (New York: Alfred A. Knopf, 1974), pp. 4, 10, 68-74, 78-79, 82-87, 163, 319. Wooldridge does admit, however, that "Parker was not all bad." cf. p. 86. Another less than complimentary portrait of Parker is given by John Tasker Howard: "His brusque manner frightened the timid, and he despised those who were afraid of him. In this he was something of a bully; he would often wilfully confuse his pupils in class, and then scoff at their confusion." cf. John Tasker Howard, *Our American Music*, 4th ed. (New York: Thomas Y. Crowell Company, 1965), p. 316.

27. John Kirkpatrick, *A Temporary Mimeographed Catalogue of the Music Manuscripts and related materials of Charles Edward Ives* (New Haven: Typed mimeograph, Yale School of Music, 1960), p. 279.

28. Ives, *Essays*, pp. 4-5, 7, and 81.

29. Henry Sturt, ed., *Personal Idealism: Philosophical Essays by Eight Members of the University of Oxford* (London: Macmillan & Company, 1902), p. 308.

30. *Ibid.*, p. 290.

31. Ives, *Essays*, p. 12.

32. *Ibid.*, p. 51.

33. *Ibid.*, p. 54.

34. *Ibid.*, p. 68. Ives is quoting Thoreau.

35. *Ibid.*, p. 51.

36. Ives, *Memos*, p. 49.

37. Paul Moor, "On Horseback to Heaven: Charles Ives," *Harper's Magazine* 197 (September 1948): 66.

38. Ives, "Some Quarter-Tone Impressions," in *Essays*, p. 117.

39. David Johnson, liner notes to Columbia recording KS 6155.

40. A particularly ingenious passage is discussed by Hitchcock. cf. *Music in the United States: A Historical Introduction* (Englewood Cliffs: Prentice-Hall, 1974), pp. 169-170.

41. John Kirkpatrick, liner notes to Columbia recording MS 7192. An excellent discussion of similar matters is found in Sondra Rae Clark, "The Element of Choice in Ives's Concord Sonata," *The Musical Quarterly* 60 (April 1974): 167-186.

42. Ives, *Essays*, p. 82.

43. Charles Ives, *The Unanswered Question* (manuscript, Ives Collection, Yale University).

44. Ives, *Essays*, pp. 21-22.

45. Charles Ives, *Central Park in the Dark* (manuscript, Ives Collection, Yale University).

46. Lou Harrison, "On Quotation," *Modern Music* 23 (Summer 1946): 168.

47. Igor Stravinsky, *Poetics of Music in the form of Six Lessons*, trans. Arthur Knodel and Ingolf Dahl (Cambridge: Harvard University Press, 1947), p. 79.

48. Ives, *Essays*, p. 3.

49. *Ibid.*, p. 55.

50. Thomson, *American Music Since 1910*, p. 25.

51. *Ibid.*, p. 30.

52. Colin McPhee, "Winter Chronicle New York," *Modern Music* 8 (March-April 1931): 43. McPhee is referring to *Three Places in New England.*

53. Perlis, *Charles Ives Remembered*, p. 150.

54. *Ibid.*, p. 221.

55. Examples of this texture may be found at the conclusion of *Putnam's Camp* in *Three Places in New England* (New York: Mercury Music Corp., 1935), pp. 50-63; in most of the second movement of *Symphony No. 4* (New York: Associated Music Publishers, 1965), pp. 15-98; and in *Robert Browning Overture* (New York: Peer International Corp., 1959), measures 39-140, 232-337, and 343-393.

56. Perlis, *Charles Ives Remembered*, p. 138.

57. Ives, *Essays*, p. 102.

CHAPTER 6

1. Twenty-three composers give varied opinions on this subject in "The Composer in Academia: Reflections on a Theme of Stravinsky," *College Music Symposium* 10 (1970): 57-98.

2. Jacques Barzun, *Music in American Life* (Garden City, N.Y.: Doubleday & Company, 1956), p. 62

3. Elliott Carter, "The Milieu of the American Composer," *Perspectives of New Music* 1 (Fall 1962): 151.

4. Virgil Thomson, *American Music Since 1910* (New York: Holt, Rinehart and Winston, 1971), p. 11.

5. Ned Rorem, *Music and People* (New York: George Braziller, 1968), pp. 211-212.

6. Gilbert Chase, *America's Music,* rev. 2d ed. (New York: McGraw-Hill Book Co., 1966), pp. 337 and 377.

7. Daniel Gregory Mason, *Music in My Time* (New York: Macmillan Publishing Co., 1938), p. 105.

8. *Ibid.,* p. 304.

9. M. A. DeWolfe Howe, "John Knowles Paine," *The Musical Quarterly* 25 (July 1939): 265.

10. John Tasker Howard, *Our American Music,* 4th ed. (New York: Thomas Y. Crowell Company, 1965), p. 302.

11. Rupert Hughes, *Contemporary American Composers* (Boston: L. C. Page and Co., 1900), pp. 145-266.

12. Many of the quotations in this chapter are from the Quincy Porter Collection at Yale University. The bulk of Porter's manuscripts and papers were donated to the John Herrick Jackson Music Library by Mrs. Porter in 1974. At the time of this writing, the papers are for the most part uncatalogued or filed according to Mr. Porter's own system. Hereafter, documentary references will be made to the Porter Collection.

13. Quincy Porter, letter to Sidney Brudick, November 24, 1958. Porter Collection.

14. Quincy Porter, preface to *Symphony No. 2* (New York: C. F. Peters Corporation, 1963).

15. The two writings are: *A Study of sixteenth century counterpoint based on the works of Orlando di Lasso* (Boston: Loomis and Co., 1948), and *A Study of Fugue* (Boston: Loomis and Co., 1951).

16. *New York Times,* April 19, 1958.

17. Aaron Copland, *Copland on Music* (New York: W. W. Norton & Company, 1963), p. 150. Copland thinks that Porter's music is derivative, an opinion he held when discussing Porter in 1936. *Ibid.,* p. 156.

18. Paul Henry Lang, ed., *One Hundred Years of Music in America* (New York: G. Schirmer, 1961), p. 34.

19. H. Wiley Hitchcock, *Music in the United States: A Historical Introduction* (Englewood Cliffs: Prentice-Hall, 1974), p. 210.

20. Quincy Porter, letter to Thomas Nee, February 4, 1960. Porter Collection.

21. Quincy Porter, "What Can Europe Offer to American Composers?" *The Musician* 37 (March 1932): 7.

22. Quincy Porter, letters to his parents: October 31, 1928; January 6, January 19, January 25, February 5, March 8, 1929. Porter Collection.

23. *Cleveland Press,* January 27, 1930.

24. Quincy Porter, letter to Richard I. Strunsky, September 21, 1949. Porter Collection.

25. Quincy Porter, letter to Jonathan Elkus, January 29, 1959. Porter Collection.

26. Quincy Porter, "The Functions of a Progressive Department of Theory," *The Musician* 32 (October 1927): 14.

27. Quincy Porter, "The Education of the American Composer," *Musicology* 1 (Autumn 1945): 29.

18. Benjamin Boretz and Edwart T. Cone, eds., *Perspectives on American Composers* (New York: W. W. Norton & Company, 1971), p. 98.

29. Porter, "What Can Europe Offer to American Composers?" p. 7.

30. Quincy Porter, papers from file of Pierson College correspondence, n.d. Porter Collection. The quotations which follow are from this source.

31. Henry Cowell, ed., *American Composers on American Music: A Symposium* (New York: Frederick Ungar Publishing Co., 1962), p. 162.

32. Porter, Pierson College papers.

33. Porter, "The Functions of a Progressive Department of Theory," p. 14.

34. Porter, Pierson College papers.

35. *Ibid.*

36. Quincy Porter, "Grief," from first composition notebook. Porter Collection.

37. Porter, Pierson College papers.

CHAPTER 7

1. Samuel L. M. Barlow, "Virgil Thomson," *Modern Music* 18 (May-June 1941): 248.

2. B. H. Haggin, *A Decade of Music* (New York: Horizon Press, 1973), pp. 45 and 47-48. Haggin is discussing Thomson's autobiography *Virgil Thomson* (New York: Alfred A. Knopf, 1966). In this book Thomson

mentions the possible conflict of interest for a composer and newspaper man. cf. pp. 348-349.

3. Kathleen Hoover and John Cage, *Virgil Thomson: His Life and Music* (New York: T. Yoseloff, 1959), p. 89. Hoover's source for this particular information is *Figaro littéraire* (May 1954).

4. Virgil Thomson, *American Music Since 1910* (New York: Holt, Rinehart and Winston, 1970).

5. Eva Goldbeck, "A Thomson Soirée," *Modern Music* 13 (November-December 1935): 51.

6. Aaron Copland, *The New Music: 1900-1960* (New York: W. W. Norton & Company, 1968), p. 136.

7. *The Baltimore Sun*, November 11, 1973.

8. *Dallas Morning News*, December 11, 1952.

9. Virgil Thomson, foreword to *The Mother of Us All* (New York: Music Press, 1947), p. 13.

10. Thomson, *Virgil Thomson*, p. 115.

11. Hoover and Cage, *Virgil Thomson*, pp. 215-217.

12. Much of the information for this essay was obtained during an interview with Thomson, held at the Hotel Chelsea in New York City on the afternoon of June 4, 1975. Unless otherwise indicated, undocumented quotations are from that interview.

13. Victor Fell Yellin, "The Operas of Virgil Thomson," in Thomson, *American Music Since 1910*, p. 91.

14. Lou Harrison, "On Quotation," *Modern Music* 23 (Summer 1946): 168-169.

15. Thomson, *Virgil Thomson*, p. 209.

16. Hoover and Cage, *Virgil Thomson*, p. 170.

17. Theodore Chanler, "All-American," *Modern Music* 10 (March-April 1933): 162.

18. Virgil Thomson, foreword to *String Quartet No. 1* (rev. version) (New York: Boosey and Hawkes, 1958).

19. Hoover and Cage, *Virgil Thomson*, p. 171.

20. A comparison with Ives's use of the word "manner" as opposed to "substance" is possible—and intriguing.

21. *The Baltimore Sun*, November 11, 1973. The quotations that follow are taken from this source, which contains an interview with Thomson concerning the upcoming first performance of his *Cantata*, a work using nonsense poetry of Edward Lear as its text.

22. Peggy Granville-Hicks, "Virgil Thomson," *The Musical Quarterly* 35 (April 1949): 211.

23. *New York Herald Tribune*, February 25, 1934.

24. Thomson, foreword to *The Mother of Us All*, p. 14.

CHAPTER 8

1. Any grouping such as this is, of course, open to questions. The author does not wish to imply that writers who were for the most part traditionalists did not experiment or did not employ a "scientific" approach to their music. Nor does he mean that the "scientific" way is devoid of any traditional qualities or any experimentation. The three categories are simply convenient generalizations that point to differences in the music of a Thomson, a Babbitt, and a Cage.

2. Gilbert Chase, ed., *The American Composer Speaks* (Baton Rouge: Louisiana State University Press, 1966), p. 245.

3. John Cage, in an interview with the author, July 10, 1975. At a question and answer session after a lecture at the Yale School of Art and Architecture on December 5, 1965, Cage spoke of it this way, in reference to the essay at the end of Ives's *114 Songs:* ". . . he [Ives] envisages the time when each person may sit in a rocking chair smoking a pipe, looking out toward the hills, the sun setting. That experience being the creation of one's own symphony." The questions and answers have been reprinted: John Cage, "Questions," *Perspecta* 2 (1967): 70.

4. *Ibid.* (interview).

5. Virgil Thomson, "The Abstract Composers," *The Score* 12 (June 1955): 63.

6. John Cage, "Experimental Music," *The Score* 12 (June 1955): 66.

7. *Ibid.*, p. 67.

8. Cage, interview.

9. John Cage, at a symposium at the University of Delaware, April 24, 1975.

10. Virgil Thomson, *American Music Since 1900* (New York: Holt, Rinehart and Winston, 1970), pp. 75 and 80.

11. John Cage, "Notes on the Program" [for Grete Sultan's Alice Tully Hall Recital, Lincoln Center, New York, January 25, 1975], *Stagebill* II (January 1975): 22-23.

12. John Cage, interview.

13. John Cage, foreword to M: *Writings '67-'72* (Middletown, Conn.: Wesleyan University Press, 1973).

14. H. Wiley Hitchcock, *Music in the United States: A Historical Introduction* (Englewood Cliffs: Prentice-Hall, 1974), pp. 249-250.

15. Chase, *The American Composer Speaks,* p. 299.

16. Milton Babbitt, "Who Cares If You Listen?" *High Fidelity* 8 (February 1958): 38-40 and 126-27.

17. "The Composer in Academia: Reflections on a Theme of Stravinsky," *College Music Symposium* 10 (1970): 79.

18. Leonard B. Meyer, *Music, the Arts, and Ideas* (Chicago: University of Chicago Press, 1967), p. 149.

19. Andrew Law, *Essays on Music* (Philadelphia: The Author, 1814), p. 10.

20. Lowell Mason, comp. and arr., *Mason's Normal Singer* (New York: Mason Brothers, 1856), p. ii.

21. George Rochberg, letter to the author, June 23, 1975.

22. George Crumb, liner notes to Nonesuch recording H-71293.

23. Donal Henahan, "Crumb, the Tone Poet," *New York Times Magazine* (May 11, 1975): 66.

24. James Drew, letter to the author, April 15, 1975.

25. *Ibid.*

26. *Ibid.*

27. James Drew, instructions for *primero libro de referencia laberinto* (Bryn Mawr: Theodore Presser Co., 1974).

28. James Drew, program notes for *West Indian Lights*.

29. *New York Times*, August 19, 1973.

30. James Drew, letter to the author, July 4, 1975.

31. *Ibid.*

32. Robert Morris, "Notes on the *Motet on Doo-dah*," unpublished essay, p. 1.

33. *Ibid.*, p. 2.

34. *Ibid.*

35. Robert Morris, "Program Notes for *Variations on the Variation of the Quadran Pavan and the Quadran Pavan by Bull and Byrd*," unpublished.

36. *Ibid.*

37. Robert Morris, in an interview with the author, July 2, 1975.

38. Rochberg, letter of June 23, 1975.

39. *Ibid.*

40. *Ibid.*

41. Shirley Fleming, "Donald Martino," *Hi-Fidelity/Musical America* 24 (September 1974): MA9.

42. Jon Appleton, at a symposium at the University of Delaware, April 14, 1975.

EPILOGUE

1. Roger Sessions, *Reflections on the Music Life in the United States* (New York: Merlin Press, 1956), p. 178.

2. Donal Henahan, "Crumb, the Tone Poet," *New York Times Magazine* (May 11, 1975): 50.

3. "Young Genius on the Rise in U.S.," *Newsweek* 78 (May 19, 1975): 56.

4. John Hubbard, *An Essay on Music* (Boston: Manning and Loring, 1808), p. 4.

5. Virgil Thomson, in an interview with the author, June 4, 1975.

6. Aaron Copland, at a symposium at the University of Delaware, April 14, 1975.

7. Tui St. George Tucker, "Notes on the Program" [for Grete Sultan's Alice Tully Hall Recital, Lincoln Center, New York, January 25, 1975], *Stagebill* II (January 1975): 22.

8. Henry F. Gilbert, "The American Composer," *The Musical Quarterly* 1 (April 1915): 180.

9. "Young Genius on the Rise in U.S.," p. 57. It is interesting to compare these words with some comments written in 1881 by Frederick Nast: "The chief hinderance to the development of a national school of music lies in the diverse character of our population. American composers may flourish, but American music can not be expected until the present discordant elements are merged into a homogeneous people." cf. Frederick Nast, "Music and Musicians in New York," *Harper's New Monthly Magazine* 62 (May 1881): 818.

10. James Drew, letter to the author, July 4, 1975.

BIBLIOGRAPHY

I. BOOKS

Alcott, Bronson. *Journals,* edited by Odell Shepard. Boston: Little, Brown and Company, 1938.

Aldrich, Richard. *Concert Life in New York: 1902-1923.* New York: G. P. Putnam's Sons, 1941.

Apthorp, William Foster. *Musicians and Music-Lovers.* New York: Charles Scribner's Sons, 1894.

Barbour, J. Murray. *The Church Music of William Billings.* East Lansing: Michigan State University Press, 1960.

Barzun, Jacques. *Music in American Life.* Garden City, N.Y.: Doubleday & Company, 1956.

Boretz, Benjamin and Cone, Edward T., eds. *Perspectives on American Composers.* New York: W. W. Norton & Company, 1971.

Brooks, Van Wyck. *The Flowering of New England: 1815-1865.* New York: E. P. Dutton & Co., 1936.

_____. *New England: Indian Summer: 1865-1915.* New York: E. P. Dutton & Co., 1940.

Butler, Francis Gould. *A History of Farmington, Franklin County, Maine: 1776-1885.* Farmington: Press of Knowlton, McLeary, and Co., 1885.

Cage, John. *M: Writings '67-'72.* Middletown, Conn.: Wesleyan University Press, 1973.

_____. *Silence.* Middletown, Conn.: Wesleyan University Press, 1961.

_____. *A Year from Monday.* Middletown, Conn.: Wesleyan University Press, 1968.

Chase, Gilbert, ed. *The American Composer Speaks.* Baton Rouge: Louisiana State University Press, 1966.

_____. *America's Music*, 1st and 2d eds. New York: McGraw-Hill Book Company, 1955 and 1966.

Commager, Henry Steele. *The American Mind*. New Haven: Yale University Press, 1950.

Cooke, George Willis. *John Sullivan Dwight: A Biography*. Boston: Small, Maynard and Co., 1898.

Copland, Aaron. *Copland on Music*. New York: W. W. Norton & Company, 1963.

_____. *Music and Imagination*. Cambridge: Harvard University Press, 1972.

_____. *The New Music: 1900-1960*. New York: W. W. Norton & Company, 1968.

Cords, Nicholas and Gerster, Patrick, eds. *Myth and the American Experience*. 2 vols. New York: Glencoe Press, 1973.

Cowell, Henry, ed. *American Composers on American Music: A Symposium*. New York: Frederick Ungar Publishing Co., 1962.

Cowell, Henry and Cowell, Sidney. *Charles Ives and His Music*. New York: Oxford University Press, 1955.

Croce, Benedetto. *Aesthetic*, translated by Douglas Ainslie. New York: The Noonday Press, 1968.

D., H. [Didimus, Henry?]. *Biography of Louis Moreau Gottschalk*. Philadelphia: Deacon and Peterson, 1853.

Daniel, Ralph T. *The Anthem in New England Before 1800*. Evanston: Northwestern University Press, 1966.

Eddy, Mary Baker. *Science and Health*, 1st ed. Boston: Christian Scientist Publishing Co., 1875.

Edwards, George Thornton. *Music and Musicians of Maine*. New York: AMS Press, 1970.

Elson, Louis C. *European Reminiscences, Musical and Otherwise*. Philadelphia: Theodore Presser, 1896.

_____. *The History of American Music*. New York: Macmillan Publishing Co., 1925.

Emerson, Ralph Waldo. *Miscellanies*. Boston: James R. Osgood and Co., 1875.

_____. *Works*. 5 vols. Boston: Houghton, Mifflin Company, 1883.

Fay, Amy. *Music Study in Germany*. Chicago: Jansen, McClurg and Co., 1881.

Gage, Thomas. *History of Rowley*. Boston: F. Andrews, 1840.

Gilman, Lawrence. *Edward MacDowell: A Study*. New York: John Lane Co., 1908.

Gottschalk, Louis Moreau. *Notes of a Pianist*, edited by Jeanne Behrend. New York: Alfred A. Knopf, 1964.

Gould, Nathaniel D. *Church Music in America.* Boston: A. N. Johnson, 1853.

Hastings, Thomas. *Dissertation on Musical Taste.* Albany: Webster and Skinner, 1822.

Hitchcock, H. Wiley. *Music in the United States: A Historical Introduction.* Englewood Cliffs: Prentice-Hall, 1974.

Hoffman, Richard. *Some Musical Recollections of Fifty Years.* New York: Charles Scribner's Sons, 1910.

Hofstadter, Richard. *Anti-Intellectualism in American Life.* New York: Vintage, 1963.

Hood, George. *A History of Music in New England.* Boston: Wilkins, Carter and Co., 1846.

Hoover, Kathleen and Cage, John. *Virgil Thomson: His Life and Music.* New York: T. Yoseloff, 1959.

Hopkins, Vivian. *Spires of Form.* Cambridge: Harvard University Press, 1951.

Howard, John Tasker. *Our American Music,* 4th ed. New York: Thomas Y. Crowell Company, 1965.

Hughes, Rupert. *Contemporary American Composers.* Boston: L. C. Page and Co., 1900.

Ives, Charles. *Essays Before a Sonata and Other Writings,* edited by Howard Boatwright. New York: W. W. Norton & Company, 1962.

_____. *Memos,* edited by John Kirkpatrick. New York: W. W. Norton & Company, 1972.

James, William. *The Meaning of Truth.* New York: Longmans, Green, and Co., 1909.

_____. *Pragmatism.* New York: Longmans, Green, and Co., 1907.

Jones, F. O. *A Handbook of American Music and Musicians.* Canaseraga, N.Y.: The Author, 1886.

Jones, Howard Mumford. *The Age of Energy: Varieties of American Experience, 1865-1915.* New York: The Viking Press, 1971.

King, Grace. *New Orleans: The Place and Its People.* New York: Macmillan Publishing Co., 1896.

Kmen, Henry. *Music in New Orleans.* Baton Rouge: Louisiana State University Press, 1966.

Kubler, George. *The Shape of Time: Remarks on the History of Things.* New Haven: Yale University Press, 1962.

Lang, Paul Henry, ed. *One Hundred Years of Music in America.* New York: G. Schirmer, 1961.

Langer, Susanne K. *Philosophy in a New Key: A Study in the Symbolism of Reason, Rite, and Art.* New York: Mentor Books, 1962.

Loesser, Arthur. *Men, Women, and Pianos: A Social History.* New York: Simon and Schuster, 1954.

Lowens, Irving. *Music and Musicians in Early America.* New York: W. W. Norton & Company, 1964.

Maisel, Edward. *Charles T. Griffes.* New York: Alfred A. Knopf, 1943.

Mason, Daniel Gregory. *The Dilemma of American Music and Other Essays.* New York: Macmillan Publishing Co., 1928.

_____. *Music in My Time.* New York: Macmillan Publishing Co., 1938.

Mason, William. *Memories of a Musical Life.* New York: The Century Co., 1902.

Matthiessen, F. O. *American Renaissance: Art and Expression in the Age of Emerson and Whitman.* New York: Oxford University Press, 1941.

Mellers, Wilfrid. *Music in a New Found Land.* New York: Alfred A. Knopf, 1965.

Meyer, Leonard B. *Emotion and Meaning in Music.* Chicago: University of Chicago Press, 1956.

_____. *Music, the Arts, and Ideas.* Chicago: University of Chicago Press, 1967.

Miller, Perry, ed. *The American Transcendentalist.* Garden City, N.Y.: Doubleday Anchor Books, 1957.

Morris, Charles. *The Pragmatic Movement in American Philosophy.* New York: George Braziller, 1970.

Mumford, Lewis. *Art and Technics.* New York: Columbia University Press, 1960.

Ossoli, Margaret Fuller. *Memoirs.* 2 vols. Boston: Phillips, Sampson and Company, 1852.

Peel, Robert. *Christian Science: Its Encounter with American Culture.* New York: Holt, Rinehart and Winston, 1958.

Perlis, Vivian. *Charles Ives Remembered: An Oral History.* New Haven: Yale University Press, 1974.

Ritter, Frédéric L. *Music in America.* New York: Charles Scribner's Sons, 1883.

Root, George. *The Story of a Musical Life.* Cincinnati: The John Church Co., 1891.

Rosenfeld, Paul. *An Hour with American Music.* Philadelphia: J. B. Lippincott Co., 1929.

Semler, Isabel Parker. *Horatio Parker: A Memoir for his Grandchildren compiled from Letters and Papers.* New York: G. P. Putnam's Sons, 1942.

Sessions, Roger. *The Musical Experience of Composer, Performer, Listener.* Princeton: Princeton University Press, 1950.

_____. *Questions About Music.* New York: W. W. Norton & Company, 1970.

_____. *Reflections on the Music Life in the United States*. New York: Merlin Press, 1956.

Seymour, Mary Alice Ives. *Life and Letters of Louis Moreau Gottschalk*. Boston: Oliver Ditson Co., 1870.

Simon, Myron and Parsons, Thornton H., eds. *Transcendentalism and Its Legacy*. Ann Arbor: University of Michigan Press, 1966.

Spillane, Daniel. *History of the American Pianoforte: Its Technical Development, and the Trade*. New York: D. Spillane, 1890.

Stevenson, Robert. *Protestant Church Music in America*. New York: W. W. Norton & Company, 1966.

Stravinsky, Igor. *Poetics of Music in the Form of Six Lessons*, translated by Arthur Knodel and Ingolf Dahl. Cambridge: Harvard University Press, 1947.

Sturt, Henry, ed. *Personal Idealism: Philosophical Essays by Eight Members of the University of Oxford*. London: Macmillan and Co., 1902.

Thomson, Virgil. *American Music Since 1910*. New York: Holt, Rinehart and Winston, 1971.

_____. *The Art of Judging Music*. New York: Alfred A. Knopf, 1948.

_____. *Music Reviewed: 1940-1954*. New York: Vintage Books, 1967.

_____. *Virgil Thomson*. New York: Alfred A. Knopf, 1966.

Thoreau, Henry David. *Journal,* edited by Bradford Torrey. 14 vols. Boston: Houghton, Mifflin Company, 1906.

Tocqueville, Alexis de. *Democracy in America,* edited by J. P. Mayer and Max Lerner, translated by George Lawrence. New York: Harper & Row, Publishers, 1966.

Upton, George P. *Musical Memories*. Chicago: A. C. McClurg and Co., 1908.

Weiss, Paul. *Nine Basic Arts*. Carbondale: Southern Illinois University Press, 1961.

_____. *The World of Art*. Carbondale: Southern Illinois University Press, 1961.

Wellek, René. *Concepts of Criticism,* edited by Stephen G. Nichols, Jr. New Haven: Yale University Press, 1963.

Whitehead, Alfred North. *Dialogues of Alfred North Whitehead as recorded by Lucien Price*. Boston: Little, Brown and Company, 1954.

II. PERIODICALS

American Journal of Music, 1844-1846.
Boston Musical Gazette, 1838-1839.
Boston Musical Times, 1860-1861.

The Columbian Magazine or Monthly Miscellany, 1786-1789.
Dwight's Journal of Music, 1852-1881.
The Euterpeiad: or, Musical Intelligencer, 1820-1822.
Modern Music, 1924-1946.
The Musical Quarterly, 1915-1975.
Perspectives of New Music, 1962-1975.
The Tocsin, 1795-1796.

III. MUSIC
(American works cited in text.)

Beach, Amy C. *Ecstasy* op. 19 no. 2. Boston: Arthur P. Schmidt, 1894.
Belcher, Supply. *Harmony of Maine*. Boston: Isaiah Thomas and Ebenezer
    T. Andrews, 1794.
Billings, William. *Continental Harmony*. Boston: Isaiah Thomas and Eben-
    ezer T. Andrews, 1794.
_____. *Music in Miniature*. Boston: The Author, 1779.
_____. *New-England Psalm-Singer*. Boston: Edes and Gill, 1770.
_____. *Psalm-Singer's Amusement*. Boston: The Author, 1781.
_____. *Singing Master's Assistant*. Boston: Draper and Folsom, 1778.
_____. *Suffolk Harmony*. Boston: J. Norman, 1786.
Cage, John. *Concert* for piano and orchestra. New York: C. F. Peters, 1960.
_____. *Etudes Australes*. New York: Henmar Press, 1975.
_____. *5 Songs for Contralto*. New York: Henmar Press, 1960.
_____. *4'33"*. New York: Henmar Press, 1960.
_____. *Music of Changes*. New York: Henmar Press, 1961.
_____. *Prelude for Meditation* for prepared piano. New York: Henmar
    Press, 1960.
_____. *Quartet for 12 Tom-Toms*. New York: Henmar Press, 1960.
_____. *Sonatas and Interludes* for prepared piano. New York: C. F. Peters,
    1960.
_____. *The Wonderful Widow of Eighteen Springs*. New York: Henmar
    Press, 1961.
Carden, Allen D., comp. *Missouri Harmony*. Cincinnati: Morgan, Lodge
    Printers, 1820.
Carter, Elliott. *Eight Etudes and a Fantasy* for woodwind quintet. New
    York: Associated Music Publishers, 1959.
Chadwick, George W. *Aphrodite: Symphonic Fantasie*. Leipzig: A. P.
    Schmidt, 1912.
_____. *Symphony No. 3*. Boston: A. P. Schmidt, 1896.
Crumb, George. *Echoes of Time and the River*. Melville, N.Y.: Mills
    Music, 1967.

_____. *Makrokosmos I.* New York: C. F. Peters, 1974.

_____. *Night of the Four Moons.* New York: C. F. Peters, 1971.

Drew, James. *primero libro de referencia laberinto.* Bryn Mawr: Theodore Presser, 1974.

_____. *West Indian Lights.* Bryn Mawr: Theodore Presser, 1974.

Foster, Stephen. *My Old Kentucky Home, Good Night.* New York: Firth, Pond & Co., 1853.

_____. *Old Black Joe.* New York: Firth, Pond & Co., 1860.

Gottschalk, Louis Moreau. *Bamboula, Danse de Nègres.* Mainz: B. Schott, n.d. [1847?].

_____. *Le Bananier, Chanson Nègre.* Boston: Oliver Ditson, n.d.

_____. *The Banjo.* New York: William Hall & Son, 1855.

_____. *Battle Cry of Freedom, Grand Caprice de Concert.* Chicago: Root & Cady, 1865.

_____. *El Cocoyé, Grand Caprice Cubain de Bravura.* Boston: Oliver Ditson & Co., 1873.

_____. *Columbia, Caprice Américaine.* 'New York: Firth, Pond & Co., 1860.

_____. *The Dying Poet, Meditation.* Boston: Oliver Ditson & Co., 1864.

_____. *La Gallina, Danse Cubaine.* New York: William Hall & Son, 1869.

_____. *La Jota Aragonesa, Caprice Espagnol.* New York: William Hall & Son, 1855.

_____. *The Last Hope, Religious Meditation.* New York: Firth, Pond & Co., 1854.

_____. *Minuit à Séville.* New York: William Hall & Son, 1856.

_____. *Morte!!, Lamentation.* New York: William Hall & Son, 1869.

_____. *Ojos Criollos, Danse Cubaine, Caprice Brillant.* New York: William Hall & Son, 1864.

_____. *O Ma Charmante, Epargnez Moi!, Caprice.* New York: William Hall & Son, 1862.

_____. *Pasquinade, Caprice.* New York: William Hall & Son, 1870.

_____. *Piano Music of Louis Moreau Gottschalk,* selected and introduced by Richard Jackson. New York: Dover Publications, 1973.

_____. *The Piano Works of Louis Moreau Gottschalk,* edited by Vera Brodsky Lawrence. 5 vols. New York: Arno Press and The New York Times, 1969.

_____. *Souvenir de Porto Rico, Marche des Gibardos.* Mainz: B. Schott, 1859.

_____. *Souvenirs d'Andalousie, Caprice de Concert.* New York: William Hall & Son, 1855.

_____. *Suis Moi!, Caprice.* New York: William Hall & Son, 1862.

_____. *Union, Paraphrase de Concert.* New York: William Hall & Son, 1863.

Griffes, Charles T. *Auf geheimem Waldespfade.* New York: G. Schirmer, 1909.

_____. *Evening Song.* New York: G. Schirmer, 1941.

_____. *Fantasy Pieces* op. 6. New York: G. Schirmer, 1915.

_____. *Five Poems of Ancient China and Japan* op. 10. New York: G. Schirmer, 1917.

_____. *Four Impressions.* New York: C. F. Peters, 1970.

_____. *La Fuite de la Lune* op. 3 no. 1. New York: G. Schirmer, 1915.

_____. *The Lament of Ian the Proud* op. 11 no. 1. New York: G. Schirmer, 1918.

_____. *Phantoms* op. 9 no. 3. New York: G. Schirmer, 1918.

_____. *The Pleasure-Dome of Kubla Khan.* New York: G. Schirmer, 1920.

_____. *Poem for Flute and Orchestra.* New York: G. Schirmer, 1951.

_____. *Roman Sketches* op. 7. New York: G. Schirmer, 1917.

_____. *The Rose of the Night* op. 11 no. 3. New York: G. Schirmer, 1918.

_____. *Sonata* for piano. New York: G. Schirmer, 1921.

_____. *Symphony in Yellow* op. 3 no. 2. New York: G. Schirmer, 1915.

_____. *Three Tone-Pictures* op. 5. New York: G. Schirmer, 1915.

_____. *Thy Dark Eyes to Mine* op. 11 no. 2. New York: G. Schirmer, 1918.

_____. *Two Sketches Based on Indian Themes.* New York: G. Schirmer, 1922.

_____. *WaiKiki.* New York: G. Schirmer, 1917.

_____. *We'll To the Woods, and Gather May* op. 3 no. 3. New York: G. Schirmer, 1915.

Holden, Oliver. *Union Harmony.* Boston: Isaiah Thomas and Ebenezer T. Andrews, 1793.

_____, rev. *Worcester Collection of Sacred Harmony,* 6th ed. Boston: Isaiah Thomas and Ebenezer T. Andrews, 1797.

Ives, Charles. *Central Park in the Dark.* Hillsdale, N.Y.: Boelke-Bomart, 1973.

_____. *Eleven Songs and two harmonizations,* edited by John Kirkpatrick. New York: Associated Music Publishers, 1968.

_____. *First Sonata* for piano. New York: Peer International Corp., 1954.

_____. *Largo* for violin, clarinet, and piano. New York: Southern Music Publishing Co., 1953.

_____. *114 Songs.* Redding, Conn.: The Author, 1922.

_____. *Orchestral Set No. 2.* New York: Peer International Corp., 1971.

_____. *Piano Sonata No. 2: Concord, Mass., 1840-1860.* New York: Associated Music Publishers, 1947.

_____. *Robert Browning Overture* for large orchestra. New York: Peer International Corp., 1959.

_____. *String Quartet No. 1.* New York: Peer International Corp., 1963.

_____. *Symphony, Holidays.* San Francisco: New Music, 1936.

_____. *Symphony No. 2.* New York: Southern Music Publishing Co., 1951.

_____. *Symphony No. 3.* New York: Associated Music Publishers, 1964.

_____. *Symphony No. 4.* New York: Associated Music Publishers, 1965.

_____. *Three Places in New England.* New York: Mercury Music Corp., 1935.

_____. *The Unanswered Question.* New York: Southern Music Publishing Co., 1953.

Luening, Otto. *Prelude to a hymn tune by William Billings.* New York: Edition Musicus, 1943.

MacDowell, Edward. *Concert-Etude* op. 36. Boston: Arthur P. Schmidt, 1889.

_____. *Concerto No. 2* for piano and orchestra op. 23. Leipzig: Breitkopf Härtel, 1907.

_____. *Woodland Sketches.* New York: P. L. Jung, 1896.

Martino, Donald. *Notturno.* Boston: Ione Press, 1975.

Mason, Daniel Gregory. *Prelude and Fugue for Piano and Orchestra* op. 20, arranged for two pianos or piano and organ by the composer. New York: J. Fischer, 1933.

McCurry, John G. *Social Harp.* Philadelphia: T. K. Collins, Jr., 1855.

Morris, Robert. *Motet on Doo-dah.* To be published in *Asterisk**, May 1976.

Paine, John Knowles. *Azara.* Leipzig: Breitkopf and Härtel, 1908.

_____. *Fuga Giocosa* op. 41 no. 3. Boston: A.P. Schmidt, 1884.

_____. *Nocturne* op. 45. Boston: A. P. Schmidt, 1889.

_____. *Oedipus Tyrannus* op. 35. Boston: A. P. Schmidt, 1881.

_____. *Symphony No. 2* op. 34. Boston: A. P. Schmidt, 1880.

Parker, Horatio. *Fairyland* op. 77. New York: G. Schirmer, 1914.

_____. *Hora Novissima.* London: The H. W. Gray Co., 1893.

_____. *The Legend of St. Christopher* op. 43. London: Novello and Co.; New York: The H. W. Gray Co., 1898.

_____. *Mona* op. 71. New York: G. Schirmer, 1911.

Peterson, Clara Gottschalk, comp. and arr. *Creole Songs from New Orleans in the Negro-Dialect.* New Orleans: L. Grunewald Co., 1902.

Porter, Quincy. *Concerto Concertante.* New York: American Composers Alliance, 1956.

_____. *Concerto for Wind Orchestra.* New York: C. F. Peters, 1959.

_____. *Dance in Three-Time.* New York: American Composers Alliance, 1937.

_____. *Day Dreams.* Bryn Mawr: Merion Music, 1958.

_____. *Little Trio.* South Hadley, Mass.: Valley Music Press, 1962.

_____. *New England Episodes.* New York: American Composers Alliance, 1972.

_____. *Poem* for violoncello and piano and for viola and piano. South Hadley, Mass.: Valley Music Press, 1957.

_____. *Quartet No. 3.* New York: G. Schirmer, 1935-1936.

_____. *Quartet No. 4.* New York: Arrow Music Press, 1936.

_____. *Quintet for Clarinet and Strings.* New York: Highgate Press, 1969.

_____. *Quintet for Harpsichord and Strings.* New York: American Composers Alliance, 1964.

_____. *Quintet for Oboe and Strings.* New York: Highgate Press, 1967.

_____. *Sonata* for piano. New York: C. F. Peters, 1966.

_____. *Sonata No. 2 for Violin and Piano.* New York: C. F. Peters, 1933.

_____. *Speed Etude* for viola and piano. South Hadley, Mass.: Valley Music Press, 1957.

_____. *Suite for Viola Alone.* South Hadley, Mass. Valley Music Press, 1937.

_____. *Symphony No. 1.* New York: American Composers Alliance, 1938.

_____. *Symphony No. 2.* New York: C. F. Peters, 1963.

_____. *Ukrainian Suite* for string orchestra. Rochester: Eastman School of Music, 1927.

Powell, John. *Natchez-on-the-Hill* op. 30. New York: G. Schirmer, 1932.

_____. *Sonate Noble* op. 21. New York: G. Schirmer, 1921.

Riley, Terry. *In C.* Reprinted in Godwin, Joscelyn, ed. *Schirmer Scores: A Repertory of Western Music.* New York: Schirmer Books, 1975 and on liner notes to Columbia recording MS 7178.

Rochberg, George. *Carnival Music.* Bryn Mawr: Theodore Presser, 1975.

_____. *Contra Mortem et Tempus* for flute, clarinet, violin, and piano. Bryn Mawr: Theodore Presser, 1967.

_____. *Quartet No. 3.* New York: Galaxy Music Corp., 1975.

Sankey, Ira D. and others. *Gospel Hymns Nos. 1 to 6.* New York and Chicago: The Biglow and Main Co., 1895.

Schmauk, J. G. *Deutsche Harmonie, oder Mehrstimmige Gesänge für Deutsche Singschulen und Kirchen.* Philadelphia: Schaefer and Koradi, 1875.

Schuman, William. *New England Triptych.* Bryn Mawr: Merion Music, 1959.

Swan, Timothy. *New England Harmony.* Northampton, Mass.: Andrew Wright, 1801.

Tenney, Samuel, comp. *Hallowell Collection of Sacred Music.* Hallowell, Me.: E. Goodale, 1817.

Thomson, Virgil. *At the Beach.* New York: C. Fischer, 1963.

_____. *Capital, Capitals* for four men and a piano. New York: New Music, 1947.

_____. *Concerto* for flute, strings, harp and percussion. New York: Ricordi, 1957.

_____. *Concerto for Violoncello and Orchestra,* arranged for violoncello and piano. New York: Ricordi, 1952.

_____. *Filling Station,* arranged for piano. New York: Arrow Music Press, 1942.

_____. *Four Saints in Three Acts.* New York: Music Press, 1948.

_____. *John Peel.* New York: Southern Music Publishing Co., 1962.

_____. *Jour de Chaleur aux Bains de Mer.* New York: Boosey and Hawkes, 1963.

_____. *Lamentations.* New York: Santee Music Press, 1960.

_____. *Lord Byron.* New York: Southern Music Publishing Co., 1975.

_____. *The Mother of Us All.* New York: Music Press, 1947.

_____. *Pange Lingua.* New York: G. Schirmer, 1962.

_____. *Pastorale on a Christmas Plainsong.* New York: The H. W. Gray Co., 1942.

_____. *Praises and Prayers* for voice and piano. New York: G. Schirmer, 1963.

_____. *Quartet No. 1.* New York: Boosey and Hawkes, 1958.

_____. *Quartet No. 2.* New York: Arrow Music Press, 1945.

_____. *Sea Piece with Birds.* New York: G. Schirmer, 1954.

_____. *The Seine at Night.* New York: G. Schirmer, 1949.

_____. *A Solemn Music.* New York: G. Schirmer, 1949.

_____. *Sonata da Chiesa.* New York: New Music, 1944.

_____. *Sonata for Violin and Piano* no. 1. New York: Arrow Music Press, 1941.

_____. *Stabat Mater* for soprano and string quartet. New York: Cos Cob Press, 1933.

_____. *Suite from "The River."* New York: Southern Music Publishing Co., 1958.

_____. *Ten Etudes.* New York: C. Fischer, 1946.

_____. *Two by Marianne Moore* for voice and piano. New York: G. Schirmer, 1966.

_____. *Wheat Field At Noon.* New York: G. Schirmer, 1954.

Walker, William. *Southern Harmony, and Musical Companion.* Philadelphia: Thomas Cowperwait & Co., 1847.

Walter, Thomas. *The Grounds and Rules of Musick Explained: Or, an Introduction to the Art of Singing by Note. Fitted to the Meanest Capacities.* Boston: F. Franklin, 1721.

White, B. F. and King., E. J. *Sacred Harp.* Facsimile of 1859 edition with an introduction by George Pullen Jackson. Nashville: Broadman Press, 1968.

Young, La Monte. *Composition 1960 #7.* Reprinted in Hitchcock, H. Wiley.

Music in the United States: A Historical Introduction. Englewood
Cliffs: Prentice-Hall, 1974.

IV. MANUSCRIPT COLLECTIONS

At the American Antiquarian Society: Timothy Swan papers.
At Harvard University: John Knowles Paine papers and manuscripts.
At the Library of Congress: Charles T. Griffes manuscripts.
At the New York Public Library at Lincoln Center for the Performing Arts:
Louis Moreau Gottschalk and Charles T. Griffes manuscripts.
At Yale University: Charles Ives, George Ives, Horatio Parker, and Quincy
Porter papers and manuscripts.

V. MISCELLANEOUS SOURCES

Anderson, Donna Kay. "The Works of Charles T. Griffes: A Descriptive
Catalogue." Ph.D. Dissertation, Indiana University, 1966.
Blom, Eric, ed. *Grove's Dictionary of Music and Musicians.* 9 vols. New
York: St. Martin's Press, 1960.
Brigham, Clarence S. *History and Bibliography of American Newspapers:
1690-1820.* 2 vols. Worcester, Mass.: American Antiquarian Society,
1947.
Brown, Francis. *An Address on Music.* Hanover, N.H.: Charles and William
S. Spear, 1810.
Chadwick, George W. *Commemorative Tribute to Horatio Parker.* New
Haven: Yale University Press, 1921.
Copland, Aaron. *The Pleasures of Music,* an address given at the University of New Hampshire, April 16, 1959. Durham: University of New
Hampshire, 1959.
Doyle, John Godfrey. "The Piano Music of Louis Moreau Gottschalk."
Unpublished Ph.D. Dissertation, New York University, 1960.
Drew, James. Letters to the author. April 5, 1975, and July 4, 1975.
Foote, Arthur. *Scrapbooks.* 3 vols. In the Library of the City of Boston,
Massachusetts.
Howard, John Tasker. *Charles Tomlinson Griffes.* New York: G. Schirmer,
1923.
Hubbard, John. *An Essay on Music.* Boston: Manning and Loring, 1808.
Kirkpatrick, John. *A Temporary Mimeographed Catalogue of the Music
Manuscripts and related materials of Charles Edward Ives.* New Haven:
Yale University School of Music, 1960.
Law, Andrew. *Essays on Music.* Philadelphia: The Author, 1814.

Malone, Dumas, ed. *Dictionary of American Biography*, vol. 14. New York: Charles Scribner's Sons, 1934.

Marquis, Albert Nelson, ed. *Who's Who in America*, vol. 20. Chicago: The A. N. Marquis Co., 1938.

Merrill, E. Lindsey. "Mrs. H. H. A. Beach: Her Life and Music." Ph.D. Dissertation, University of Rochester [Eastman School of Music], 1963.

Offergeld, Robert. *The Centennial Catalogue of the Published and Unpublished Compositions of Louis Moreau Gottschalk*. New York: Ziff-Davis Publishing Co., 1970.

Pratt, Waldo Selden. *The New Encyclopedia of Music and Musicians*. New York: Macmillan Publishing Co., 1924.

Rider, Daniel. "Musical Thought and Activities of the New England Transcendentalists." Ph.D. Dissertation, University of Minnesota, 1964.

Rochberg, George. Letter to the author. June 23, 1975.

Stevenson, Robert. *Philosophies of American Music History*. Washington, D.C.: The Lewis Charles Elson Memorial Fund, 1970.

Yellen, Victor Fell. "The Life and Operatic Works of George Whitefield Chadwick." Ph.D. Dissertation, Harvard University, 1957.

INDEX

About the Author

Garry E. Clarke is an associate professor and the chairman of the Department of Music at Washington College, Chestertown, Maryland. A composer and pianist, he specialized in American music and music theory, and is the coeditor of Charles Ives's *Varied Air and Variations.*